LIFETIME ENCYCLOPEDIA OF LETTERS

Revised and Expanded

Harold E. Meyer

PRENTICE HALL
Paramus, New Jersey 07652

Library of Congress Cataloging in Publication Data

Meyer, Harold E.
    Lifetime encyclopedia of letters / Harold E. Meyer.—Rev. and
expanded.
        p. cm.
    Includes index.
    ISBN ISBN 0-13-529546-7 (c)   ISBN 0-13-8948747-7 (p)
    1. Letter-writing. I. Title.
PE1483.M43 1992
808.6—dc20

Printed in the United States of America

20 19 18 17 16   10 9 8 7 6 5 4 3 2 1

To Linda and Patricia

ISBN 0-13-529546-7 (c)   ISBN 0-13-8948747-7 (p)

ATTENTION: CORPORATIONS AND SCHOOLS

Prentice Hall books are available at quantity discounts with bulk purchase for educational, business, or sales promotional use. For information, please write to: Prentice Hall Special Sales, 240 Frisch Court, Paramus, New Jersey 07652. Please supply: title of book, ISBN, quantity, how the book will be used, date needed.

PRENTICE HALL
Paramus, NJ 07652

A Simon & Schuster Company

On the World Wide Web at http://www.phdirect.com

Prentice Hall International (UK) Limited, *London*
Prentice Hall of Australia Pty. Limited, *Sydney*
Prentice Hall Canada, Inc., *Toronto*
Prentice Hall Hispanoamericana, S.A., *Mexico*
Prentice Hall of India Private Limited, *New Delhi*
Prentice Hall of Japan, Inc., *Tokyo*
Simon & Schuster Asia Pte. Ltd., *Singapore*
Editora Prentice Hall do Brasil, Ltda., *Rio de Janeiro*

How You Will Benefit from This Book

Do you sit down to write a letter and wonder, "Just what is it I'm trying to say and how should I say it?"

Is your letter clear enough that you can confidently omit the popular last sentence that reads, "If you have any questions, please call me?"

How do you reprimand an employee, to "put him in his place," and still inspire him to improve?

When you have to terminate an employee, how do you write a letter that does that job and still remains a model of fairness?

Can you apologize appropriately to your boss after behaving shockingly at the company party?

If your lifelong friend were to die, what would you write to his or her spouse?

When your church asked you to write a fund-raising letter did you panic?

Complete Range of Categories

These and many other questions are answered in the *Lifetime Encyclopedia of Letters*, which covers 554 separate categories of letters, including:

Thanking a person
    For being our customer
    For helping my career
    For doing a job well
    For accounting help

Congratulating a person
    Upon graduating
    Upon receiving a promotion
    Upon exceeding a sales goal
    Upon marrying

Selling
    A sales promotion book
    A loaf of bread
    An executive search service

Raising funds
    For churches
    For hospitals
    For schools
    For the mentally retarded
    For runaway children
    For disadvantaged girls

Hunting for a job
    Using résumés
    Using acceptance letters
    Using rejection letters
    Using resignation letters
    Using performances reviews

Collecting accounts
    By reminding gently
    By appealing to fear
    By taking legal action

Requesting favors
    To alleviate a fear
    To find a job for my relative

Requesting information
    About a warranty
    About a claim
    About a pollution check
    About an investigation
    About a chemical hazard

Providing information
    For claims against the city
    For instructions not being followed
    For a price increase

Answering complaints
    About a misunderstanding
    About a faulty product
    About a foreign object in food

Making complaints
    About transit damage
    About billing errors
    About misrepresentation

Reprimanding an employee
  For uncleanliness
  For misconduct

Refusing
  A request for credit
  A job applicant
  A donation or gift
  A volunteer's help

Apologizing
  For ignoring a customer
  For failure to complete a project
  For behaving indiscreetly

Expressing sympathy
  To an accident victim
  To the spouse of the deceased
  To a relative upon death of an employee
  To a mother of a defective child

If you need help with your writing in these or any other areas, this encyclopedia gives you that help.

We Can All Use Help

Many writers of business letters and reports need direction because their compositions are too often disorganized, wordy, and unclear.

Note the lack of clarity in the following true example written by a college graduate employed by a manufacturer:

Subject: Special instructions regarding order No. 98227.
In order to complete orders 99411 and 99412, please ship 98727 as close to equal amounts of A, B, and C as possible.

What was the shipping clerk to do? Obviously call the writer of the instructions—valuable production time spent clarifying a written communication. The growing emphasis on speed in communication requires letters the reader can understand clearly the first time through.

Among the many aids to easier and better writing, the *Lifetime Encyclopedia of Letters* shows you how to write an interest-arousing first sentence, to write a persuasive closing sentence, to be polite yet positive, to solve the problem of saying "no," to be encouraging, to complain, to make a sales letter sell, to open the pocketbook of a potential contributor, to collect money, to organize your thoughts, to retain the reader's goodwill, to fire an employee, to express true sympathy, to take your guilt out of an apology, and to get action from your request. Just locate your topic, read the lead-in comments and follow the model letters.

Easy-to-Follow Models

All the model letters in this encyclopedia are written in current, up-to-date language. Letters of long ago that were once considered standards of good writing but contain outdated expressions do not appear here.

Many of the examples can be nearly copied. Only the change of a name or a few words is required to turn a sample into your own personal letter. You may want to take a sentence or two from one letter and additional sentences from others, creating a letter you prefer to any of the models.

But what can you do if you want to create your own letter? For each type of letter there is a basic outline called "How to Do It."

"How to Do It" Outline

One special feature of this encyclopedia that helps you organize your thoughts is the "How to do It" section preceding each group of model letters. This feature is a step-by-step outline for your letters. Using these steps, you will be able to include all the essential parts of your message and eliminate any unnecessary digressions.

For example, the "How to Do It" section for a letter of encouragement lists these four steps:

1. Admit that an adverse condition exists.

2. Name the condition or problem.

3. Indicate your conviction that the condition can be overcome.

4. Suggest how to overcome the condition.

Notice how smoothly the letter below fits the outline—without sounding as if it were chopped into four separate and unrelated pieces.

> Teaching at P.S. 24 is a difficult assignment for any teacher and even the most seasoned instructors often find the integration process takes time. Thus, it comes as no surprise that you have spoken of submitting your resignation at the end of the school year.
>
> Discipline remains a problem for many new teachers here, as you have discovered. Students tend to "test" a teacher. However, once the test is passed, teachers often find themselves responding with enthusiasm to the challenge.
>
> Please take a little time to reconsider your decision, then see me to discuss the matter at your earliest convenience.

If you can't find a model letter or a topic outline for the subject of your letter, this book will still help you.

How to Use This Book When You Can't Find Your Topic

The first step is to determine exactly what your subject is. Are you confusing a thank you with a congratulation or providing information with sales? Read the introduction and the "How to Do It" section to a related or similar topic. Then, after reading a few model letters, you will have a clear understanding of how to write your letter.

When writing to a politician or public office holder, ask yourself which topic in the table of contents most nearly covers the *subject matter* of your letter.

A common question at this point is how do I start? This book suggests many beginning and ending sentences.

Beginning and Ending Sentences

A special feature of the *Lifetime Encyclopedia of Letters* is the 334 suggested beginning and ending sentences for letters. Often just getting started on a letter is all it takes to get you into the swing of it and then to carry you through. The starting sentences provided will accomplish this.

Chapter 2, "Declining Requests," suggests that one way to decline a request is to start with a thank you. For example:

> Thank you for your recent request for a charge account at Liberty House.
> Thank you for your interest in Inland Steel.
> We appreciate your asking us to participate in your budget meeting.

This chapter offers statements of refusal, and the last step in the "How to Do It" section suggests offering help or encouragement to the reader. Some encouraging statements are listed:

> I know you will find a suitable position soon.
> I believe the Abbot Company could give you more detailed information.
> We wish you great success.

In many letters, the last paragraph or sentence is a summary of the letter, an expression of appreciation or a call for action, as illustrated by these sales letter endings:

> Your credit is good. Just tell us what you want.
> We cut all the red tape—simply mail the card.

> If for any reason you're dissatisfied, simply return it ... and owe nothing.
> Our supply is limited. Act now!

Hard hitting sentences like these, while usually productive, do not appeal to all readers.

Hard Sell Versus Soft Sell

The variety of approaches within each category is a unique feature of the *Lifetime Encyclopedia of Letters.* One fund-raising letter (which is a sales letter with a heart tug) consists of three short sentences:

> You make the differences between mediocrity and excellence.
> Think about it.
> Your considered gift to the Dartmouth Alumni Fund supports the Campaign for Dartmouth.

More common is a two-to-four page letter listing numerous reasons to make a donation, one of which the writer hopes will elicit a response from the reader.

Another contrast in presentations included in this book is the soft sell versus the hard sell, different approaches directed to different audiences. One real estate sales letter begins:

> Once in a lifetime there is a special place. Reaching a gentle rise overlooking a flowering meadow...

A different realtor starts off:

> Another home SOLD at 0000 Windmill Way...

Contrasts in presentation offer you an opportunity to reach specific audiences. Analysis of appeals to human emotions can also help in directing your letter to a particular audience.

Model Letters Analyzed

For most situations, the explanations, suggested outlines and analyses will make adapting the model letter easy. The fund-raising letters, for example, may not fit individual needs as precisely as many of the sympathy letters. Sympathy letters are short and general, while fund-raising letters are long and specific. In the latter, money is requested for a particular cause, and many separate reasons to donate can be included in one letter so that at least one will touch the pocket book of the reader. Fund-raising letters are outlined, then analyzed to point out what techniques are used in each case. This enables the writer to list appeals, set them into the outline and write the letter using one or more of the attention-getting techniques shown in the analysis.

One quick way to locate a model for the letter you want to write is to consult the index.

Easy-to-Use Index

In this reference work, all the information found in the Table of Contents can also be found in the Index. Many letters are indexed in several ways: by topic, category within the topic, alternate names for the topic and the category, geographic location, and company name. Having read a letter once, you can locate it in the index by referring to one of several words. Double indexing is also used. For example, *reader's viewpoint* is indexed under both *reader's* and *viewpoint*.

Lifetime Reference Work

Through the use of suggestions and model letters, this book shows you how to write a letter that accomplishes your intended purpose.

Because the model letters in the encyclopedia are standards and can be adapted to your requirements for many years, this book will become a long-term investment and companion. The range of topics and the variety of treatments within each topic make the *Lifetime Encyclopedia of Letters* a reference work that will last a lifetime.

Harold E. Meyer

Contents

How You Will Benefit from This Book   iii

Chapter   1   REQUESTING FAVORS
                                                                        1

How to Do It   5
Closing a Request with Confidence Examples   5
Additional Information   5
Answering Questions   5
Questionnaire   6
Consumer Survey   7
Response to Inquiry   7
Procedural Change   7
Rescheduling Order   8
Time Extension   8
Meeting Deadline   9
Shorten Deadline   9
Office Visit   10
Manufacturing Plant Visit   10
Share Experience   11
Financial Statement   11
Business Guidance   11
Business Statistics   12
Business Forecast   12
Business Location   13
Business Opportunities   13
Sample Letter   14
Quote from Article   14
Obtaining Interview   14
To Speak   15
Getting Speakers   16
Entertaining a Friend   16
Alleviating Fear   17
Board a Relative   17
Job for a Relative   18

Chapter   2   DECLINING REQUESTS   **19**

How to Do It   23
Begin by Agreeing   23

Begin with a Thank-You 23
Begin with an Agreement and Apology 24
Statements of Refusal 24
Close with Encouragement 25

INVITATIONS 25
Invitation to Dinner 25
Invitation to Speak 26
Join a Group 26
Victory Celebration 26
Football Game 26

REQUEST FOR INFORMATION OR MATERIAL 27
Information Not Available 27
Item Not Available 28

APPLICATION FOR PERSONAL CREDIT 29
Lack of Information 29
Lack of Work Record 30
Short Employment 30
Slow Pay 31
New in Area 31
Current Information Lacking 32

APPLICATION FOR BUSINESS CREDIT 32
Financial Condition 33
Credit Limited 33
Company Procedure—Late Payment 33
Guarantor Needed 34
Previous Poor Pay 34
Bad Risk 35
Bad Risk—No Hope 35
Franchise Refused 36
Will Not Change Prior Understanding 36
Credit Information Available Elsewhere 37

DONATION 37
Funds Limited 37
Use of Name in Fund Raising 37
Company Policy 38
Budget Limitation 38
Disagree with Charity Project 39

CUSTOMER ADJUSTMENTS 39
Damaged Product 40
Cash Discount 40
Special Product 41
Poor Workmanship 41

Slow-Selling Product 41

OTHER LETTERS OF DECLINATION 42
Untested Sample Letters 42
Special Assignment 42
Business Meeting—Unnecessary 43
Magazine Subscribers Limited 43
Publication—Too Specialized 43
Publication—Editorial Program 44
Publication—Needs Reworking 44
Refusing a Volunteer 45
Freight Claim 45
Miscellaneous Request 45
Financial Aid 46

Chapter 3 SALES   47

How to Do It 51
Model Openers 51
Model Closings 53
Investment—Real Estate 54
Business Magazine 56
Magazine—Elitist 56
Mortgage Insurance 57
Homeowner's Insurance 57
Health Insurance 58
Dentistry 59
Book Club 59
Real Estate—Homes 60
Real Estate—Mountain Property 62
Wrist Watch 62
Camera 63
Computer System 64
Specific Customer—Roofing Tile 65
Sales Promotion Book 65
Gift of Food 67
Bakery 67
Income Tax Consulting 68
Service Contract 69
Inactive Customer 69
Collection Service 70
Public Official 70
Executive Recruiter 71
Personal Credit 72

Furniture, Retail 73
Art Object 73
Life Insurance 74
Cost Savings 75
Store Sale 76

FOLLOW-UP SALES LETTERS 76
How to Do It 76

Chapter 4 FUND RAISING   **79**

How to Do It 84

CHARITABLE HELP FOR THE DISADVANTAGED 84
Runaway Children 84
Disadvantaged Girl 86
Troubled Boys 87
Destitute Children 88
Mentally Retarded 88
Crippled Children 89
Handicapped Children 90
Hungry Children 90
Homeless Boys 91
Heart Fund 92
Heart Disease 92
American Veterans 93
Cerebral Palsy 94
United Way 95
CARE 96
Sponsor a Child 98
Lung Disease 100

LIBRARY 100

CHURCHES 104
Secular Appeal 104
Preparation for Fund-Raising Campaign 105
Every Member Canvass 107
Budget Can Be Met 107
Delinquent Pledge 108
Appeal to Faith 108
Love Is a Reason for Giving 109

HOSPITALS 110
Updating Facilities 110
Success Story 111
Equipment for Senior Patients 112

Need for Continuing Support 113
Expansion Costs 113
Maintain Quality Service 114
Doctors Join in Giving 115
Doctors as Business Persons 115
Last Appeal to Doctors 116
Using a Specific Example 116
Replace Equipment 117
Appeal to the Ego 118
Join Hospital Foundation 118

SCHOOLS 119
Give More Than Last Year 119
Library Needs 121
Alumni Solicitation 122
Haven't Given Yet 122
Minorities Program 124
Operational Funds 125
Building Fund 125
Student Union Building 125
Religious Appeal 126
Financially Disadvantaged Students 127
Every Little Bit Helps 127
Pledge Not Received 128
Request for Small Gift 128
Worthy Projects 129

Chapter 5 COLLECTION 131

How to Receive a Prompt Reply 135
How to Do It 135
Attention-Getting Openings—Humorous 136
A Strong Close 137
For Prompt Action 137
To Build Goodwill 138
To Soothe 138
To Apologize 138
To Reassure 139
To Repeat 139
To Promote the Future 139
Series of Collection Letters 140
Series One, Three Letters: Reminder 140
Series Two, Three Letters: Business Charge
  Account 141

Series Three, Three Letters: Past Due Freight
Bill 142
Series Four, Four Letters: Make Account
Current 143
Series Five, Four Letters: Loan Past Due 144
Series Six, Four Letters, Charge Account 145
Series Seven, Five Letters: Charge Account 146
Series Eight, Five Letters: Charge Account 148
Series Nine, Six Letters: Slow Pay Business
Account 150
Series Ten, Six Letters: Business Account
Delinquent 132
The First Collection Letter Is a Reminder 154
Credit Union Loan 158
Middle Stages of Collection Letters 158
Slow Pay—Terms Explained 164
Final Collection Letters 164

**Chapter 6 INFORMATION—PROVIDING
AND REQUESTING**   **169**

PROVIDING INFORMATION 171
How to Do It 172
Shipping Instructions 173
Procedural Change 173
Price Increase 173
Purchasing Policy 174
Bid Price 175
Complying with Request 175
Data No Longer Required 175
Lease Instructions 175
Action Taken 176
Confirmation 176
Payment Instructions 177
Continue Procedure 177
Number Code Changes 177
Repeated Instructions 178
Distribution of Reports 178
Claim Against City 178
Effects of Strike 179
Insurance Policy Transfer 179
Layoff 179
Statement of Future Occurrence 180

Test Run Assigned 180
Policy Change 180
Change in Items Used 181
Address Change 181
Address Correction 181
Will Contact You Again 182
Reason for Cooperation 182
REQUESTING INFORMATION 182
How to Do It 183
A Report 184
Accounting System 184
Acknowledgment of Gift 184
City Information 184
Recent Sales Activity 185
Strength Analysis 185
Data for Newsletter 185
Review of Claim 186
Credit Information 186
Credit Card 187
Warranty Questions 188
Making an Appointment 188
Old Equipment 188
Pollution Check 189
Corporate Name 189
Please Investigate 190
Incomplete Files 190
Office Furniture 191
Life Insurance Questions 191
Correct an Error 191
Restricting Receiving Hours 191
Using Credit Memo 192
Procedural Change 192
Keep Records 193
Reporting Period Changed 193
Personnel Evaluation 193
Safety News 194
Price Quote 194
Where Is the Report? 195
Chemical Hazards 195
Physical Inventory 196
Opinion Asked 196
Survey of Consumption 196
Claim Follow-Up 197
Suggestions 197
Record of Address Change 198

Claims Service Evaluation 198
Medical Facility Evaluation 198

**Chapter 7 COMPLAINTS: MAKING
                AND ANSWERING**   **201**

MAKING COMPLAINTS 203
How to Do It 204
Transit Damage 204
Cost of Purchases 204
Incorrect Mailings 205
Inadequate Explanation 205
Messy Work Area 206
Low Sales 206
Sales Forecast 206
Manufacturing Errors 207
Manufacturing Problem 208
Shipping Errors 208
Billing Error 209
Computer Error 209
Catalog Order 209
Labor Law Violation 210
Misrepresentation 210
Parking in Driveway 211
Noisy Driver 211
Meetings Out of Control 211
Muddy Newspaper 212
Delivery Person 212
Barking Dog 212
No Stop Light 213
Gardening Problem 213

ANSWERING COMPLAINTS 214
How to Do It 214
Opening Sentences 214
Closing Sentences 215
Disturbed Retail Customer 215
Our Mistake 216
Misunderstanding 216
Incomplete Instructions 216
Misdirected Mail 217
Late Delivery 217
Shipping Error 218
Delayed Order 218

Delivery Method 218
Damaged Merchandise 219
Merchandise Guarantee 220
Wrong Style 220
Unsatisfactory Chair 221
Unsatisfactory Recorder 221
Foreign Object in Food 221
Declining Responsibility—Frozen Food 222
Pricing Error 222
Billing Error 223
Statement Error 224
Complaint Handling Procedure 224

Chapter 8 EMPLOYMENT   **227**

*SECTION I—LETTERS WRITTEN BY JOB
APPLICANTS* 229
Cover Letters for Résumés 229
How to Do It 230
Sales Representative 230
Chief Accountant 230
Buyer Trainee 230
Cover Letters for Job Applications 231
Plant Accountant 231
Secretary 231
Résumés 232
Advertising Executive 234
Senior Accountant 234
Assistant Staff Manager 236
Systems Administrator 237
Job Application Letters 239
How to Do It 239
Answering Ad for Accounting Manager 239
Answering Ad for Market Research Trainee 240
Cold-Call Application Letter for Private
  Secretary 240
Cold-Call Application Letter for Computer
  Systems Manager 241
Application Letter for Job Suggested by a Present
  Employee 242
Thanking an Employer 243
How to Do It 243
Accepting Offer of an Interview 243

Thank You for the Interview 244
Thank You for Your Recommendation 246
Accepting Job Offer 246
Rejecting Job Offer 248
Resignation 249
SECTION II—LETTERS WRITTEN BY EMPLOYERS 249
How to Do It 249
Tentatively Accepting Applicant 249
Requesting Data from References 250
Requesting Data from Applicants 251
Providing References to Another Employer 251
Invitation to an Interview 253
Rejecting Tentatively Accepted Applicants 254
Rejecting Applicant 255
Accepting Applicant 256
How to Do It 257
Welcome to New Employee 258
Performance Appraisal 259
How to Do It 259
Performance Evaluation 260
Job Performance Review 260
Recommendation for Promotion 262
Notice of Promotion 263
Congratulations on Your Promotion 263
Reprimand 264
Termination Warning 266
Termination 266
Accepting Resignation 266
How to Do It 267
Notice of Employee Leaving 267
Retirement Congratulations 268
SECTION III—LETTERS INVOLVING
THIRD PARTIES 270
Thanks for Helping Me Get a Job 270
Recommending a Job Applicant 270
Rejecting Applicant Recommended by
  a Third Party 271
Congratulations on Promotion 272
Congratulations on Retirement 274

Chapter   9   TERMINATION AND RESIGNATION   **275**

TERMINATION 277
How to Do It 277

Plant Closed 278
Company Cutbacks 278
Company Merger 279
Financial Problems 279
Indiscretions 280
Project Completed 280
Personal Friend 280
Performance 281
Classroom Procedures 281

TERMINATION WARNING 281
How to Do It 282
Personal Problems 283
Poor Performance 283
Classroom Performance 285
Tardiness 285
Absentee Record 286

RESIGNATION 286
How to Do It 286
New Position 287
Seeking New Challenge 287
College Training 288
Ill Health 288
Heart Problem 289
Allergies 289
Personal Problems 289
Disagree with Goals 290
Want Less Travel 290
Credit Union 290

RESIGNATION ACCEPTANCE 291
How to Do It 291
Acknowledgment of Separation Pay
  and Release 292

Chapter 10   SYMPATHY AND CONDOLENCE   **293**

How to Do It 296
Sentences Expressing Sympathy 296
Sentences Thanking the Reader for an
  Expression of Sympathy 297
Letters to Hospitalized People 298
Other's Illness 299
Death of Business Associate 300
Death of a Business Friend 300
Death of Spouse 301
Death of Relative 303

Death of Others 306
Belated Condolences 307
Death by Suicide 308
Death—from a Business Firm 308
Birth Defect 310
Divorce 311
Marriage Separation 311
Misfortune 311
Personal Reverses 312
Unnamed Tragedy 312
Thank You for Your Sympathy 312

Chapter 11 APOLOGY   315

How to Do It 317
Sentences of Apology 318
Reasons for an Apology 318
Bad Behavior 319
Billing Error 320
Company Procedure 320
Confusing Word Usage 320
Declining Dinner Invitation 321
Delayed Answer 321
Delayed Credit 323
Postponed Dinner 323
Delayed Order 323
Delayed Paper Work 324
Delayed Return of Borrowed Item 324
Delayed Thank You 325
Indiscretion 325
Ignoring a Customer 326
Incomplete Instructions 327
Incomplete Project 327
Late Report 327
Missed Appointment 328
Missed Meeting 328
Missing a Caller 329
Project Failure 329
Quote Error 330
Shipping Error 330
Slow Payment 331
Small Reward 331
Statement Error 331
Wrong Information 332

Chapter 12 CONGRATULATIONS   **333**

How to Do It 335
Sales Volume 336
New Customer 336
Job Well Done 337
Top Salesperson 337
Exceeding Goal 337
Graduation 338
College Degree 338
Specialized Teacher 339
Handicapped 339
New Position 339
Service Award 339
Golf Tournament 340
Industry Award 341
President of Rotary 341
Anniversary 341
Honorary Sorority 341
President of Association 342
Opening Store 342
City Councilman 342
Loan Paid 342
Marriage 343

Chapter 13 THANK YOU AND APPRECIATION   **345**

How to Do It 349
Gift 349
Pamphlet 350
Information 350
Materials Received 350
Advice 351
Recommendation 351
Dinner Invitation 352
Recognition 352
Going Away Party 352
Companionship 353
Friendship 353
Appreciation 353
Illness 354
Job Well Done 355
Being Our Customer 356

Charge Account Request 357
Sales Presentation 358
Accounting Help 358
Payment 358
Referral 359
Attending 359
Visiting 359

Chapter 14 OTHER BUSINESS LETTERS   **361**

GOODWILL 363
How to Do It 364
Season's Greetings 364
Good Work 365
Free Bulletin 365
Golf Invitation 365
To a Salesperson's Spouse 365
Sales Agreement Ended 367
To Parents of Young Employee 367
Enjoyed Meeting You 367
Fishing Trip Invitation 368
Real Estate Service 368
Gift Received 368
Requested Information 369
Sending Information 369
Making Contribution 369

INTRODUCTION 370
How to Do It 370
New Sales Representative 370
Friend for Sales Position 371
A Friend 371
Academic Assistance 372
New Employee 372

INVITATIONS 372
How to Do It 373
Luncheon for an Old Friend 373
To Do Advertising 373
Use Company Hotel Room 373
Ball Game 374
Dinner Guest 374
Accepting Invitations 374
How to Do It 375
To Speak 375
Football Celebration 375

Retirement Dinner 376
Dinner Invitation 376
Join a Group 376
Declining Invitations 376

ACCEPTING A POSITION 376
How to Do It 377
Committee Chairperson 378
Lions Club 378

COVER LETTER 378
How to Do It 379
Expenditures Request 379
Lists 379
Agreement for Signature 380
Warehouse Report 380
Certificate of Incorporation 380
Statement Requested 380
Commodity Codes 381
Savings Statement 381
Insurance Renewal 381
Price Increase 381
Valuable Document 382

FOLLOW-UP 382
How to Do It 382
Correct an Error 383
Additional Information Requested 383
Additional Information Provided 383
Inactive Charge Account 384
Power Lawn Mower Purchase 384

QUERY LETTERS SEEKING PUBLICATION 384
How to Do It 385
Book 385
Magazine Article 386

Chapter 15 OTHER PERSONAL LETTERS 389

WELCOME 392
How to Do It 392
To New Resident 392
To New Member 393

GOOD WISHES 393
How to Do It 394
Season's Greetings 394

Convalescing 395

ENCOURAGEMENT 396
How to Do It 396
Sales Contest 397
Low Productivity 397
Promotion 398
Research Paper 398
Fund Drive 398
Teaching 399

COMPLIMENTS 400
How to Do It 400
Staff Help 400
Expert Assistance 400
Orientation Help 401
Better Truck Loading 401
Unusual Help 401
Finding Error 402
Getting the Facts 402
Construction Bid 402
Good Salesman 403
Sales Volume 403
Sales Increase 403
Vote Getter 404

RECOMMENDATION 404
How to Do It 405
Customer 405
Domestic Service 406
Inexperienced Worker 406
High School Graduate 406

REPRIMAND 407
How to Do It 407
Outside Activities at Work 408
Lack of Cleanliness 408
Bad Behavior 408
Travel Expense 409
Lack of Cooperation 409
Unsafe Conditions 410
Exceeding Budget 410
Trespassing 410

PRESENTING GIFTS 411
How to Do It 411
Companionship 411

Friendship 411
Advice 411
Funeral Officiating 412
Baptismal Officiating 412
Hospital Patient 412
Eightieth Birthday 413
Illness 413
Retirement 413

ACCEPTING GIFTS 414
How to Do It 414
Chess Set 414
Food Snacks 415
Book 415
Money 416
Oil Painting 416
Watercolor Painting 417
Art Object 417
Statuette 417
Free Product 418
Cooler 418

DECLINING GIFTS 418
How to Do It 419
Company Policy 419
Must Maintain Image 419
Duplicate Gift 420
Gift Too Valuable 420
Expensive Gift 420

TRIBUTE 421
Tribute to a Wife 421
Tribute to a Husband 421

INDEX 423

Chapter 1

REQUESTING FAVORS

Many people find it difficult to make a request that seems to impose upon others. Often, the person asked feels complimented that he is considered capable of helping to solve a problem, so you should not be reluctant to ask—assuming the request is reasonable. When making requests of a sensitive nature, such as for a favor or for cooperation, you must indicate clearly and persuasively why the request is being made. Let the reader know why you came to him or her for help and how that help will be used.

A letter requesting only information can be short and direct. For example:

> We need quarterly SEC reports, our form C-140, for the year 19__. Submit these by the 20th of the month following each quarter.

A more willing response, however, would be received if the letter were expanded just enough to include an explanation of why the request is being made. A word or two, such as "please" or "would appreciate" is helpful in eliciting the desired response. This is illustrated in the following request that is also short and direct, but adds the reason for the request in a polite tone:

> The year-end Tax Requirements report unintentionally omitted charitable contributions.
>
> We would appreciate it if you would provide us with a schedule of donations made during the year showing the donee and the dollar amount.

The key to getting results from a sensitive letter of request is having a persuasive and convincing explanation of the reason for the request. Think before you write: what will appeal to the reader? how are the writer's wants tied to the reader's interests? A request is more willingly granted if the practical psychology of give-and-take is recognized. The reader may ask, "What's in it for me?" Whenever possible, offer something in return.

One of the model letters asks for financial statements and offers prompt deliveries of future orders upon receiving them. Other letters ask for information, implying that the reader knows more than the writer, and all readers like compliments. One letter requests a stepped-up delivery date for part of an order, " . . . because we don't want to split the order with another supplier." This is not a threat of taking away promised business, but a suggested practical solution to a business problem, and of much interest to the reader. Another letter requesting a favor suggests an exchange of information about manufacturing plant operations. The reader of this letter is interested because he has an opportunity to receive information in exchange for giving information. In one letter a request is made by an alumnus doing research. Being an alumnus and doing research are both topics of interest to the college president to whom the letter is addressed. These offers of something in return or topics of personal interest to the reader can induce the reader to participate willingly.

When asking several questions in one letter, make the response easier by listing and preferably numbering the questions. In this way each specific question will result in a specific answer.

Another technique for getting a positive response is to write to an individual rather than to "Gentlemen." (The names of corporate officers can be found in reference libraries. Another method is to call the office of the person to whom you wish to write.)

When the request is mentioned early in a letter that includes an appeal of more than two sentences, repeat the request at the end. Make the reply easy for the reader by making the request specific and by providing an envelope or an address or a due date.

Never end a letter by saying, "Thanking you in advance" or the shorter "Thank you" or "Thanks." These phrases leave the reader with the feeling that the writer is terminating all interest in the request and that the reader is left to struggle on alone. Rather than ending with a curt "Thank you," make the reader happy to grant your request by clothing it with politeness and appreciation for the expected action. This can be done by using such phrases as, "It would be helpful," or "We would appreciate," or "Please."

Close the letter with confidence. Make no apologies. A letter ending with the statement, "I know you're awfully busy and I hate to ask you this, but maybe you could find time to check this report for me," is likely to draw the response, "You're right, I don't have time." The ending should indicate confidence that the request will be granted, and it must be stated politely.

How to Do It

1. Make the request specific, using a polite tone.
2. Explain persuasively the reason for the request.
3. Offer something in return.
4. Show appreciation for the granter's help.

Closing a Request with Confidence—Examples

Your answer will be gratefully received.

We appreciate your cooperation.

Please mail the financial statements today.

Receiving a sample drawing would be greatly appreciated.

Please let us know when you can do this.

We will expect your answer soon.

Even a short visit with you will be truly appreciated.

Your answers to the above questions will be of great help to us.

Your filling in the blanks below and returning this letter in the enclosed envelope will be greatly appreciated.

Additional Information

Dear Mr. Hoskins:

Thank you for the operating schedule you made for conducting the market survey we discussed in April. All the bases seem to be covered.

I would like, however, to have you add calendar dates and costs for the various steps you have listed. As we discussed, timeliness is essential. The cost is also important because we have a definite and limited budget for this project.

With the added information on dates and costs, we can make a prompt decision on how to proceed with the survey. We hope to hear from you soon.

Sincerely,

Answering Questions

Dear Ms. Carpenter:

Could you help us with a favor? We are considering the installation of a small computer to replace hand posting of our accounting records and the typing of financial reports and monthly statements. We have been told that you have experience with the Conrad 103 system. Could you help by answering the following questions? A brief answer is all we need.

1. How frequently does this system require adjustments or repairs to the machine?
2. Has the use of this system reduced your office staff?
3. Do reports and financial statements get to your managers at an earlier calendar date than before the system was installed?

We will greatly appreciate your answers to these questions.

Sincerely,

Questionnaire

Dear Mr. Dawson:

Because you are one of our past trainees who has become successful, we recently sent you a questionnaire asking about your work and personal background, your work experience, and your opinions on several related matters. We are eager to have your reply in order to better understand the characteristics of those entering our training program, and to improve our program for future trainees.

If you have already returned your questionnaire, many thanks. If not, we hope you will do so soon.

Sincerely,

Dear Ms. Walker:

We are compiling a guide to the employment of women in top firms in the nation and would appreciate your cooperation in filling out the enclosed questionnaire.

Given the timeliness of the subject, and the involvement of both the Government and women's groups, the answers to our questions will be valuable to women seeking responsible positions.

Since we are already informally aware of your company's progressive policy, your response will be particularly encouraging.

Any additional information and comments you might provide will be appreciated.

Sincerely,

Consumer Survey

Dear Mr. Summers:

Thank you for taking the time to talk with us on the phone recently and for agreeing to participate in our survey.

We have sent one questionnaire to be filled out by each member of your household, twelve years of age and older. Please fill out the enclosed material and return it in the envelope provided as soon as possible. No postage is necessary.

We hope that you will enjoy participating in this survey. Your answers will become an important part of our scientific study.

Please accept the enclosed token of our sincere appreciation for your cooperation.

Sincerely yours,

Response to Inquiry

Dear George:

You should receive a phone call next week from our Washington headquarters. Please make every effort to supply them with the information they have requested from your branch.

The main office is drawing up a company profile. The exposure provided by our data should be beneficial for both the branch image and the individual personnel involved.

I look forward to seeing your responses.

Regards,

Procedural Change

Dear Andy:

It seems there is a breakdown in procedures between our departments. We are not getting all the receiving records for scrap that your department receives after our department orders it. When inquiries are made directly to your receiving clerk, he complains that apparently he doesn't get all the copies of our orders to match with his receipts.

We have learned that our orders are sent through the company mail with the receiving clerk's name written in no particular place on them. Now we have instructed our order clerk to mail these in an intracompany envelope. This should eliminate misdirection of the mail.

Could you have your receiving clerk mail the receiving records to our department in an intracompany envelope? Please send them to the attention of Bob Smyth.

Sincerely,

Rescheduling Order

Dear Carl:

On July 24 we sent you our purchase order number AC 3341 for 100,000 tomato boxes. The requested delivery date, which you confirmed, is September 4.

Due to forecasted changes in the weather, tomatoes will ripen a month earlier than expected, and we will need 50,000 of these boxes before August 4 and the balance by September 4. Could you reschedule your production line to work in at least half our order to meet the earlier delivery date? I know your production schedules are full at this time of the year, but a profitable harvest depends upon boxing the tomatoes as soon as they are ready. We would certainly appreciate your help because we don't want to split the order with another supplier. Please let me know immediately if you can do this for us.

Best Regards,

Time Extension

Dear Mr. Mullen:

Enclosed is a copy of our option on rental space at the Furniture Mart. The option expires March 23.

The decision to renew must be made by our Board of Directors, and it is not possible for them to meet until March 28.

Would it be possible, therefore, to extend the option renewal date to March 29? We will have the decision then.

Sincerely,

Dear Ms. Bradley:

Is it possible for us to obtain an extension of the initial trial leasing contract for the 150 copier?

I am aware that the three-month trial period was provided at a reduced rate. Unfortunately, we could not take full advantage of testing the copier because the office was shut down for three weeks of the lease period.

The performance of the machine has, thus far, been satisfactory. There is, however, one special run to be made next week that will determine our decision either to buy the copier or to return it to you and end the agreement.

Please respond as soon as possible.

Sincerely,

Meeting Deadline

Dear Mr. Hartfeld:

Because of an audit by the Internal Revenue Service on September 27, I will need a transaction-by-transaction listing of all my stock purchases and sales made through Sanders and Sanders, Inc. for the calendar year 19__. Each transaction must include:

Name of stock   Date of purchase
Date of sale   Purchase price
Sales price   Brokerage purchase fee
Brokerage sales fee

I know it will be a tight schedule for you, but I must have the report no later than September 26.

Your prompt attention will be greatly appreciated (by Uncle Sam as well as by me).

Sincerely,

Shorten Deadline

Dear Mr. Mays:

When we sent you the flat stock for 7000 formed steel channels, we told you that you could have 36 days in which to do the job.

We now find, however, we cannot allow you that much time, due to the rescheduling of a U.S. Government bridge contract.

Can you get the job done by March 28? This cuts off 11 working days, unless you work Saturdays. Could you help us by shortening the deadline on this project? We really would appreciate it.

If this revised schedule is not possible, please ship back to us what you have completed and the remaining flat stock by March 18.

We hope you can do this favor for us. Please let me know immediately.

Sincerely,

Office Visit

Dear Ms. Jorgenson:

I understand you have a TM600 computer installed for use in your accounting procedures. We are considering several computer systems including the TM600.

I will be in Los Angeles September 25, 26, and 27. Would it be possible to visit your office then? I can arrange to come at any hour convenient for you. Even a short visit with you would be helpful, and greatly appreciated.

Sincerely,

Manufacturing Plant Visit

Dear Mr. Patterson:

We have had the Adenhaur starch-making system in operation at our plant for five months, and understand you have used this system for about two years.

I will be in Memphis during the week of November 19, and would like very much to visit your operation. We have found interesting solutions to some of the problems posed by the installation of this system, and we could exchange information that would benefit us both.

I can arrange to visit any day during the week of November 19. Please let me hear from you.

Regards,

Share Experience

Dear Ms. Wallen:

Your firm has the reputation of having a workable and fair personnel policy. We are revising some of our personnel policies and are rewriting our personnel manual.

Could you share with us a few of your successful procedures? I would like to discuss this with you within the next two weeks. A short interview at your convenience, during which time we could exchange information, would be greatly appreciated. Please call me.

Sincerely,

Financial Statement

Dear Mr. Bangor:

Thank you for your order dated August 20 for 5,000 pen and pencil sets. We especially appreciate orders from new customers. It will be shipped to arrive September 6 as you requested.

I would like to ask a favor of you before we fill your next order. We need a copy of your latest financial statements. It will take only a few minutes and will ensure prompt delivery of your future orders.

Next month we will have pen and pencil sets available for a promotional program. Our salesman, John Harvey, will show you these soon.

I would appreciate your mailing your financial statements today.

Sincerely,

Business Guidance

Dear Allen:

With the recent reduction in our staff that resulted from current economic conditions, we are finding it impossible to complete the monthly reports required by our headquarters office on time. Several steps have been taken to consolidate scattered information, to redistribute work loads, and to eliminate duplicated efforts. Our staff members realize the importance of making every minute count and of continuing to discover quicker ways to complete our reports.

In spite of all our efforts, we are continually falling behind. I would like to ask a favor. I believe you can help us. Would you come here for a day, or even half a day, to review our reports and to suggest some that might be eliminated? Some reports can probably be combined. Then, perhaps you could persuade the headquarters office that these reductions on our reporting workload would not eliminate any necessary management information. We would certainly appreciate your coming here, and hope that the whole company will benefit. Please let me hear from you soon.

Sincerely,

Business Statistics

Dear Mr. Winters:

Our Manager of Marketing, Mr. Aaron Smith, asked me to write you for two statistics that he would like to incorporate in a marketing trend report for *Western Apparel* magazine. You will, of course, be given credit in the magazine for the information you provide.

To meet the magazine's deadline, we will need these figures by October 1.

What we would like is the following:

1. Number of leather jackets you shipped in 19__.
2. Number of plastic and simulated leather jackets you shipped in 19__.

Your help will be greatly appreciated. May we hear from you by October 1?

Sincerely,

Business Forecast

Dear Mr. Peterson:

Thank you for your help in making the year 19__ the most successful in our history. As you know, our sales exceeded all previous records, and because of the increased business we expanded our order assembly and shipping departments. We also added four delivery trucks to our fleet. With this, we will be able to offer even faster service than before. Your business played a big part in our expansion.

To help us continue our fast service, could you provide us with an estimate of your needs for 19__?

Please accept our best wishes for a prosperous 19__.

Sincerely,

Business Location

Dear Andy,

After listening to you at the Retail Hardware Association convention last fall, I have given serious consideration to our expansion plans. Your point about the price advantages of volume purchasing really struck home because our markup is low when we meet our competitor's prices.

I opened a branch store shortly after last fall's convention and it shows promise of turning a profit in a few more months.

I am now considering a third store in a new shopping development, but I can't decide definitely to go ahead with the project. I am bothered by the store space available for expansion and the projected population growth in that area.

Could I ask an extraordinary favor of you? Could you possibly come here for a day or two to look over the situation and give me your opinion? Or make it three or four days and enjoy a mini-vacation. I want you to stay with us, and of course bring Ethel with you. The lake and two golf courses are nearby.

Just talking over this decision with you would be a tremendous help to me.

Beth and I are eagerly awaiting your reply.

Best regards,

Business Opportunities

Gentlemen:

Please send me information regarding business opportunities in the Jacksonville area for an unfinished furniture store.

I am looking for a small but growing business community—and a place in which to live as well as work.

Any information you can provide to get my investigation started will be greatly appreciated.

Sincerely,

Sample Letter

Dear Mr. Hogness:

Could you do a small favor for an alumnus (1969)?

I am doing a research paper on charity contributions. What I need is a sample of a letter asking for a contribution to a worthy cause. You have probably written such a letter asking for money for the University of Washington. Any names and dates should be deleted from the copy or transcript sent to me.

Receiving a sample letter would be truly appreciated.

Sincerely,

Quote from Article

Dear Ms. Sanderson:

The immediate nature of your recent article on the subject of anxiety and performance makes it highly quotable. I would like permission to quote several paragraphs in my paper for the Psychology Association Workshop on psychological disorders most prevalent in affluent women.

As you are aware, too much misinformation has been common in the field. Thus, a well-written, logical evaluation of anxiety, such as you have produced, is extremely valuable.

Should you consent, full credit for your ideas will be given.

Your permission and any suggestions will be appreciated.

Sincerely,

Obtaining Interview

Dear Tim,

Can you help me obtain an interview with Dr. Jerson? I know you've worked closely with him for six months now, and you might at least be able to put in a good word or two for me.

The article I am writing is highly important to me because if it is successful, it will show that I really can handle investigative reporting. In addition, Dr. Jerson might feel relieved, at long last, to have the opportunity to tell his own story in his own way.

I'll be on edge until I receive your reply.

Sincerely,

To Speak

Dear Ms. Nylund:

You have taught a work-study course for legal secretaries for several years and have talked to me about it many times.

Would you be interested in sharing your obvious enthusiasm with the Alamo Business Women at their monthly dinner meeting? We will meet Friday, March 21, at the Sheraton Hotel at 6:30 P.M. A twenty- to thirty-minute talk would be well received by the group.

Please let me know. I can pick you up on the 21st shortly after 6:00.

Sincerely,

Dear Mr. Blackwell:

You are known in this area as a top salesman. Would you be willing to help some young people become better salespersons, to tell them some of the methods and techniques that have earned you your reputation?

The carriers for the Marin County Times are having a sales meeting Friday, February 22 at 7:30 P.M. at the Times office, 333 Silvera Way.

They would be thrilled (and I am sure educated) if you could speak to them for fifteen to twenty minutes and then answer questions.

I'm sure you will find the carriers an enthusiastic group. Please call me.

Sincerely,

Getting Speakers

Dear Jean,

Our seminar on the executive woman is scheduled for April and I'm in the process of putting together the list of speakers. Can you assist me here?

With your executive experience and your contacts with other women in the field, would you be willing to contact a few of them to speak at the seminar?

I would really appreciate it if you could use your influence to help me out. The more diverse our speakers, of course, the more productive the seminar.

My fingers are crossed in hope of your assistance.

Sincerely,

Entertaining a Friend

Dear Pete:

I would like to ask a tremendous favor of you.

Could you possibly spend part of a day with Jack Herald, who is one of our best customers as well as a personal friend of mine? He mentioned yesterday that he will be spending a week or more of vacation time in San Francisco, starting October 7. Jack is production manager for Aames Company here. He is still a bachelor, though I don't know how he manages to stay that way. Jack is an outgoing type but modest and extremely pleasant. He would just about match you in golf. He is a camera bug like you and will surely bring along his new Nikon. I'm sure he would like to take pictures from such spots as Coit Tower, Harding Park's 17th green, the Cliff House, and Twin Peaks. Jack would also enjoy one or two of the tourist-type nightclubs, but that is not his strong suit.

Can I have him call you when he gets to San Francisco? I realize this is asking a lot, but you know I will return the favor whenever I can do something to help you.

Sincerely,

Alleviating Fear

Dear Mrs. Miles,

I am sending this letter to your office for the obvious reason that Mr. Miles should not see it.

In my opinion, and the opinion of Doctors Agnew and Danis, whose reputations as diagnosticians are excellent, Mr. Miles requires surgery as soon as possible.

It is understandable that you feel the way you do about surgery, Mrs. Miles. You expressed yourself clearly when we first met. We feel there isn't any other treatment, however, if you want your husband to recover his good health. Surgery isn't what it was forty years ago, or even ten, and you can be reassured by knowing the mortality rate for this particular operation, when performed in time is less than 5 percent. The mortality rate for neglect of this condition is a certain 100 percent.

Please try to stop by my office with your husband Tuesday evening so that I may talk with both of you. If this is not convenient, please call my secretary this week for an appointment.

Sincerely,

Board a Relative

Dear Sue,

Is there any chance that you and Tom could have Jane stay with you for a month this summer? You've offered in the past, but the need has never been so great. I have the chance to take on a really big account that requires a month-long stay in Israel shooting fashion layouts and generally supervising the whole scene.

Jane has often talked of visiting with you, and I have felt that you would like to see more of her. If it can be arranged, count on me to take time off (I'll be due some if this goes through) to help you with the wedding in January. I already have some ideas.

Call me - even collect!

Sincerely,

Job for a Relative

Dear Tom,

Please review the enclosed résumé of my nephew, John Wentling.

John is an intelligent and ambitious young man whose college performance and initial work experience have been admirable. His work with Grande Company should prove beneficial to you.

Could you check around a bit to see if there is a place for John in the company in the areas of interest he has indicated. Anytime I can return the favor, or assist you in further contacts, you know you can just call.

I look forward to some good news.

With regards,

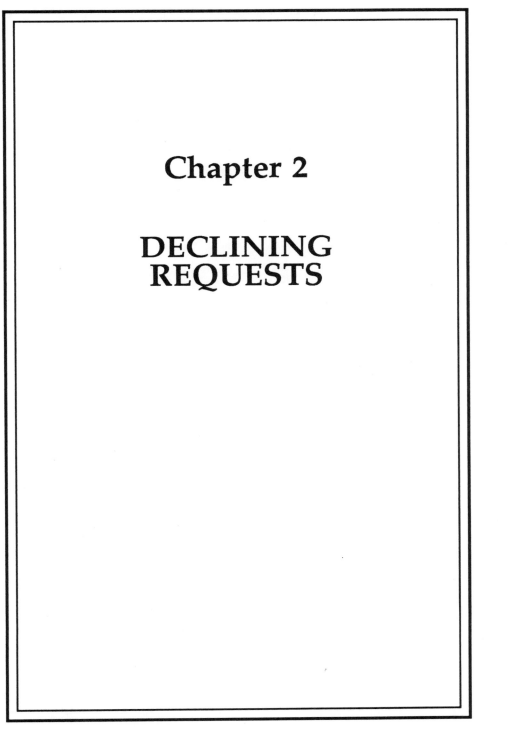

Chapter 2

DECLINING REQUESTS

It is difficult to refuse or say "no." The key to the successful "no" is tact. In a letter of refusal, the goodwill of the reader must be retained, and if the letter is tactfully written, the reader's disappointment will be lessened.

A customer receiving a flat "no" to a request for an adjustment will often not complain: he will quietly take his business elsewhere. The customer has bought a product or service and now asks for an adjustment. He or she receives a rejection. The disappointment that started with the unsatisfactory product or service deepens into distrust and then anger. This lost goodwill must be salvaged. The writer's task is to explain the rejection in a tactful way and to offer an alternative. He or she must combine the refusal with help for the customer. This will not please the customer all of the time, but the chances of alienating the customer all of the time are considerably lessened.

One good way to start a letter of refusal is to agree with the reader on some point. This establishes a feeling of working together as opposed to an "I'm-right-you're-wrong" confrontation. For example:

> We agree that a watch running only part of the time is useless.

Another recommended opening statement is a thank you. This sets a tone of courtesy, pleasantness, and consideration for the reader. An example:

> Thank you for your recent letter requesting a donation to the Redwood Girl's Club.

A combination of agreement and apology is a third introduction to model refusal letters. The message to be conveyed is that "we would like to help, but we can't." The use of this opening requires a reasonable and sincere explanation of why the request is refused. A strong alternative suggestion for obtaining help should follow the apologetic opening as in this example:

> We wish it were possible to provide door prizes for your second annual meeting . . . Perhaps we can help by advertising it in our store window.

After letting the reader know that you are aware of his or her request and have considered it from the reader's point of view, explain the reason for the refusal. Explain the refusal before making it. This takes the sharp edge off the refusal, and prepares the reader for the disappointment which, to some extent, all refusals bring. The statements, "It is not company policy," or "For various reasons we cannot comply," are only slightly better than completely ignoring the request. If it is not company policy, the reader would like to know why it is not company policy. Perhaps it is that "Children under 12 years of age are not allowed to visit our plant because the safety hazards are too great to be covered by a reasonable insurance premium, " or "We cannot continue in business if we extend our free delivery policy to purchases under $100." A request for credit may be refused because of lack of information or not meeting certain qualifications. A request for a contribution may be denied because of lack of budgeted funds. Company procedures may not provide the data requested. A job applicant may be rejected because there is no opening, he or she is underqualified, or overqualified. A pamphlet may be out of print. A request for a refund may be turned down because of an obvious condition excluded by the warranty. Whatever is being refused, the explanation to the reader must be straightforward, definite, and reasonable.

The next step is to state the refusal. The reader has been prepared by the explanation, and there is no reason to smother the refusal in a barrage of words. A few examples:

> I regret that we must decline this opportunity to help the Girls Club.

> I am sorry to inform you that we cannot supply the information requested.

> We hate to say "No" to your credit application but we do not have enough information to say "Yes."

Because the ending of a letter is the most emphatic position, a tactful letter of refusal should end on a positive or upbeat note. Consideration for the reader suggests that a sincere effort to offer at least some help or encouragement would be appropriate in offsetting the unavoidable disappointment. This helps the reader to save face, gives him or her an out, offers an alternative course of action, and reinflates the reader's ego. Closing statements like the following are encouraged:

We wish you great success.

We are interested in your business venture.

Please keep us in mind for other ideas you may develop.

Many adjectives can be used to describe the proper tone of a letter refusing a request, but they are all brought together when the writer uses the persuasive power of a soft denial.

How to Do It

1. Agree on some point with the reader or offer thanks for the reader's interest.
2. Present reasons for the refusal.
3. State the refusal.
4. Offer a suggestion or an alternative that will help the reader.

Begin by Agreeing

Here are some agreeable beginnings for a letter of refusal:

As you requested, we are enclosing a tally of the monthly purchases you made during 19__.

Your Junior Chamber of Commerce *Sports Annual* is a commendable project.

A copy of the first quarter 19__ issue of *Semiconductor Science* is being mailed to you today.

We like your approach to the consumer survey on garden tools.

Your questions are most interesting.

Begin with a Thank-You

Using a thank-you is another good way to start a letter of refusal:

Thank you for your recent request for a charge account at Liberty House.

Your enlightening comments on our Direct Mail selling series of letters are greatly appreciated.

Thank you very much for giving us the opportunity to consider you for employment.

Thank you for your interest in Inland Steel.

We are pleased that you thought of us as a source of information.

We appreciate your asking us to participate in your August meeting.

Begin with an Agreement and Apology

Agreeing with the reader while at the same time apologizing for not granting a request is a third beginning for a letter of refusal:

We would be happy to comply with your request for a sample of our new loan forms. May I suggest you write directly to our headquarters office.

We would like to grant your request for a copy of our booklet *Animal Husbandry* but our supply has been exhausted. More will be available next year. To help you now, may we suggest you write to the Superintendent of Documents in Washington, D.C. asking for publications on this subject.

We are sorry to learn that the paint work on your car was not to your satisfaction. I have talked to Bob Anderson and he suggests you bring your car in next Saturday for a complete inspection.

Statements of Refusal

Direct but polite statements of refusal include these:

At present, however, your financial condition does not quite meet Barrow's requirement.

He believes that meeting would not be helpful.

We do not have a position open that fits your qualifications.

I am sorry that we cannot accept the chairs for credit.

I am sorry we cannot provide the information you requested.

We hate to decline granting you credit but we need additional information from you.

We regret declining this opportunity to help the Bay Area Youth Council.

I am sorry we cannot grant your request.

Close with Encouragement

A statement of encouragement for the reader is an effective goodwill gesture to offset the natural disappointment of a refusal. Some examples:

Thank you for thinking of Carl & Henderson.

I know you will find a suitable position soon.

I believe the Abbott Company could give you more detailed information.

Have you thought of asking Tom Anderson?

We will be glad to receive other ideas from you.

We are interested in your proposed new business.

We wish you great success.

We wish you continued success.

INVITATIONS

An acceptable declination of an invitation includes three important points. The first is brevity. Long explanations turn into excuses that become confused and hard to believe. The second is a polite thank-you for the invitation. Let the inviter know you are pleased to have been considered worthy of an invitation. The third is a plausible reason for not accepting—a reason that is believable by the person you are refusing.

Invitation to Dinner

Dear Andy,

Thank you for your personal invitation to attend the Old School dinner meeting on October 22. I regret that only yesterday I accepted an invitation to a meeting with a business group to which I have belonged for the past few years. Perhaps I can join you and our Old School gang next year. Thanks again for your invitation.

Sincerely,

Invitation to Speak

Dear Jon Larson,

Thank you for your invitation to speak before your fund-raising committee about our success last year. Unfortunately, I have been scheduled to lead our sales meeting in Atlanta that week. I would have enjoyed discussing our problems, solutions, and eventual success of last year's campaign. Perhaps Ron Lentler can help you. He was involved in all the details and could offer many suggestions. I sincerely appreciate your asking me.

With regards,

Join a Group

Dear Mr. Adams:

I appreciate your asking me to join the Morgan Hill Toastmasters. I was a member of the Toastmasters a number of years ago but dropped out because of conflicts with my tax work.

I am new in town, am buying a new house, and have a new job. With all this piling up on me, I don't believe I could do my fair share as a participating member.

I will keep your kind invitation in mind, and hope to join you at a later date. Thank you for asking me.

Sincerely,

Dear Mr. Rogers:

Thank you for inviting me to join the Delta Cost Accountants group. I am sure the monthly meeting to discuss mutual problems and solutions would be most helpful.

I have been on the job here for only four weeks and am up to my ears learning the job and clearing up the backlog of work. I would like, therefore, to decline your invitation at this time. After another year, please contact me again. I think the group is an excellent idea.

Sincerely,

Victory Celebration

Dear Joan,

Thank you for your invitation to Dan and me to celebrate the Viking's conference victory at your house.

If we had not promised the AOPI sorority that we would chaperone their ski club that day, we would be there.

Sincerely,

Football Game

Dear Bob,

I am sorry Barbara and I cannot attend the Cal-Stanford big game with you this year. We have a previous commitment in Los Angeles that weekend, but I will have the radio tuned in. I am sure you can find another couple to share the excitement and tickets you won.

Again, we appreciate your thoughtfulness.

Sincerely,

REQUEST FOR INFORMATION OR MATERIAL

Refusing a request for information, of whatever nature, should be done politely. The request may be inconvenient or seem useless or silly to the receiver of the request, but the fact that the requester has gone to the trouble to single out one company or person indicates that the request is of importance to the person making it. Respect for and a show of interest in the person asking for information can go a long way toward building goodwill for the organization or person answering the request—or refusing the request.

Information Not Available

Dear Mr. Newton:

At the present time, Tractor Mechanics, Inc. does not have an accounting system program for its members, but we did in the past and would certainly recommend it for your review. If you are interested, contact Mr. Robert Strong at Menson Accounting Systems. Their address is 000 Wescott Way, Portland, MA 00000.

We are in the process of compiling the type of data you requested. Initially, this information will be made available only to those who participated in the survey. It is hoped that the survey will be completed by the end of the year.

Sincerely,

Dear Ms. Darlington:

We are enclosing a tally of the monthly purchases you made during 19__. We are sorry we cannot provide details of the monthly totals, but our accounting system does not retain itemized purchases beyond one month.

I am sorry the information is not as complete as you asked for, but I hope it will be of some help to you.

Sincerely,

Item Not Available

Dear Mr. Johnston:

We would be happy to comply with your request for a sample letter asking for contributions. However, Honourman Medical Center has just now received its full tax-exempt status, making us eligible for tax-deductible donations. Because we were not tax-exempt until now, we have not had an active fund-raising program and are only now reaching the final stage of our plans.

I would suggest that you contact Mr. George Appleton, Foundation Director, Boulder River Hospital, for sample letters. Boulder River has had an established and active fund-raising program for several years and could provide you with several examples. The address is: 111 Round Plaza, Boulder, California 00000.

If I may be of further assistance, please let me know.

Sincerely,

Dear Miss Conrad:

We would like to grant your request for twenty-five copies of our booklet, *Live Oak Tree Diseases*, but we have run out and will not print any more this year.

To help you now, we suggest that you write to the Superintendent of Documents, Washington, D.C. and ask for publications on this topic.

Cordially,

Dear Professor Roland:

Your enlightening comments on our series of sales letters are greatly appreciated. We plan to use many of your suggestions as we continue the series.

This series was planned for a list of advertisers with only a few allocated to instructional institutions. The value of these letters as teaching material rather surprised us. We therefore do not have available the number of copies you requested, but two copies have been mailed to you today. Perhaps you can circulate these or make copies for your students.

After using these letters in class, we would appreciate your views on how to improve them for use as teaching material.

Very Sincerely,

Dear Mr. Woodward:

I have read your letter requesting copies of drawings for the Number 5543 Ward Press. I am sorry we no longer have these drawings.

I would suggest you contact Mr. Leonard Brown, Managing Director, Society of Historical Businesses, 000 - 15th Street, Washington, D.C. 00000. His telephone number is 000-000-0000.

The Society has many drawings of machinery manufactured in the 1800s.

Sincerely,

APPLICATION FOR PERSONAL CREDIT

Always show an interest in the person applying for credit. Even if credit is refused now, potential future sales should never be overlooked. Let the customer know that thorough consideration was given to the application. Then state the reasons for refusal, clearly but politely. End with the fact that cash purchases or layaway plans are available or that credit will probably be available later.

Lack of Information

Dear Mr. Ames:

Thank you for your interest in Rankin's and your request for a line of credit.

Based on the information you supplied us and that from our normal sources, we are unable to grant you the open credit you requested. If you can supply us with additional references, however, and current financial statements, please do so, and we will be happy to reconsider our disappointing decision.

While waiting for this additional information we will welcome any orders accompanied by a cash payment.

Sincerely,

Dear Mrs. Lawn:

Thank you for requesting a Capper's charge account. We appreciate this expression of your goodwill.

As you probably know, a routine credit investigation is the usual procedure before new accounts are opened. Since the available information in support of your credit application is incomplete, we shall appreciate your assistance.

When you have a convenient moment, will you please call at the Credit Office on the second floor? No doubt you can furnish the information we need to reconsider your request.

We are looking forward to talking with you, and welcome this opportunity to meet you personally.

Yours sincerely,

Lack of Work Record

Dear Ms. Alward:

We appreciate your interest in Bowen's Department Store and your application for a credit card.

Your lack of a permanent work record at this time prevents us from approving your application. Your part-time work references are good, and as soon as you establish a permanent work record, we will be happy to reconsider granting you credit.

Sincerely,

Short Employment

Dear Ms. Lindstrom:

Thank you for your recent application for a charge account at Fordham's. Your application has received careful consideration and we find the information furnished by you does not meet our requirements for granting credit. Perhaps in the future, when circumstances have changed, we can again consider your request for a charge account. Our decision is based on the following reasons:

Length of employment
No credit file

I regret we could not be more helpful at this time. Meanwhile, our quality selections are available for cash, and you can take advantage of our layaway service.

Sincerely,

Slow Pay

Dear Mr. Snowden:

Thank you for your credit application. We appreciate your interest in Abbott's.

For your own protection, however, we feel that your credit approval should be delayed for another six months. By then you should have less difficulty making prompt payments on your open accounts.

Until then, remember that cash purchases have no monthly interest charge.

Please contact us again in February.

Sincerely,

New in Area

Dear Mr. Lawrence:

Thank you for your interest in Matson's Department Store and your request for a credit account.

We notice that you have been in this area only a few weeks and have just begun to work here. When you have lived and worked here a little longer and have established a bank account, we will be happy to review your application. We hope to open a credit account for you when you apply again in another two months.

In the meantime, please take advantage of our Annual Sale next month. We carry many lines of quality merchandise, and are especially proud of our men's shop.

Please let us hear from you again.

Sincerely,

Dear Mrs. Ballard:

Thank you for your recent request for a charge account at Ford's. Your confidence in our store is appreciated.

Although we are not in a position to open an account for you just now, perhaps we will be able to do so when your residency has been established for another six months.

Meanwhile, please visit us often and enjoy the many conveniences of shopping at Ford's. Every effort will be made to serve you well.

Sincerely,

Current Information Lacking

Dear Ms. Esthers:

We appreciate your request for a Golden credit card.

It is a standard procedure with all companies issuing credit cards to check on the applicant's past payment record. We have found that you usually require more time to pay than our 25-day terms allow.

If we have not received current information, perhaps you could furnish us with the names of two or three firms from which you are now buying on credit. We will be happy then to reconsider your request for a credit card.

Meanwhile, we find that more and more of our customers prefer to pay cash and thereby avoid the high cost of interest on unpaid balances.

Sincerely,

APPLICATION FOR BUSINESS CREDIT

Future business must not be lost when refusing business credit. Be appreciative of the applicant's request. State any favorable elements in the application before explaining clearly the reasons for refusal. End with encouragement and suggestions that he or she may use to qualify in the future.

Financial Condition

Dear Mr. Colson:

Thank you for your application for credit at Barrow's. We appreciate your interest.

Your personal references are exceptionally good, and your record of hard work indicates that your business prospects are good for the near future. At present, however, your financial condition only partially meets Barrow's requirements. Therefore, we cannot extend the $5000 open credit you requested.

Please come in and talk to me at your convenience. I am sure we can set up a program of gradually increasing credit that will benefit both of us. Meanwhile, remember that deliveries on cash purchases are made within two days.

Let me hear from you soon. We are interested in your business venture.

Sincerely,

Credit Limited

Dear Mr. Snelling,

We appreciate receiving your order of January 29 for 50,000 boxes.

This is our slack season and we would like to receive several orders of this size. However, you have been in business only since October, and we feel that until we have had a little more experience with you, your open line of credit should be limited to $5000. This limit can be raised as your business improves and expands.

We hope this is satisfactory as a starter, and we thank you for the opportunity to be of service to you.

Sincerely,

Company Procedure—Late Payment

Dear Ms. Arthur:

We received the copy of the past due freight bill No. 278-089799 that you sent Wednesday, November 21. We have matched it with our purchase order and will mail it today to Central Freight Payment, Inc. in Atlanta, Georgia for payment.

Although the bill is overdue because we did not receive the original bill, our corporate procedure requires that Central Freight pay the bill. This procedure speeds payment in practically all instances and includes an audit of all paid freight bills. We cannot write you a check from our local plant as you have requested.

We are sorry for the delay. You should have your money in less than a week.

Sincerely,

Guarantor Needed

Dear Mr. Almond:

We greatly appreciate the order you gave our Mr. Robbins. You will find that we have reason to be proud of our quality products.

We want to work with you and help you get established, but from the information we have been able to gather, you appear to be undercapitalized, which would make it difficult for you to meet payments on our terms.

One temporary solution we might suggest is for you to find a person or firm that would guarantee your open account with us. We have found this arrangement to work well with other customers until they become established. This could take care of your immediate needs. Later, we can work together on other arrangements.

Please let us hear from you soon.

Sincerely,

Previous Poor Pay

Dear Mr. Pappas:

It is pleasing to learn that you are still interested in Allen's high quality tools. We received your order on October 22.

You may recall that when you last purchased goods from us, we had a difficult time getting payment from you. In fact, some of your account was turned over to Dun & Bradstreet's collection department.

We realize, however, that times and conditions change, and we should probably not be concerned. To relieve the concern we do have, please send us a few current credit references and a recent statement of your financial condition.

If you are in a rush for the tools you ordered, please send us a check for $928.50. We still maintain the prompt delivery service you are familiar with.

Thank you for considering us again, and we hope to hear from you soon.

Cordially,

Bad Risk

Note that this letter follows an outline nearly the reverse of that suggested in the **How to Do It** section.

Dear Mr. Bankhead:

I am being completely honest when I say that many of our customers prefer to pay cash. This relieves them of any anxiety about having to make late payment charges. I would like to suggest this method to you, because, as hard as I have tried, I just can't find a way to add you to our list of credit customers at this time.

The information we have gathered indicates that your payments have consistently been getting further and further behind during the past year. This may have been a bad year for you, but we cannot see adding to your outstanding debts. We hope that conditions soon improve for you.

We do, however, appreciate your considering us as a supplier. We will be most happy to do business with you on a cash-with-order-basis. You will find both our service and products outstanding.

Sincerely,

Bad Risk—No Hope

Dear Mr. Blair:

We appreciate your interest in Sampson's and your desire to establish credit with us.

However, based upon reports from our numerous sources of credit information, we can make shipments to you only when cash is received with the order.

We are sorry for this, but we are sure you understand. If we can be of any further service to you, please let us know.

Sincerely,

Franchise Refused

Dear Mr. Goodall:

We greatly appreciate your interest in obtaining an American Chicken franchise. Our present expansion rate exceeds our most optimistic expectations.

We, of course, make credit checks on all potential franchisers, and our information indicates that you might have difficulty meeting our payment terms for merchandise and supplies to be purchased from us. These payment terms must be met as well as those for the expected loan on the purchase price.

Past experience can be temporary, and we hope your financial condition improves soon. Perhaps we can review another application from you in the near future.

Sincerely,

Will Not Change Prior Understanding

Dear Mr. Donaldson:

We are very sorry to learn of your unsatisfactory experience with our Mr. Hanson's letters, but the bearings that we manufactured and delivered to you in Waterford became your property.

When Mr. Hanson and I visited you on February 17, 19__, there was no question that these bearings were left on consignment at your Waterford warehouse until 19__ and were used at that time by your customer, Central Trailer. The only unanswered question on your part was the problem of your pending bankruptcy and when you would be able to settle all the outstanding items. This was stated in your letter of February 24, 19__.

As far as we are concerned, Mr. Donaldson, these bearings were purchased by you and used by your customer. Our position has not changed, and this invoice, No. 43332, in the amount of $3,459.90, is still outstanding.

Sincerely,

Credit Information Available Elsewhere

Dear Mr. Bagley:

Referring to your letter of May 25, 19__, if you phone Mr. Apply at our Billings, Montana plant (000-000-0000) he will be able to give you general information about our credit experience with Zenno Corporation. He has credit responsibility for that account.

It is our policy not to provide written information about our customers. However, I am sure Mr. Apply can help you.

Sincerely,

DONATION

Start this type of refusal with a thank-you, apology, or complimentary statement about the organization or event you are asked to help. Offer a plausible reason for the refusal, and end with alternative help or at least best wishes for success.

Funds Limited

Dear Mrs. Alberts:

I am sorry I cannot contribute to the Children's Fund this year.

I am involved in several charities, including some for disadvantaged children. Your needs are real, I recognize, but my funds are limited and I have to make my own choice about the distribution of those funds.

I wish you well on your program to help these children.

Sincerely,

Use of Name in Fund Raising

Dear Mrs. Lansing:

Please accept my sincere regrets for having to decline the use of my name as a sponsor of Belmont Boys Home. I feel a little insincere about sponsoring something I am not actively involved in. I work with a number of charities now and just don't have the time to consider any more at present.

Your cause is worthy, I know, and I wish you well in your endeavor to obtain prominent names for your sponsor's list. Thank you for asking me.

Sincerely,

Company Policy

Dear Ms. Wells:

Thank you for your recent letter requesting a donation to the Redwood Girls Club. In a company like ours, with fifty-five divisions throughout the country, it is impossible to support the many worthy causes in each area. Instead, the company makes an annual contribution to the United Way Fund, which in turn sponsors many organizations.

I am sorry to have to tell you that because of this policy we are unable to contribute locally to the Redwood Girls Club. It is a fine project, and we wish you great success.

Cordially yours,

Dear Mr. Sundston:

We wish it were possible to provide door prizes for your fund raising meeting. Your cause is commendable. We find, however, that as a national company, we are asked quite often for donations of merchandise for worthy organizations. We feel that if we give to one good cause, we should give equally to all good causes. I am sure you recognize that this is not practical, and therefore we do not make door prizes available.

Perhaps we can help in another way: by advertising in our store window or preparing an advertisement for the newspaper. Let us know if we can help in this way.

Sincerely,

Budget Limitation

Dear Mr. Bates:

Your Junior Chamber of Commerce *Sports Annual* is a commendable project. We do budget for special advertising, but unfortunately, the money has been spent for this year. I am sure you can understand that we must operate by our budget to stay in business.

If you plan to make this publication an annual event, contact us earlier next year. We will try to consider you in next year's budget. The Junior Chamber of Commerce will receive our full help and cooperation.

Sincerely,

Disagree with Charity Project

Dear Ms. Eggmont:

I agree that St. John's University is badly in need of a new gym. I think, however, that this is an inappropriate time to request contributions for a building fund. The basketball team has not won a local conference championship in twelve years. I recognize that the gym is used for many activities besides basketball, but basketball is all the public hears about—and they haven't heard much about that in recent years.

When the team has won a local conference championship and a state championship and is headed for a national meet—then you can go to an enthusiastic public and meet little resistance. Big donors will also give more willingly at that time. Everyone loves a winner.

This may seem an unkind attitude toward a school in need of a new gym, but I feel a team must earn its right to a new facility. Best wishes for success in your campaign.

Sincerely,

CUSTOMER ADJUSTMENTS

Customer adjustments must be made with tact. It is difficult to refuse the customer's request while retaining his or her goodwill. Open with something agreeable, a point you can agree upon or a thank-you for letting you explain your point of view. The explanation that follows must be clear and definite but not curt. Take enough time and space to make a complete and logical explanation. Completeness is important to the reader. Then let the reader know what he or she can do, or what you will do to make an adjustment satisfactory to the reader.

Damaged Product

Dear Miss Gerald:

We agree that a watch running only part of the time is useless. And we guarantee trouble-free operation of Serra watches for a year from the purchase date.

Your watch has been thoroughly examined by our service department. They report a dent near the winding stem, perhaps too small for you to have noticed. This indicates physical damage to the case which is not covered by our guarantee. The dent is deep enough to touch the main spring regulator when it expands in warm weather. This can cause the occasional stopping of the watch.

Although not covered by our guarantee, we can repair your watch at factory cost and extend the warranty for a year from the repair date. The cost to you is only $15.00.

If you wish to have the repairs made, please return the enclosed card and attach your check for $15.00. We will repair your watch and return it promptly.

Sincerely,

Cash Discount

Dear Mr. Allsworth:

Thank you for your letter of February 28. You asked about our billing you for the 1 percent cash discount you took with your payment on February 17.

As you know, our terms for several years have been 1 percent 10 days, net 30 days. We offer these terms because we save interest on borrowed capital when we receive cash within 10 days. This is a savings we can pass on to our customers, but we have no savings to pass on when payment is received after the 10-day period.

The dollar amount involved in this case is small, only $32.10, but when multiplied by the number of our customers, the total is significant.

Our policy has always been to treat all customers equally, with discounts as well as service and reliable merchandise. I hope that you will see the consistent fairness in our bill for $32.10, and that we can both benefit from our 1 percent 10-day cash discount policy.

Sincerely,

Special Product

Dear Mr. Mills:

Your memo requesting credit for the gear housing we made for you in October has been given to me by our sales engineer.

Although we realize that machinery rebuilding plans are sometimes changed at levels above that of the purchasing agent, we are sorry we cannot accept the gear housing for credit. It was cast to your specifications and there is no market for it among our other customers.

If we do get an inquiry for this type of casting we will get in touch with you immediately. I'm sorry we can't do more for you.

Cordially,

Poor Workmanship

Dear Mr. Wilson:

We are sorry to learn that your application of Thickwall to your house was not completely to your satisfaction.

Applying Thickwall is a specialized job, and that is why we request all our dealers to make this part of our warranty clear to each customer. Mr. Bob Johnson, salesman at your dealer, Appley Building Supplies, recommended application by John Sanders, a specialist who works with Appley Building Supplies. Our warranty states clearly that Thickwall must be applied by a specialist.

I have talked to Bob Johnson and he suggests that John Sanders inspect your house and make recommendations for correcting the work. Mr. Sanders can then make the necessary repairs at a reasonable cost or perhaps suggest how you can make the repairs yourself.

Please talk to Bob Johnson at Appley Building Supplies. I am sure you can work out a satisfactory arrangement for getting the application of Thickwall corrected.

Sincerely,

Slow-Selling Product

Dear Mr. Lunsford:

Thank you for writing us about the Country Gentleman chairs you purchased on September 3, and wish to return for credit.

These are the chairs you ordered. In fact, you paid for them early and took our 2 percent cash discount.

As I understand the situation, you wish to return them because of slow sales. I am sorry that we cannot accept the chairs for credit. We discontinued this line six months ago, but most of our dealers found them to be good sellers during the winter promotion we sponsored. We are sending you additional promotional material and ideas that proved successful with others. If there is anything else we can do to help you sell these chairs, please let our salesman, John Ballard, know. He will be calling on you next month, and will have some helpful suggestions.

With regards,

OTHER LETTERS OF DECLINATION

The following letters cover a variety of refusals, from sample letters to a church volunteer. They follow the general outline: agreeing with the writer or showing appreciation for the writer's interest, offering a plausible reason for refusing, and ending with an alternative or expression of goodwill.

Untested Sample Letters

Dear Mr. Adams:

We have received your request for sample fund-raising letters.

Even though Emerson Society has had an ongoing development program for several years, it is only recently that we have developed direct mail fund-raising letters. Since these letters have not been thoroughly tested in terms of response, I would be reluctant to offer them as teaching material.

Thank you for your interest.

Sincerely,

Special Assignment

Dear Mr. Wilshire:

I deeply regret the amount of time that has passed before responding to your letter of November 26, 19__.

After careful consideration and the exploration of some possibilities, I find that we cannot handle this particular assignment.

Please accept my best wishes for your success in this endeavor.

Sincerely yours,

Business Meeting—Unnecessary

My Dear Mr. Ames:

Mr. Sanders has carefully considered your request for a meeting to discuss a change in your property settlement. If a personal meeting would be of benefit to you, he would be happy to arrange an appointment. He has asked me to write and tell you that he believes another meeting at this time would not be of any help to you.

With regards,

Magazine Subscribers Limited

Dear Mr. Ludwig:

A copy of the first quarter 19__ issue of *Semiconductor Science* is being mailed to you. Please accept it with our compliments.

Your interest in our publication is appreciated, but we discourage subscription by those who are not directly engaged in the production of semiconductors. This quarterly manual is highly technical and expensive to produce. We find that those outside the industry do not continue their subscriptions, and this makes the printing difficult to schedule and unduly costly.

I am sure you understand our position, and we sincerely thank you for your interest in *Semiconductor Science*.

Sincerely yours,

Publication—Too Specialized

Dear Mr. Saunders:

Thank you very much for giving us the opportunity of considering your manuscript, "Tombs of Egypt."

We regret that we cannot extend publishing interest in your material because it is too specialized to fit into our present publishing program.

We wish you success in finding the right publishing house for your work and do appreciate your thinking of Wilson Publishers.

Sincerely,

Publication—Editorial Program

Dear Mr. Smythe:

Thank you very much for inquiring about Wilson Publishers' possible interest in you proposal for a textbook: *Essentials of Psychology*.

I very much regret that we must decline the opportunity to publish this interesting work. Our editorial program is, unfortunately, unable to accept an addition of this kind.

Please understand that this response to your idea is the reaction of only one company. Opinions vary widely among publishers, and I hope you will continue to develop your material towards a successful publication. I also ask you to keep Wilson Publishers in mind for any other textbook ideas you may have.

Sincerely,

Publication—Needs Reworking

Dear Professor Nelson:

Enclosed are three reviews of your proposed *Cost Accounting* text. I share them with you for the benefit of the text's development.

Based on the reviews, you have the basis for a fine text. While the concept of a brief book is sound, it is my opinion that it does not go far enough, which limits the value and marketability of the text.

Should you be willing to expand the text's coverage and appeal, I would be pleased to reconsider the text for publication. I would also appreciate receiving more information on how your text would compare to existing competing books.

Cordially,

Refusing a Volunteer

Dear Ms. Lester,

We appreciate very much your volunteering to head the Junior Youth Fellowship for the coming year. Looking at the overall program, however, we believe you could serve the church better working with Mrs. Holbrook and the Senior Youth Fellowship. She is in need of someone with your background and willingness.

We hope you will consider working with Mrs. Holbrook. The Seniors need your helping hands.

Yours in Christ,

Freight Claim

Gentlemen:

Please refer to your Claim No. 00000:

Our records show your bill of lading 0000 signed August 29, 19__. Your claim is dated June 20, 19__.

Section 2(b) of the Bill of Lading Contract Terms and Conditions requires that claims be filed in writing within nine months from the date of delivery or, in case of failure to make delivery, within nine months after a reasonable time for delivery has passed.

We are sorry we cannot honor your claim. We have checked all possible sources for a prior filing, and can find no record of an earlier claim related to this shipment.

If, however, you can provide proof of an earlier filing, we will be happy to reconsider your claim.

Sincerely,

Miscellaneous Request

Dear Mr. Walkup:

In reply to your recent letter, while we wish you success with your project, we must decline the opportunity to participate.

We appreciate your interest in Smith Company, Inc.

Sincerely,

Dear Mr. Stofer:

Your letter of March 3 has been referred to me.

In the past, we would have been pleased to accommodate your request. However, due to the increasing volume of inquiries from governments, universities, and other parties, plus requests for data not readily available through our current reporting network, we regret we have found it necessary to discontinue discretionary reporting services. Your understanding of our situation is appreciated.

Thank you for thinking of National Plumbing Contractors.

Sincerely,

Financial Aid

Dear Mr. Ohlsen:

Thank you for your letter describing the need of Sandia Youth Homes. I am sorry that we will be unable to assist you at this time with your farm project. I would, however, be interested in hearing more about the vocational training program which you mentioned.

I am enclosing a copy of our Grace Foundation annual report which includes our guidelines for financial assistance proposals. I think it will be helpful to you in sending us more information on your program.

Our next cutoff date for new proposals is June 30. The board meeting is scheduled for the early part of September.

If you have any questions after looking at our guidelines, please do give me a call. I hope everything is going well with you and the boys and girls, and I wish you success with your farm project.

Sincerely,

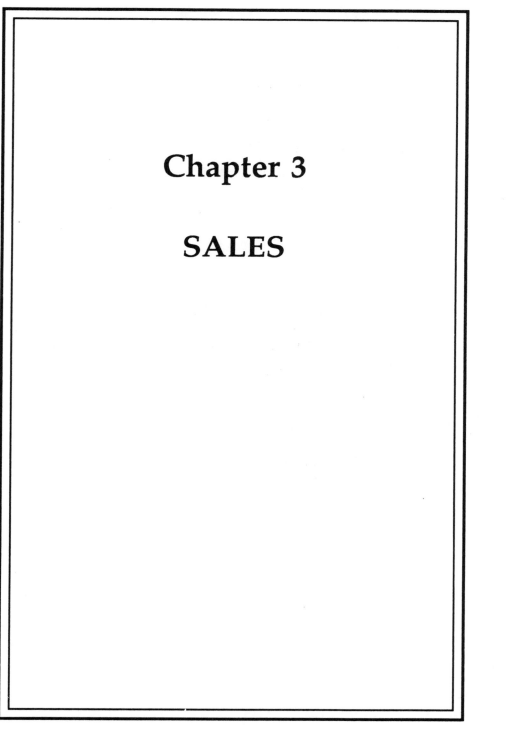

Chapter 3

SALES

$\mathbf{A}$ sales letter is only one of many factors in the sale of a product or service. A need must exist—or be imagined; the customer's interest must be aroused and a choice must be made among competing sales-persons and products. A sales letter probably won't accomplish all these things, but it can persuade the reader that he or she will be helped by buying the product or service.

One technique for persuasion is to use POWER words. Using words to make people DO things is the key to business success. Listed here is a sampling of power words, effective in pepping up a sales letter:

able	free	powerful
absolute	great	professional
advantage	guarantee	proved
brilliant	hard-sell	quality
confidence	help	quickly
controlled	immediate	results
delighted	impelling	satisfaction
detail	insight	scientific
different	instant	solved
economical	know	stunning
effective	largest	successful
electronic	latest	super
emphasis	lowest cost	today
expert	money-making	tremendous
extensive	new	value
fact	now	volume
fair	oldest	you
flare	persuasive	yours

As will be observed in the models, sales letters also take advantage of visual aids. These include such devices as CAPITAL LETTERS, "quotation marks," underlined words, dashes—, dots..., short paragraphs, phrases tuated as sentences, indented paragraphs, exclamation points, and postscripts.

The purpose is to hold the attention of the reader, who, thus becomes eager to read on to find out what is interesting enough to deserve this special presentation.

Insurance sales letters and advertisements often emphasize fear—fear of what *could* happen—so you had better be prepared with *our* insurance coverage. Fear is one basic appeal. Other basic appeals, which are general themes or topics running through the letter, include love, pride, greed, ambition, sex, hate, and loyalty. An emotional appeal is usually more effective than an intellectual presentation.

A word of caution when appealing to these various emotional feelings; don't belittle the reader, exaggerate, trick the reader, be flippant, or abuse competitors. A little puffing of your item or service is good, but respect the intelligence of your reader.

However intelligent the reader, he or she has a limited attention span. Cover only a few selling points in each letter (or preferably only one). Trying to tell everything only confuses the reader.

What you say should be directed toward the audience you have chosen. Sell an elitist magazine to college educated people, sell farming equipment to ranchers, sell wrenches to mechanics. Your audience can be targeted geographically down to specific postal Zip Code numbers.

The reader will want to know *why* he or she should buy; not what the product or service can do, but what it will do *for the reader*. This statement can be strengthened by a guarantee. Present a testimonial from a well-known person, offer a free trial period or a money-back guarantee. Let the reader know you are interested in his or her welfare.

The proper length of a sales letter is debatable. One theory is that no one reads past the first page, so don't make it any longer. Another theory is that if the first page gets the reader's attention, the fourth page will clinch the sale. One standard suggestion is to tell the story and then stop, regardless of length. Another standard is to tell only enough to make the reader ask for more information. The proper length, in the final analysis, will be determined by the writer's best judgment of the presentation to which the majority of the selected readers will respond.

Selling the reader must begin with a strong statement of interest to your particular audience, be he or she a druggist, accountant, housewife, business executive, dog lover, or doctor. Also, the first sentence must relate to the statements that follow.

There are many types of attention-getting opening sentences:

— Reference to a previous personal contact
— A sentence encompassing who, what, when, where, why
— A question
— An unusual remark
— A story
— Invoking a well-known personality
— A well-known quotation
— Using the reader's name (if not obviously inserted into a blank space that doesn't fit the name)
— Use of gimmicks, such as enclosing a stamp, pencil, or address labels; or a question on the envelope that is answered inside

Endings are also important. Having presented your sales story and gotten readers interested, he or she must be moved to action. Tell the reader exactly what to do and when: "Mail the enclosed card today"; "This offer ends June 30"; or "Phone us right now at 888-888-8888." Of most importance, make the action easy: "Phone us toll-free at 800-000-0000"; "Use the enclosed postage-paid envelope"; or "We are open 7 days a week."

When reviewing your written letter, a few checkpoints may be helpful:

— Are sales points presented clearly and simply?
— Are enough *facts* presented to make the letter convincing?
— Are the strong points emphasized in short, two-or-three-line paragraphs?
— Is the appeal enthusiastic? A great salesperson is one who sets into motion the contagious emotion of enthusiasm.

How to Do It

1. Use an effective attention-getting opening.
2. Develop a central selling point.
3. Be vivid and specific in talking up the product.
4. Present proofs of your statements.
5. Close by moving the reader to specific action.

Model Openers

The following are ideas and suggestions for sales letter openers:

It's your money that's involved, and the stakes are HIGH!
Here's an indispensable invention for anyone who . . .

Strength in numbers may be good for the military, but not for the fashion-conscious woman. Barbara's Exclusive Fashions promises what the name implies.

This letter is unlike any we have written before.

Select any three books from the list below. I'll send you two of them *free*.

If you're not sure you want _____, I can understand.

If we have selected our prospects as carefully as we think, you qualify on two accounts.

Have you looked at mountain property and failed to buy because . . . ?

We would like you to select any three important professional books—value to $93—for only 99¢ each.

We nurses can never know enough about IV therapy, can we?

I wonder if you have ever had an experience like this one—

Here are nine hard-sell secrets to triple your advertising results.

This may be your last chance to . . .

You're hard to find, Mr. Anderson.

Levitz has opened a great new store in . . .

Just a little note to say HELLO, and to let you know what's happening at Todd Valley.

A mortgage is a wonderful thing.

You don't know me from Eve.

Today I feel like a salty sailor.

I feel like the flinty old mule skinner.

Has your eye ever been caught by a picture so beautiful you couldn't look away?

Mark Twain once remarked, "Always do right. This will gratify some people and astonish the rest."

The two most abused words in manufacturing sales are *quality* and *service*.

This letter will keep you form being fined . . . severely penalized . . . or deprived of your livelihood under the 19__ Tax Reform Law.

You can well imagine the kind of quandary we are in.

Would you like an estimate of the present value of your home?

The average home is now for sale every three or four years.

You couldn't have chosen a better time to request the enclosed booklet.

I am most grateful to loyal customers like you who have made 19__ the greatest year in our history.

We live in an age where there seems to be a club for just about every purpose you might imagine.

The San Francisco area has long been known for its cosmopolitan tastes.

You probably get a lot of mail like this—and it goes in the round file—but don't be too hasty!

Do you know Socrates' chief attribute? Pertinacious curiosity—and with it he came to represent the highest achievement of Greek civilization. This quest for answers has drawn Zellwell Chemicals into the search for relief from the common cold.

You can buy a Stone's lifetime battery today, next month, or probably ten years from now. But not at our special price of $55.20. That price ends February 28.

Have you ever looked in the mirror in the early morning and said, "There has to be a better way"? We have said that too. And we can help you. Jones Correspondence Courses can prepare you . . .

Did you know that the average person uses a mere 10% of his or her brain power? Why not double that, or even triple it? You can. Our new book tells you how.

So many of us are tired of the day-to-day dull routine of a salaried job. Now you can do something about it! Chicken Little Franchises offers . . .

Too many expenses have doubled in recent months. Why not double your income? Our training course has doubled the salaries of a great many men and women. It can do the same for you.

As chairman of the Board of Trustees, I'd like to personally invite you to . . .

When General Electric calls on us for information, that is something to be proud of.

Wilcox and Associates has changed its name. We thought you might be interested in the story.

Model Closings

Here is a list of suggestions to spark the reader into action:

So do the right thing for yourself—mail the card today.
Your credit is good. Just tell us what you want.

Won't you take advantage of it *now*—to put a quick stop to costly losses?

Save yourself some time. Just initial this letter and return it in the business reply envelope enclosed.

Allen Albright, a fellow you are going to like, will be around Tuesday morning to show you samples and to write your order.

Your copy of this interesting publication is ready for you. Just initial and mail the enclosed card.

Send no money. Simply mail the card.

We take all the risk. You enjoy the food.

This letter is your guarantee. Keep it but send us the card—today.

The enclosed order blank should be mailed immediately.

Do not delay—send the order blank now.

Simply check the card and put it in the mail today.

Remove the coupon below and mail it with your order at once.

Mail your check today in the convenient envelope enclosed.

We've cut all the red tape—simply mail the card.

Break out of the summer slump. Return the order blank right away.

Don't write a letter. The enclosed check-off card is for your convenience.

Before you put it aside, sign and return the card.

Just sign the card and have your secretary mail it promptly.

Our supply is limited. Act now!

Send no money. If not satisfied, don't pay.

There are no strings attached to this offer. It is simple. Just mail the enclosed, postpaid card.

Put the card in the mail to start the ball rolling.

It's your move. Telegraph orders are filled overnight.

If for any reason you're dissatisfied, simply return . . . and owe absolutely nothing.

When it comes to service, ABC Corporation produces results.

We will be happy to assist you. Please give us a call.

Investment—Real Estate

Dear Friend:

Although their incomes have climbed during the passing years, many people today are living beyond their means. Some try to help themselves by taking on extra work, but there is a limit to what a person can earn in an eight- or even twelve-hour day.

An excellent solution is to make a sound investment that will provide enough READY CASH for increasing future needs. Listed below are a few of the more popular types of investments:

STOCK MARKET	Considered somewhat unstable, a speculation on the general economy
SAVINGS BANKS	Yields up to __% annually: the bank then often takes YOUR money and invests it in Real Estate
REAL ESTATE	One of the safest, surest investments that can offer substantial profits if the following rules are observed!
1. LOCATION	As close to a MAJOR CITY as possible
2. POPULATION	City requires a past and present history of growth
3. HIGH GRADE PROPERTY	Not desert or swamp, but good, usable land
4. UTILITIES	Water, roads, electricity, gas, phones
5. PRICED RIGHT	Buy UNDER comparable land prices, if possible

We would like the opportunity to prove to you that even as little as $__ monthly may bring substantial returns over the years. Billions have been made with land located in the path of progress. In these days of high taxes, the opportunity *to keep big profits* is due to the many favorable tax concessions allowable in Real Estate.

Mailing the enclosed card may open your eyes to a new path leading to attractive long-range profit opportunities for you and your family in years to come.

Sincerely,

Business Magazine

Dear Executive:

How does your business compare with similar ones? What are you doing right? What are you doing wrong?

Read the monthly *Business Journal* and know where you stand—and why.

This magazine contains a wealth of information to help you operate more efficiently.

We feature interviews and profiles of business people, your peers—and also your competitors. Are they doing better than you? Why?

Articles about individual businesses reveal successful as well as not so successful policies and strategies. Are you placing too much emphasis on one aspect of your operation and neglecting others to the detriment of the company?

Business Journal keeps you abreast of governmental activities that affect your business, international business opportunities, financial markets, business statistics with special emphasis on trends, political changes and investment strategies.

Business Journal is a monthly magazine with complete economic and business coverage. The competitive advantages of reading this publication are yours for only $30 a year. We have enclosed a copy for you to examine. Do you want to continue in business without being this well informed? Please mail the enclosed card now.

Sincerely,

Magazine—Elitist

Dear Mr. Deskins:

World Journal reveals the influence of the world's best minds on our politics, science, environment, cities, and the couple next door.

Become a part of this intriguing world by learning what the great thinkers are accomplishing.

True, ideas from the world's greatest minds will conflict, but that stimulates other minds—including yours—when you read this exceptional magazine. Even with its sophistication, it is well written and easy to read.

What subjects does *World Journal* embrace? They vary from written portraits of great people and their ideas to what you as an individual can do to improve our environment. The articles and departments cover Books, Art, Poetry, Short Stories, Essays, Commentary, Medicine, Environment, Politics, Humor and the great dissenters who write letters to the editor.

This entertaining and stimulating magazine is yours for only $24 a year. Please mail the enclosed card today. We will bill you later.

Sincerely,

Mortgage Insurance

Dear Mr. Hodges:

A mortgage is a remarkable obligation.

Do you have a mortgage? Most families do. Few families could afford to live in their comfortable homes without a mortgage and its monthly payments spread out for twenty to thirty years.

You are making regular payments from your salary and your family is secure. But what would happen if suddenly you were no longer there? Who would continue the payments? Would the family continue to feel secure?

We have the answers. We can provide you with a simple insurance plan that in the event of your death will pay off the mortgage. Your family can continue living in their home. They can retain their feeling of security.

All this is available for only about one percent of your mortgage annually.

Surprising? Yes.

Simple? Yes.

Your neighborhood representative, Mr. Al Hoerner, will phone you soon to arrange a time to allow you to see how this plan works—how simple it is—and how inexpensive—especially when you consider the potential benefits.

Sincerely,

Homeowner's Insurance

Dear Neighbor:

Your homeowner's insurance is due to be renewed next month. Before you renew, please ask yourself these questions:

IS MY AGENT A NEIGHBOR AND FRIEND?
AM I UNDER INSURED—OR OVER INSURED?
DOES MY COVERAGE MEET MY PARTICULAR NEEDS?
AM I PAYING MORE THAN NECESSARY?

If you are unsure of any of your answers, please call me at 000-0000. You can become better informed with absolutely no obligation.

Sincerely,

Health Insurance

Dear Mrs. Ashland:

Perfect health and never an accident! A wonderful dream, but unreal for most of us.

That is why Total Health Plan was started. If you have no hospitalization insurance or a policy that pays less than $1000 a day, Total Health can help you. Current hospital stays cost closer to $2000 a day, and intensive care can be many times that.

TOTAL HEALTH PLAN PAYS FULL COVERAGE

We do not limit you to 80% of the cost, as many health plans do. When costs go up our payments go up to cover those increases.

Your entire family can receive full coverage, maternity benefits are included, and we cannot refuse your application or cancel your policy—only you can do that. You can count on our being here when you need us because our service has continued uninterrupted since 1931. In support of our financial stability, we are rated A+ (Superior) by A. M. Best Company, an independent insurance analyst.

To introduce you to our plan, just mail the enclosed enrollment form with a check for only $7. When we receive your check, you will be enrolled and covered for 30 days.

Our guarantee: you have those 30 days to read your policy in detail and decide if you wish to continue at our normal rates. If you wish to cancel after 30 days, your $7 will be refunded.

It is your health. We are here to help you keep it. Please mail the enrollment form today—for your peace of mind.

Sincerely,

Dentistry

Dear Mr. French:

Professional dental care is the first step to a lifetime of healthy teeth, overall health, and an appearance you can be proud of.

Doctor Samoto, D.D.S. and I, Doctor Hardwich, D.M.D. are established dental practitioners in this area, having worked as a team in one location for 14 years.

We can do cosmetic dentistry to repair chipped or broken or darkened teeth or to repair unsightly gaps. Small but significant changes in appearance can often be made without anesthesia. We will be happy to discuss in detail how these techniques can be used in your particular case.

Of course we are professionally trained to help you with general dental care including cleaning, cavities, gum care, crowns and the old fashioned toothache.

As part of our service for you, we will obtain your dental records and request from your previous dentist any medical problems or special care you require. This eliminates unnecessary examinations and X-rays.

We have a pleasant office with soft music in the background, a relaxing decor, and tropical fish aquariums for your viewing interest. You will find our staff helpful and friendly.

Sincerely,

Book Club

Dear Reader:

Book club selections still on best-seller lists?

Many of them are when you enroll in the PRIMUS BOOK CLUB. Keep up with what is going on in the world and what your friends are talking about. And the price is right.

For only $10 you can choose three books currently or recently on best-seller lists. If not completely satisfied, return the books and we will refund your $10—OR—you may select another three and retain your membership. You will be pleased to find that PRIMUS BOOK CLUB gives you about 40 percent off the normal retail price.

Every month you will receive a newsletter describing the First Selection and up to 40 other books of current interest. Do nothing to receive the First Selection. If you prefer another title, indicate your preference on the accompanying card and mail it to us. You will have 14 days to make your selection or to notify us that you do not want the monthly First Selection. If the newsletter is delayed, you may return unwanted books. To retain your membership you are required to purchase only one book in each six-month period.

Be informed. Don't let the world pass you by. Read the latest of fiction, humor, biography, economics, politics, science and more. Enroll now in the PRIMUS BOOK CLUB.

Another cost savings: If you send your payments in advance, we will pay shipping and handling charges.

Please fill in and mail the enclosed enrollment card. Start right now to become entertained and enlightened.

Sincerely,

Real Estate—Homes

Dear Mr. and Mrs. Henshaw:

Another home SOLD . . . at 0000 Windmill Way, Saratoga. Please stop by and welcome your neighbors.

SOLD by Nolan Associates, your neighborhood realtor.

We offer top $$$ for our SELLERS—Speedy sales for our SELL-ERS—Personalized, professional service for our SELLERS—98% of homes listed are SOLD!!—We don't just collect listings...We service what we list!

We offer speedy sales—courteous service—and a free evaluation of your home.

Please use the enclosed GOLD MARKET ANALYSIS CERTIFICATE for a market evaluation of your home.

Please phone today: NOLAN ASSOCIATES, 000 Hamilton Ave., Saratoga, FL 00000. Phone 000-000-0000

Sincerely,

Dear Mr. and Mrs. Sutherland:

Once in a lifetime there is a special place.

Just beyond the gentle rise overlooking a flowering meadow you come upon a secluded setting of prestigious homes. The tree-covered slopes are fenced and guarded, ensuring protection and peace of mind.

The custom-built homes are designed by A. I. A. architects and are priced from $695,000. Homesites of from two to five acres are also available from $250,000.

These are the Wallingford Estates of Saratoga—telephone 000-000-0000.

                                        Sincerely,

Dear Property Owner:

Within the next year over two million people in the United States will sell their houses, some successfully, some at a sacrifice.

Backed by Pacific Real Estate's 22 years of success in selling real estate in this area, you can depend on a most satisfactory sale. We know that home buyers compare and look for charm, comfort, convenience, location and "the best deal." We will help you prepare your house for these "fussy" buyers. We have learned much during the past 22 years.

We were the first realtors to establish a training school offering state-accredited courses in real estate in this community. All our sales people attend this school.

We initiated the local board of realtors which started the community multiple listing service, which vastly expands the visibility of our sales efforts.

A free appraisal of your home's value and marketability is available just by phoning us at 000-0000.

Pacific Real Estate is here to help you whether you are buying or selling or both. Give us a call.

                                        Sincerely,

Dear Mr. Sommers:

All fired up.
Desk piled high. Morning gone. Energy too.
Day pushes on. One last call and out the door.
Goodbye traffic. Goodbye smog. Honking horns turn to silence.
Quiet mountains. Skittering quail. Quiet time.
Scampering rabbits. Time to think. Time to breathe.
Relax. Unwind.
        Regroup.
            Recharge.
                At Tatum Ranch, Phoenix
                A master-planned community.

                        (signature)

(Reprinted from a magazine advertisement, with permission from SunCor Development Company.)

Real Estate—Mountain Property

Hi Folks,

Just a friendly note to let you know that we aren't really in the high mountains. More like nestled in the foothills. But you can see the mountains from your back porch and the wildflowers, and hear the birds chirping, and the afternoon breeze whispering through the trees.

Property values are rising monthly, so don't wait too long. The number of homes Rancho Verde has built now exceeds 600, and our qualified, local sales staff has increased to meet the growing demand. We know you want to talk to sales people who own cabins and houses here and who know this area. John was born only ten miles to the north. Tim has owned a cabin here for seven years. Sarah has lived for twenty years adjacent to our estates, and just can't bear to move next door. I tramped through these woods as a child and live in the third house to the left down there. You are not dealing with strangers when you drop in to visit us.

If you are interested in buying a lot for future development, a comfortable cabin or a completed home, any of our sales people will be glad to help.

Write your name and address on the enclosed card and we will mail you a few pictures of these foothill estates. Or just call us at 000-000-0000.

Your friends at Rancho Verde,

Wrist Watch

Dear Mr. Farnsworth:

Your watch: elegant yet rugged, an exciting possession with proven Swiss quartz accuracy and dependability—for discriminating men and women.

The Aargo watches in either classic or contemporary designs, including slimline and water resistant, are not ordinary. They have hand crafted, precision movements. The crystals and hands are scratch proof, and so well made you may never see an indication of wear.

Prices range from $1,500 to $14,500.

From our vast collection in gold or stainless steel or the combination of both, you will find the exceptional masterpiece you are proud to wear—an Aargo. Impressive.

A color brochure will be mailed when you return the enclosed card.

Sincerely,

Camera

Dear Ms. Won:

Accept no limitations.

A horse and jockey breaking from the pack, stopped at full speed by the autofocusing Minolta Maxxum 8000i. Because both rider and camera rose to the challenge.

Here, Maxxum's Predictive Autofocus anticipates the horse's charge for exact focus in a split second. While our Sports Action Card, one of 14 unique, computer-like Creative Expansion Cards, automatically pre-programs Maxxum to take advantage of its unsurpassed shutter speed. Freezing every detail, even at the pace of a wire-to-wire winner.

Maxxum, the world's most comprehensive autofocus system, offers more than 30 lenses to help you unleash your creativity as never before.

The possibilities are as limitless as your imagination.

For details or product information, see your Minolta dealer or write: Minolta Corporation, 101 Williams Dr., Ramsey, NJ 07446. In Canada: Minolta Canada, Inc., Ontario.

Sincerely,

((c)1990 Minolta Corporation. Used with permission.)

Dear Mrs. Vaught:

Action Pictures! Beautiful color!

If you can see it, you can capture it with your Auto-10 camera—simply. Why simply?

Because your Auto-10 sets the exposure *and* the focus. The results rival those of the professionals: rich colors and clear details, even as the amount of light changes.

The Auto-10 is a precision instrument for beautiful photography, compact, light weight and easy to handle.

You can enhance the range of your creativity with any of Auto-10's 30 precision ground lenses from telephoto to wide angle, a motor drive for quick action sequences, automatic flash, and other accessories to make your photography more precise and more convenient for you.

See your local dealer today. Dealers are listed in the accompanying brochure.

Action photos make lasting memories and are fun with your Auto-10.

Sincerely,

Computer System

Dear Mr. Graham:

Quick letters; instant revisions and updates while on the road; no wasted time. That is the Mercator Laptop computer.

Take a look at it: small enough to fit in your briefcase, only 9"x11"x1.5" and weighs only 5 pounds. The Mercator is a high performance instrument with a hard disk and a 40-column, nonglare screen—all for an easily affordable price.

The Mercator gives you instant access to files and programs, offers desktop publishing capability and easy transferability between your laptop and your office computer.

A Mercator portable printer is available. It is lightweight, compact and provides quality output on plain paper.

For further details and technical data, please call 1-800-000-0000.

Sincerely,

Dear Mr. Bowers:

No longer need haste make waste.

The Xerox 0000 electronic printing system is both amazingly fast and precise.

That is why the Xerox 0000 is used by such companies as Fast-Tax, a computer firm that processes hundreds of thousands of income tax returns each year. Up to a million pages of returns are processed in one day. The Xerox 0000 converts the input data and uses laser beams to precisely print the tax forms—and even collates the forms automatically.

That is managing information the way it should be managed: accurately, with a minimum of waste and a maximum of haste. It is all done with the Xerox 0000 electronic printing system.

Call your local representative, Mr. Alvin Goodman, today at 000-000-0000. He can explain this and other Xerox systems—one of which will meet your needs and do a better job of managing your information.

Sincerely,

Specific Customer—Roofing Tile

Dear John:

This confirms our conversation concerning real estate developer Allen Company's plan to close down their roofing tile operation in Oakland, California and go to the open market for their tile requirements.

The Johnson Corporation is in a very good position in the Bay Area to be a dependable long-range source of supply for roofing tile. Johnson has two tile plants in the immediate area of the Allen Company's housing developments. One plant is in Dublin, which is 30 miles east of your development, and the other is in San Jose, which is 35 miles south of your current operation. These two tile plants are under one Resident Manager who correlates the two operations to give the best possible service to our customers.

At your convenience I would like to arrange a tour of our Bay Area operations for you and for anyone else from your company who would be interested in seeing what Johnson has to offer as a source of supply.

You stated that your National Director of Purchases will visit Oakland the week of December 6 to discuss with you the procedures and guidelines for acquiring quotations on your tile requirements. You also asked me to contact you the following Monday, December 13 to further discuss what our next steps should be.

If, during your Director of Purchases' visit, he would like to see some of Johnson's operations, we would be more than happy to make any arrangements that would be convenient. If not, John, I look forward to talking to you on December 13.

Best regards,

Sales Promotion Book

Dear Mr. Elender:

Would you like to make big money using the incredible power of the hard-sell approach that gets ACTION from your prospects? . . . actually doubling or tripling the effectiveness of your ads, sales talks or merchandising techniques?

You will quickly learn from *The Ten Keys to Money* the clues to advertising—and selling—and be ahead of your competitors whether in retailing, wholesaling, manufacturing or servicing. You will learn the hard-sell approach that it takes to get ahead these days. Immediately, you will write powerful and absolutely persuasive ads and promotional materials.

You will be able to look at the ad you or your associate—or your competitor—wrote and know that, "this is a selling ad," or that, "this needs reworking, and I know *exactly* how to change it."

You want to be skeptical? The *10 Keys* are time-tested, scientifically sound and success-proved techniques used for over twenty years by the country's few most highly successful—and rich—sales people.

The *10 Keys* are explained in simple language by Tom Morlick, a successful salesman himself, in his book *The Ten Keys to Money.*

The book is yours for only $14.95. Money back if not absolutely delighted beyond your wildest expectations.

Rush the enclosed postpaid card today!

Sincerely,

Dear Mr. Capel:

You can Boost Sales . . .Slash Selling Costs . . . Perk up Profits . . . with this rich storehouse of tested and proven sales promotion ideas!

Modern marketing places more and more emphasis on effective sales promotion as a sure way to boost sales volume and reduce the cost of selling. And, one of the best sources of good promotion ideas is a close working knowledge of what others in creative sales promotion are actually doing. This handbook brings that goal within your reach.

The *Sales Promotion Handbook* is virtually brimming over with hundreds of practical techniques for getting ideas, training dealer personnel, measuring results, exploiting every possible sales outlet for your products and services. For example, if you are looking for ways to build up stronger selling effort on the part of your salesmen—your own or dealer representatives—you will have at hand some of the best motivational programs ever developed.

If your daily problems involve old sales territories, allocating budgets, or writing effective promotion copy, this handbook will provide you with many examples to stimulate your own thinking and imagination.

Without cost or obligation, see how the new Dartnell *Sales Promotion Handbook* can help you boost sales and profits.

Read the *Sales Promotion Handbook* for 15 days with no obligation. The all new 6th edition contains 1206 pages of stimulating sales promotion ideas. It is fully illustrated and indexed.
The cost is $45.50.

Just fill in and mail the enclosed card today.

Sincerely,

Gift of Food

Every year 'bout this time . . .

we start feeling downright sentimental . . . start taking time
to think of the special ladies in our lives. Lots of other folks do,
too—and that's why we put together this special booklet of
gifts for Moms of all kinds, on their day.

Harry and I picked these gifts especially for Mother's Day.
We think there's something special here to please every Mom
you want to remember at this special time of year. You'll find
truly original gifts of the finest quality—such as our tangy Royal
Gala Apples, imported fresh from New Zealand . . . flowers and
exotic foliage plants she can grow in her home . . . our new
Sweets and Sentiments, a delicate hand-crocheted pouch filled
with a box of our luscious Mint Truffles . . . and our famous
homemade food gifts from the kitchens here at Bear Creek!

Best of all, our prices include everything . . . all the extras you
usually pay for at stores. Harry and I will gift pack and deliver in
the nicest way . . . and every gift will be sent with your own personal
greeting.

Mother's Day is May 11 this year . . . and that's just around
the corner. Harry and I need your instructions just as soon as
you can get them to us. So please fill out your order right away
. . . and return it in the special postage-paid envelope enclosed.
We guarantee *you'll* be pleased . . . and so will *she!*

David

(Reprinted by permission of Harry and David, Medford, Oregon.)

Bakery

Greetings:

San Francisco has long been known for its fine foods.
Barocchio's Bakery will become a part of this tradition. We
recently moved into a most modern bakery with a team of

exceptional baking specialists whose two concerns are quality and taste.

Our bread line is complete with varieties from bleached to black, from white enriched to 12-grain, from extra sour to honey bran.

Each day we bake a selection of cookies, pies and sweet rolls. Choose cakes from white angel food to German chocolate fudge.

The enclosed sheet of coupons will enable you to sample a wide range of our products at a 50% discount.

We value our customers and are certain that once you have tasted our bakery goods you will know they are a part of San Francisco's tradition of fine foods.

Sincerely,

Income Tax Consulting

Dear Mr. Tiffany:

You're probably going to pay too much in personal income taxes this year.

You are, if you're the kind of totally involved executive we think you are.

With everything else on your mind, there's a good chance you may fail to take some perfectly appropriate steps to minimize your taxes.

This makes it all the more important that you get the advice and counsel of the professionals at Deloitte, Haskins & Sells.

To start with, we'll systematically review your current financial picture and your returns for previous years. (Who knows? We may very well find refunds you've overlooked.)

Then we'll go further, and help you devise financial strategies to meet your long-term business and family needs—your needs for trust arrangements, perhaps, or the sale of a family business, or exercising some stock options.

At Deloitte, Haskins & Sells, we think income tax and estate planning is a very personal matter.

When we say we don't stop at the bottom line in serving clients, we include thousands of businessmen and professionals among them.

They're individuals who look to us for planning for the years to come—just as much as for our help in filing this year's return.

Of course, not everybody requires our kind of help. But if you do, perhaps we should talk.

The sooner, the better.

Call our local office at 212-790-0500, or write 1114 Avenue of the Americas, New York, New York 10036.

Sincerely,

(Adapted, with permission, from a magazine advertisement.)

Service Contract

Dear Mr. and Mrs. Cody:

Just a reminder that your Service Contract will expire soon. Don't let it!

Actually, your service contract is more valuable to you as your set gets older. That is when repairs get more complicated and are therefore more costly. One service call may cost as much as the annual contract.

Renew your contract now. You will save time and money and be assured of fast, efficient service from Terry's Appliances.

We are enclosing a renewal contract for one year. You can sign and return it in the enclosed, postpaid envelope. You pay only $__ for our low cost renewal policy.

Don't worry any longer about uncertain appliance repairs— that are always needed at an inconvenient time. You may use your Master Card or VISA card for easy payment.

Why not sign and return the contract today?

Sincerely,

Inactive Customer

Dear Andy,

The loss of a business friend may not seem as tragic as the loss of a personal friend, but still a part of one's self fades away when a friend is gone.

We seem to have lost you as a business friend, and we feel the loss. Is there something we have done, or something we have *not* done? As a personal favor, could you give us, briefly, the reason for apparently leaving us. Just a short sentence or two on the back of this letter is all we ask. You can mail it in the postpaid envelope enclosed.

We have recently expanded our warehouse capacity and increased the variety of paper and stationery items to serve you better. A request for a quote or an order for a carton of Scotch tape would be most welcome. We will do everything possible to become a business friend of yours again. Please let us hear from you.

Sincerely,

Collection Service

Dear Mr. Caplan:

Tylenol may be replacing aspirin as a headache remedy—but headaches remain. Especially collection headaches. Perhaps your collection remedy should be changed.

If you are plagued with "headache" accounts, let us help you. We have many years of experience and an outstanding track record of clearing up old accounts.

Our method is as simple as it is effective. First, we send out a letter that is both imaginative and skillful. It commands respect. And it gets results. Most collection problems are solved at this point.

For more reluctant debtors, we send a trained expert who is tactful and persuasive and can hold your goodwill.

Give us a try. Send us a list of your past due accounts. If the first letter succeeds, you pay us nothing. We must, however, charge a modest fee for sending our personal service representative. If we collect nothing, you pay nothing.

With nothing to lose but your "headache" accounts, and the probable recovery of your inactive assets, give us a call today at 000-000-0000.

Cordially yours,

Public Official

Dear Mr. and Mrs. Baker:

I would appreciate your serious consideration of my candidacy for City Council when you vote on April 8 this year. You have been among the few who take the time and interest to vote in Municipal elections, which indicates your concern about local government.

Forecasts show that I have an excellent chance of winning a seat in this forthcoming election, as my years of volunteer involvement in community affairs and present position of Planning Commissioner have provided the name recognition and background that is necessary to be a viable candidate in _____.

As it is physically impossible to contact every voter personally, and as the press gives only equal and therefore minimum coverage to any candidate, I have to communicate by using signs and mailed campaign literature. To reach every voter with just one message requires over $7,500.

I hope to be able to provide each voter with sufficient facts upon which to base his or her selections on April 8. If I miss your house, it's because I did not have the funds to supply all the literature and postage necessary to mail it to you. If this happens, please understand. I cannot spend any campaign funds unless they are donated by supporters who want to see me on the City Council.

If you really want to help me and yourself for the next four years, $1 or more now and your vote on April 8 will do it.

I have always said that the way to keep an elected public official honest is to have his campaign financed by $1 each from 7,500 people rather than $7,500 from 1 person. I am sure you share that opinion.

Sincerely,

Executive Recruiter

Dear Mr. Butler

Is your valuable time wasted in interviews and background checks of potential executives who later prove unqualified for the job? Has questionable information by a candidate slipped through the hiring procedure only to surface when the performance record of an executive is called into question weeks or even months later? Do you find too few qualified individuals from which to choose?

James and Jordan can assist you in recruiting qualified candidates for your available positions—and often with less cost to you in both time and money.

Here is why:

— James and Jordan's executive search service covers the nation.
— We have referral agreements with other recruiting agencies.
— We are on top of the current salary market: what is being asked and what is being offered.
— We know the latest labor and fair employment laws, rulings and court decisions.
— We refer to you only qualified and motivated candidates.

— We practice complete confidentiality.

— We approach our work from our client's viewpoint.

— We have a large number of satisfied clients to whom you may refer.

In taking over the search for executives, James and Jordan completely eliminates one of your business problems.

Further information is available by returning the enclosed postpaid card. We look forward to working with you.

Sincerely,

Personal Credit

Dear Mr. Nordstrom:

Very likely you have heard about Individual Financing. This is our bank's special finance service created for people with an above average income and credit standing. It occurred to me that you might be interested in hearing a bit more about it.

With Individual Financing you enjoy the remakable independence of administering you own long-term credit needs. If your annual net income is $25,000 or better and you also qualify in other respects, you'll have a credit line of somewhere between $5,000 and $25,000. Use it whenever you want to for personal, family, or household purposes simply by writing a special check of $500 or more.

Individual Financing can give you the flexibility you want through these valuable benefits:

1. There is no charge until you use it.
2. You can pay more than the minimum monthly payment, if you wish, thereby reducing the amount of future financial charges.
3. No collateral is required.
4. There are no prepayment penalties.
5. No bank visits are necessary each time you need a loan.
6. Credit life insurance of up to $25,000 is available.

Please take this opportunity to complete and sign the enclosed application and financial statement. You can be sure this information will be handled in confidence. By signing this application, you are under no obligation. Mail it in the prepaid return envelope provided. Soon after we receive your application, either a loan officer or I will call you.

Cordially,

Furniture, Retail

Dear Mr. Mosland:

Parsons has opened a great new store in Phoenix at 00000 Camelback Road. Although we're new to this area, Parsons has been satisfying home furnishing needs since 1919. These years of experience have shown us that when you shop, you want selection, availability, and value. Parsons can offer you all that, and more!

We have expanded our selection of 200 room groupings to include our new Formal Gallery. This collection features American of Martinsville, Hibriten, the Burlinghouse Globe Collection, Thomasville, and the many other famous name brands that complete our three million dollar inventory.

As an introduction to our new Phoenix store, we're offering you a 20% discount on ALL regularly priced merchandise. In addition, we have a get-acquainted gift for you. It's a beautiful piece of native Indian pottery, absolutely FREE with any purchase of $200 or more.

To make shopping at Parsons even more convenient, we're inviting you to open a charge account today. With this card you can charge your purchases and never have to worry about a down payment, or tying up your credit lines on other charge cards. And your card will be welcome at any of our ninety-eight locations nation wide.

All you have to do is complete the coupon below and return it in the enclosed postpaid envelope. It's so easy, why not do it today?

Sincerely,

Art Object

Dear Alumnus:

We are pleased to announce that the University of Washington Alumni Association has commissioned world-renowned Reed & Barton Silversmiths to create in rich and precious metals a Limited Edition Damascene Insculpture (metal etching) of our famous landmark—the Rainier Vista.

This uniquely beautiful metal etching, handcrafted in pure silver, 24kt. gold electroplate, burnished copper and bronze is being produced exclusively for Washington alumni—and for no one else. It is being offered at this time only, through this single announcement, and will never be issued again.

Each richly detailed Damascene etching of the Rainier Vista will be faithfully recreated by skilled artisans in Reed & Barton's famous patented process. The rare art medium of Damascene involves more than 20 separate hand operations in the creation of each metal etching through the painstaking blending of silver, gold, copper, and bronze.

Mounted to produce a handsome three-dimensional effect, each Insculpture will be in an antiqued gold and silver leaf frame, dramatically displayed against a rich velveteen background, as depicted in the attractive brochure enclosed.

A Certificate of Registration will be affixed to the reverse side of the Rainier Vista frame, and will bear your name, your class year, and your limited edition number.

Since this is the only time that the Rainier Vista Damascene Insculpture will ever be offered—and since only Washington alumni will receive this information—these exquisite works of art are almost certain to become collector's pieces.

Reed & Barton will honor all orders postmarked on or before March 31. They cannot guarantee to honor orders postmarked after that date.

The original issue price of this framed etching is just $125, including delivery. We have made arrangements to have all orders entered directly with Reed & Barton Silversmiths. You may pay for your University of Washington Insculpture with a $25 deposit, if you prefer. After you have received your Insculpture, the unpaid balance of $100 will be billed at the rate of $25 a month for four months. All of these details are described on the enclosed postage-paid Reservation Form.

Please mail it before March 31.

Sincerely,

Life Insurance

Dear Wells Fargo Master Card Customer:

As you know, Wells Fargo Bank, known for its service to Californians since 1852, makes available to you many financial services including your convenient Master Card account. We are pleased that Wells Fargo has selected us to add to these services by making available to you a product design for the protection of your estate and the future security of those dependent on you.

You are undoubtedly aware that what you can buy with one dollar today is hardly more than half of what you could buy with that same dollar ten years ago. The other half has been lost to inflation.

With this in mind, we offer you a unique Term Life Insurance Plan that is competitively priced, has a special anti-inflation Benefit Protection Option, and features convenient premium payment through your Wells Fargo Master Card account.

Let me tell you about the highlights of this special plan:

Adults under 60 can select up to $50,000 of Term Life Insurance benefits.

You and your spouse, if under age 60, can protect your insurance benefits against inflation by including the Benefit Increase Option in your coverages. This option will automatically increase your insurance benefit until the total benefit doubles.

You can cover the balance in your Master Card account with your insurance benefit.

You have the convenience of having the monthly premiums billed to your Wells Fargo Master Card account.

Medical examinations are not required to apply for this insurance.

You will own your policy—it is your personal property.

You can have lifetime protection, regardless of any change in your health, because at any time prior to age 60, while your coverage is in force, you can convert this policy to a whole life or endowment policy without evidence of insurability and without a medical examination.

We are proud to offer this Term Life Insurance Plan to you and to support it with the strength of our company, a member of AMEX Life Assurance Company group which, for 127 years, has provided Californians with quality insurance plans at competitive rates.

I urge you to read the enclosed material which further explains the Plan, then evaluate your insurance needs, complete the enclosed application, and mail it to us today.

                                         Sincerely,

Cost Savings

Dear Customer:

Valley Truck Supply is now in a position to reduce the cost of your truck replacement parts. This is due to our growing number of satisfied customers over the past few years.

Volume discounts are available to customers buying as few as six of an item with, however, a dollar minimum per order.

Please refer to the enclosed sheet for a list of commonly purchased parts and the discount rates.

We hope this program will help you provide faster service to your customers. We look forward to continuing to serve you in the future.

Sincerely,

Store Sale

Dear Mr. and Mrs. Letterman:

Just a note to let you know that we at Staples' Family Store are already having our After Christmas Sale—before Christmas—so you may enjoy your savings before the holidays.

These will include shoes, shirts, blouses, slacks, and everything in the Children's Department.

This is Staples' way of wishing you the best Christmas ever.

We look forward to meeting you during this season of good cheer.

Sincerely,

FOLLOW-UP SALES LETTERS

A successful salesperson is likely to be one who uses follow-up letters. They are effective because they generate orders from current customers and new prospects, build goodwill, iron out misunderstandings and provide written records that may forestall future disagreements.

Additional purposes of follow-up letters are to thank buyers, to remind customers that it is time to reorder, and to introduce new products.

Because the ending of a letter is the most emphatic position, close your letter in a pleasant manner.

How to Do It

1. State the reason for the letter.
2. Explain the subject of the letter.
3. Indicate the steps you are taking to assist the reader.

Dear Policy Holder:

As you know, it's almost time to renew your Comair Service Policy. It has been a pleasure serving you this past year. Enclosed you'll find a new contract form with simple instructions. Please read it carefully, then sign and return it with your check to ensure uninterrupted service coverage.

We are enclosing one of our current brochures with all of the options and prices listed. If you have any questions please feel free to call, and one of our representatives will be glad to stop by your home and assist you.

Again, it has been a pleasure serving you this past year, and we look forward to doing so for many years to come.

Sincerely,

(Reprinted with permission from Bob Unruh of Comair Service Systems, Peoria, Arizona.)

Dear Mr. Tucker:

It is with genuine pleasure that I thank you for your purchase of our Model VII tractor. Choosing Normans as your dealer represents your faith and trust in us, and I, personally, would like you to know that that is a matter of great importance to us.

Please be assured that we shall endeavor to deserve your confidence and friendship. It is our company policy to conduct our business in a manner that gives full attention to providing the best service to our customers. Our personnel are chosen for their enthusiastic and pleasant attitudes and are trained to give courteous and efficient service on which you can depend.

I hope it never happens, but should Normans ever fall short of your expectations, I would consider it a personal favor if you would let me know about it.

Sincerely,

Dear Mrs. Spencer:

It has been some time since we have been in touch with you. I hope this note finds you well and ready to enjoy the holiday season.

We have been busy at Sun Ridge. You may have noticed our dramatic landscaping and seen ads locally for our many special events. Rio Salado College is now located on our campus, and Sun Ridge is bustling with activities.

We would be delighted to have you stop by for a new look at our community. I look forward to hearing from you. In the meantime, I wish you the happiest of holidays!

Cordially,

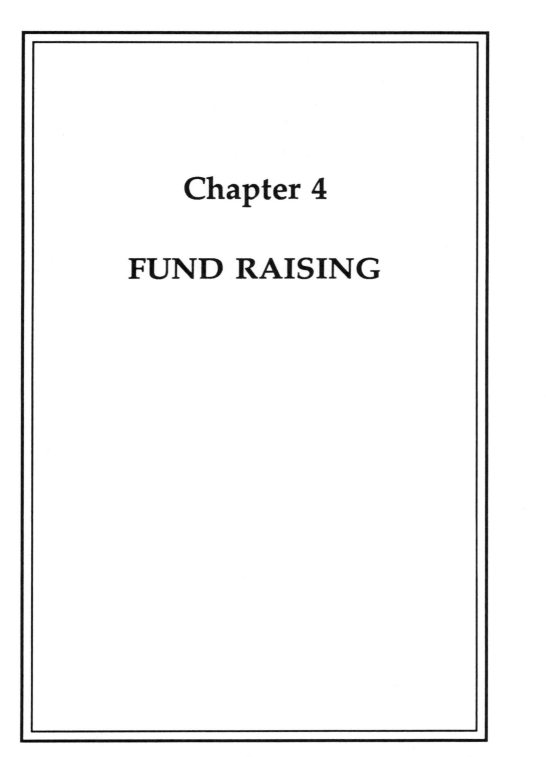

Chapter 4

FUND RAISING

A written request for a contribution to a charity is a sales letter with a heart tug. Like a sales letter, the fund-raising letter first arouses the interest of the reader, then convinces the reader of the need for buying the product or service (or making the contribution), next tells how the product or service will help the buyer (or giver), and finally makes positive action by the buyer (or contributor) easy. The heart-tugging part is the second step—convincing the reader of the need to give.

Let us follow the steps in order, using the first letter in this chapter to explain them. The opening sentence excites the reader's interest with the intriguing statement:

> Right now, the people best equipped to help runaway kids are pimps.

The first three phrases are straightforward and suggest a problem of interest to many people, but the surprising last word of the statement snaps the reader awake and arouses his curiosity. The reader is eager to read on.

Another letter begins:

> This is the story of Ella.

Because the stories hold the promise of being interesting, the reader looks for that promise and finds:

> Ella is lonely.

Now the reader wants to know *why* she is lonely. A startling first sentence is not mandatory in a good fund-raising letter, but the reader's interest must be aroused if the writer expects the letter to be read. Here are more interesting first sentences:

> 3:00 A. M. is a rough time to be needing a ride to work . . .
> CARE hasn't shipped a food package in twenty-five years.
> Put a "little" life in your life.

Why should you give $25 to the Heart Fund?
Difficult choices must be made during difficult times.

Having captured the reader's interest, the heart-tugging second step begins. The reader must be convinced that the cause is good and just, and worthy of opening his or her checkbook. Referring again to the first letter in this chapter, how a pimp can help is mentioned, as well as why the children seek anyone's help. What happens to the child is described, arousing the sympathy of the reader, who also becomes emotionally involved with the helplessness of the runaways. Here are children as young as nine, searching for love, but hooked on drugs, selling their bodies, cast off by society, beyond the reach of family or government, helpless in the hands of brutal pimps. Any one of these treatments is reason enough to open the pocketbook of the reader.

The third step in a fund-raising letter is a statement of the benefit for the giver. The community problems of juvenile prostitution and pornography will be alleviated through the organization REFUGE. Most fund-raising letters, including this one, indicate that one of the reader's benefits will be the personal satisfaction of helping someone in need. Many letters mention the deductibility of the gift for tax purposes—definitely a direct benefit.

Making positive action by the giver easy is the fourth step. In our model letter, the chore of deciding how much to give is done by the writer when he suggests five or ten dollars. The assumption is that less will be gladly accepted and that more is hoped for. The *postscript* requests that the contribution be mailed in the enclosed envelope and states that the postage is prepaid. Envelopes and stamps are small items, but they can be exasperating inconveniences when not provided. The giving must be made easy.

Positive statements should be used in any request. Imagine the potential giver's lack of enthusiasm when reading, "We can't build a new Intensive Care Unit if you don't contribute something." It would be better to say, "Your contribution, added to those of our other donors, will assure starting our Intensive Care Unit early next year." A positive attitude in the letter promotes a positive attitude in the giver.

The first model fund-raising letter may seem emotional—and it is intended to be that—but in it, several unemotional techniques are used to induce the reader to give. A friendly, conversational tone is carried throughout the letter. Three devices are used to accomplish this: informal language, short sentences and questions, and contractions. Some contractions used are *it's, isn't, we're, can't,* and *won't.*

The short sentences and questions include *It's ironic, isn't it? It really doesn't have to be that way;* and *We need your financial support.* Informal language also adds to the conversational tone: the use of the word *kids,* phrases such as *maybe get hooked on drugs, it's an ugly scene,* and *beat the pimps on their own turf.*

Additional sales techniques are used in other letters, and some recommended techniques even contradict others. How effective any particular one is depends on the audience to which it is directed. Here are some examples:

- Be brief.
- Fully state the need.
- Avoid gimmicks.
- Attract attention with an unusual letter layout.
- Prod the reader into fulfilling his pledge.
- Remind without undue pressure.
- Have the letter signed by the highest official of the organization.
- Make examples specific.
- Make the request specific.
- Have a specific use for the donation.

As these persuasions are used in the model letters, they will be mentioned in the introductions to the various sections.

Many of the model letters have a *postscript.* This is not an after-thought, but a planned part of the letter. The reason for using a *postscript* is to attract attention. This is accomplished by placing the added remarks outside the body of the letter and at the end, where emphasis is strongest. Just how much emphasis is added is a matter of choice. Some writers of sales letters use it constantly and some not at all, but it does add a little punch to the end of a letter.

One fact of direct mail solicitation should be noted: it is one of the least effective solicitation methods. If five percent of the letters elicit a response, the mailing is highly successful. This fact does not diminish the dollar importance of this method, however, because a large number of small donations can add up to as much as a few large donations. The return percentage can be improved by directing specific letters to specific groups. For example, a series of three letters in this chapter were sent to doctors who work in the hospital making the solicitation, and the appeals were directed toward the doctors' involvement in that hospital. Many solicitations by colleges are addressed to alumni with the appeal made to their interest in the college.

In spite of limitations, fund-raising letters do bring in large sums of money.

The following are thoughts from successful fund raisers. Keep them in mind when preparing a campaign or a letter:

- In general, ninety percent of giving is done by ten percent of the donors; therefore spend ninety percent of your time on that ten percent.
- Always assume that your prospect has more money than you estimate. Flattery may get you somewhere.
- It is reported that when one millionaire was asked by an alumnus why he gave a large donation to one college but only a small one to his own alma mater, he replied, "Because no one from your school asked for a large donation."

How to Do It

1. Start with an interest-arousing first sentence.
2. Explain convincingly the need for the donation.
3. Indicate how the giver will benefit.
4. Make positive action by the giver easy.

CHARITABLE HELP FOR THE DISADVANTAGED

Runaway Children

The letter to Mr. Longworth from REFUGE appeals to the reader's sympathy. The sales (or pleading) techniques, describing the dangers to runaways, tax deductibility, and informal language have been described above. The letter is directed toward a wide, general audience, as indicated by the conversational style and the mention of many reasons for the reader's being sympathetic, at least one of which should appeal to any reader.

My Dear Mr. Longworth:

Right now, the people best equipped to help runaway kids are pimps.

A pimp can come off like a father figure to a kid who never had much love at home, particularly when she's scared, lonely, and right off the bus.

All he needs is a week to break her in, maybe get her hooked on drugs, and put her out to work on the street. It's an ugly scene, and it's getting worse all the time.

Keep in mind that these are kids we're talking about, both boys and girls as young as nine who sell their bodies in the squalid marketplace of commercial sex.

It's wrong for these kids to leave home, of course, at least for most of them. Some can't really be blamed: they leave separated parents, alcoholic parents, or drug abusing parents. Sometimes the child just can't cope with the inconsistent confusion of present-day pressures. Is it any wonder they run off, searching for the love many don't even know they're seeking?

They're society's castoffs, beyond the reach of family, church, school, or government. It's ironic, isn't it? In the richest nation on earth, the people best equipped to help runaway kids are pimps.

It really doesn't have to be that way. We think it's time to take the responsibility for their futures out of the hands of the pimps, and put it where it belongs: in the hands of the people who care enough to give them a second chance—people like you.

With your help, REFUGE can make the difference. REFUGE is a nonprofit program to help communities cope with the growing problem of juvenile prostitution and pornography.

REFUGE is based on a simple idea. Every community has at hand right now the resources to help runaway children. Through REFUGE, these resources can be integrated into a network of critically needed services that will start these kids back toward useful lives.

Given enough support, we can beat the pimps on their own turf, with street-work counselors, crisis housing, professional guidance, medical care, and psychiatric care. The point is to reach these kids before they fall prey to the pimps, advocate for their rights, and get existing institutions to take an interest.

We need your financial support.

Five or ten dollars won't make much difference in your life, but it will make a big difference in the life of some runaway child.

Do it now, please! You'll be giving us a weapon no pimp will ever have on his side: simple human decency.

Sincerely,

P.S. Please mail your tax-deductible check in the enclosed envelope. It is for your convenience, and we pay the postage.

(With thanks to the National Office for Social Responsibility, Alexandria, Virginia.)

The following letter about Ella is an intriguing story of a teenage tragedy. The story technique leads the reader easily to the last two paragraphs, where the request for help is made. Requests for contributions using teenagers as the basis of the appeal are most effective when directed to people who have or work with teenagers.

Disadvantaged Girl

Dear Mr. and Mrs. Wallan:

This is the story of Ella and a teenager's loneliness. Ella does not feel isolated from her friends, but she feels trapped—as though confined inside a crowded bus: the doors are locked, the driver is missing and no one speaks. Each turn of her head reveals only blank faces. Confusion swells inside her mind, struggling desperately to release itself when she hears voices at the other end of the bus. For a moment hope dawns—but each word is contradicted by the next. The voices seem to say one thing but obviously mean quite another.

Ella's life is like that. She is no longer a child, but not yet an adult. She is experiencing the struggle of an adolescent for identity. Actually, she is searching for a solid base upon which to make her own decisions. But in this era the search is so often in vain. Her father tells her to attend college and find a career she can happily follow, but he implies that a woman's place is in the home. Her parents say, "We'll teach you to drink in our home," but the obvious message is, "Stay away from bars and drinkers." Her mother says, "I'll help you get birth control pills," but the thought is clear: "Sex is sinful."

Because a solid base for decisions cannot be found at home, Ella turns to her peers and friends. They have a simple solution: if it feels good, do it. She tries alcohol, she tries sex, she tries marijuana. These become intriguing, then comfortable, then compulsive.

Ella is still locked inside a crowded bus with strangers talking only in contradictions, but she is coping—she thinks.

You are the one who can help unlock the doors. Youth Service Groups has psychologists and counselors, some volunteer and some paid, working with adolescents like Ella. Your dollars are needed to help these youths who are trying so desperately to find a solid base upon which to build their lives—lives that will become self-rewarding and self-supporting. Well-chosen guidance for Ella now will forestall a future of institutionalized care.

Please use the enclosed, postage-paid envelope to make your contribution to Youth Services Groups. Even a small donation helps.

Ella is waiting.

Sincerely,

Troubled Boys

Dear Friend:

While our youngsters prepare to observe our fortieth birthday in December, those of us privileged to actually live and work with them have been looking back with fond memories at Hanna Boys Center's past and ahead with great hopes for its future.

I assure you that we have thought with affection and pride of the more than 1,700 troubled boys who found a measure of love and care here, and we have thought with gratitude and admiration of the literally thousands of warm-hearted people who have made our home possible through their support.

The boys who come to us are troubled and face problems too difficult for them to resolve without help. They are going through hard times. They are struggling with feelings of worthlessness, confusion, frustration, sadness, and anger. Successes are few and far between. The danger of their developing a delinquent behavior pattern is real. Unaided, they will have difficulty moving from childhood, through adolescence, and into manhood.

Our job here is to provide assistance—to extend the helping hand our boys and their families need at a crucial moment. The help we offer is available around the clock, provided by a skilled and understanding staff working to develop an effective program for each boy and his family. It is help that they have been unable to find in their home communities. The staff has worked closely together to improve the quality of child care, counseling, academic and vocational education, and recreation.

We have the capability of providing a large measure of love and badly needed special care for some lads who few other individuals and organizations can help. This is true only because of the support given to us over these many years by so many people having compassion for these children. This support is principally in the form of modest gifts and bequests. Any contribution you could make to our work would be most welcome and most appreciated.

Sincerely,

Destitute Children

Dear Friend,

All parents love their children—some just don't do it very well. A child's tears cannot replace parental love. Month-old Cindy wouldn't stop crying. Her father couldn't stand the "irritating noise" any longer. He left, leaving Cindy's mother without funds.

Young Todd cries because he is hungry and he misses his daddy who left seven months ago. Todd's mother is struggling to make ends meet, but she cannot provide the food and clothing her son needs. She just told him Santa Claus would not visit this year. Hardly a way to dry the tears.

The Crisis Center gave temporary relief to these two children, but what about the hundreds more who seek our help?

We provide warm shelter and food for a few days, a caring person to act as a "mother" and freshly laundered clothing.

Donations of clothing, food and money are needed to carry on these desperately needed activities. Even small amounts help—and larger amounts help even more. You will receive God's blessing and the deep down feeling that you have really helped someone in need.

Your donated food and clothing will be a big help. Or use the enclosed envelope to mail your tax-deductible contribution—today please.

The children thank you,

Mentally Retarded

Dear Mr. and Mrs. Conrad:

Your past generosity has been most helpful in continuing the Young People's Center. The fight against mental retardation is long and hard and neverending. Recent research breakthroughs, however, do give us some hope that future generations of children may be spared the handicap of birth defects.

We have done much with the funds available. We have a day care center, and a training center for those who respond to our heartfelt assistance, and although slow, the results are so rewarding.

We sincerely ask you for another generous contribution to continue this essential work. Please use the postage-paid envelope enclosed.

If they could, these retarded youngsters would give you a most appreciative thank-you.

Cordially,

Dear Mr. and Mrs. Cantrell:

Mentally retarded children may have no braces, no scars, no physically observable defects. But these handicapped children desperately need our help.

With proper training, many can be helped to perform small tasks and thus become more useful citizens of our community. Our training center has done much in the past and will continue to do as much as our funds permit.

Another need is research. That is the only hope for future generations. Much more needs to be learned about the causes of birth defects, and progress is being made.

I know you must consider many requests for donations, but the needs of the mentally retarded are greater than ever.

Please give this request serious thought. Your contribution, added to that of our many other contributors, can add up to real help for those otherwise so helpless.

The enclosed envelope is for your convenience. Please use it today.

Sincerely,

Crippled Children

Dear Mr. and Mrs. Jackson:

Sameness can be monotonous; it can also be wonderful—when it is the same people each year giving to the Crippled Children's Home.

You gave last year, and we feel sure you will want to give again this year. Perhaps you can give more than last year. We have more children to care for and operating costs just won't stay down.

In addition, we are expanding our physical therapy program. We have some new equipment and need more. We need another professional therapist as well as more volunteer assistants.

All this takes more of that same commodity: money.

The children respond well to our help and their parents are appreciative of the benefits from your contribution.

Please be as generous as possible, and use the enclosed envelope for your tax-deductible gift. Do it today.

Cordially,

Handicapped Children

Dear Friend:

This is our fiftieth year of continual assistance to the needy handicapped children of Contra Costa County. Our help is available when there is not any other.

As has been our custom for the past fifty years, our All Volunteer Nonprofit organization now asks for your financial support.

Your entire contribution, except for our expenses of postage, printing, and telephone, provides:

EQUIPMENT	—corrective shoes, braces, wheelchairs, walkers, crutches, glasses, hearing aids.
TREATMENT	—speech and physical therapy, medications, eye, dental, and surgical care.
CAMPERSHIPS	—for the Blind, Diabetic, Mentally Retarded, and other disadvantaged.

We are counting on your contribution to help us help an unfortunate child.

Memorials may be contributed throughout the year.

Very Sincerely,

P.S. Checks, tax-deductible, may be made out to C.C.C.C. Soc., Inc. (Contra Costa County Crippled Children's Society, Inc.)

Hungry Children

Dear Mr. and Mrs. Addison:

Two ragged children sharing a can of creamed corn for dinner. A photo of that scene was printed alongside a recent, local newspaper article.

Joseph, Manuel and Jose were left with a kindly aunt due to a family tragedy. The aunt was a widow surviving on meager social security payments, and although she appreciated the children's needs, she could not buy enough food for them.

Joan was seven months old. Her abusive father disappeared leaving her and her mother with no income. Until the mother could find work and a place for her child, Riverside Food Bank provided their food.

The sole mission of Riverside Food Bank is to feed the hungry. We distribute up to 1,000 nutritionally balanced food boxes each week to those who have nowhere else to turn.

To continue this aid to the needy, we require donated food, and money to buy additional food. Children who go to bed hungry cannot study. Parents who go to bed hungry cannot work well. They need YOUR help. For your concern and generosity, they and the community thank you.

Please use the enclosed return envelope for your thoughtful sharing.

Sincerely,

Homeless Boys

Dear Mrs. Heinman:

Jed Tomkins, age 16, was overwhelmed by life, if you could call it life. His mother was dead; his father continually beat him. He left home for the streets of a large city where he met Debbie, a 15-year-old cocaine addict. Before the year was over, Jed was a father. Not wanting to care for a baby, Debbie disappeared, leaving the baby girl to Jed.

Like many boys living on the streets, Jed washed cars, shined shoes, made deliveries for businesses and occasionally for drug dealers. Also like many other street boys, he turned to prostitution to feed himself and his baby, until he was able to leave her with an orphanage. As a male prostitute, he contracted AIDS.

One social administrator said that homelessness is primarily related to extreme poverty and lack of support from families and government programs.

Boys Haven strives to provide the family-type support these boys so desperately need.

We offer room and board for up to three months for 12 boys at a time—all that our current resources will allow. We offer a healthy diet, consultation, as much job and skill training as we can and, of most importance, the love and caring these boys

had never known. Jed was with us for nearly three months;
then we were able to get him a job with Goodwill Industries.

Obviously, these efforts require money. All tax deductible
contributions, small or large, are most welcome. We trust you
will help.

Sincerely,

Heart Fund

Dear Mr. and Mrs. Gooderham:

Why should you give $25 to the Heart Fund?

If you have had heart trouble you already know why. If you
have relatives or close friends with recent heart problems you
will appreciate our request for money.

If you have been fortunate so far, let me explain our need
for your $25 donation.

Over 670,000 people each year in the United States have
heart attacks, more of them men than women. One-fourth of
all heart attacks hit people under the age of 65. Preventative
measures, however, can reduce the possibility of a heart attack.
These preventative measures include elimination of smoking,
regular exercise, controlled diet, and regular checkups by a
doctor.

This knowledge is the result of research that requires money,
and your $25 donation (or more if you can) will assure contin-
uation of this research.

When your contribution is received, we will send you an illustrated booklet outlining steps that can be taken to reduce
the chances of a heart attack, how to recognize the symptoms
of a heart attack, and what should be done when the symptoms
appear.

It's your life we are concerned about. Please use the enclosed envelope so we can help you.

Sincerely,

Heart Disease

Dear Ms. Trail:

How much is your life worth? Consider the odds:

Heart and blood vessel disease claims an American life every
32 seconds, almost a million lives a year—including about
180,000 under retirement age.

In fact, cardiovascular disease claims more than twice as many lives as cancer. And almost as many lives as all other diseases and causes of death combined.

When it comes to giving, you're one in a million.

Your distinctive financial standing makes you one of those rare individuals who can help shape history by influencing the course of medical research. Research that has already reduced the age-adjusted death rates from coronary heart disease by 28.7% and the stroke mortality rate by 36.6%—both since 1977.

Yet as encouraging as this progress is, worlds of work still need to be done. Simply stated, we need to intensify ongoing, primary research if we are to understand, control, and ultimately prevent the underlying causes of this insidious and complex disease.

That is why we so urgently need your help now. Because far more than the average person, your generous financial support can help us unravel the mysteries that still confound us. Moreover, your gift can help give you and your family a lasting legacy of life and health—today and for years to come.

Heart disease is a monumental problem.

For instance, in the United States alone, nearly 66 million people have one or more forms of heart or blood disease. *That's more than 1 out of every 4 Americans—people just like you and your family.*

The cost is staggering: More than 88 billion dollars this year in lost wages, productivity and medical expenses.

Sincerely,

(Reprinted with permission. How Much is Your Life Worth, 1989 Copyright American Heart Association.)

American Veterans

Dear Friends of AMVETS:

Today you and I—all Americans—have reasons to be thankful. The guns of war are silent. Our nation is at peace.

But walk the wards of any VA Hospital. Visit the men who served those agonizing years in Vietnam—in Korea—in World War II. Then you'll know why their battle is not over.

Time does not cure what a mortar shell does to a man's legs—or what two years of P.O.W. interrogation does to his mind.

— AMVETS offers a nationwide counseling service to any veteran, widow, or dependent *entirely without charge*.

— In 48 of the 50 states, there are AMVETS Service Officers, and their job is to help veterans. Whatever the problem involves, hospitalization, compensation, vocational re-habilitation, or any of a hundred other things, AMVETS is ready to give them the hand they need.

— AMVETS volunteers reach the 75,000 veterans who are hospitalized today. More than tax dollars are needed to fill the lonely hours that sometimes stretch into years.

As Americans, we must remember and be willing to help, even beyond tax-supported hospitals or a pension check. The support you give to AMVETS is one way to show how much you care.

Whatever you can give—$5, $10, $25 or more—means so much to those who gave so much, and please remember, YOUR CONTRIBUTION IS USED DIRECTLY BY VETERANS TO SERVE VETER-ANS—and our nation.

Please don't forget. These are the ones who paid a high price for the peace we enjoy today.

Sincerely,

Cerebral Palsy

Dear Friend:

You probably don't think of a trip to the market as anything special, but for my friend Sue, it is a learning experience.

Sue and I are attending the Cerebral Palsy Center for the Bay Area where we are learning skills to help us lead more independent lives. Through these classes, my friends and I are learning how to travel, cook, manage money, and shop—things common to you perhaps, but that are new horizons for us.

The funds raised during Capella Auxiliary's annual Carrousel Capers helped make it possible for us to attend these classes. Now in its fourteenth year, Carrousel Capers is three days of fun, carnival rides, family entertainment and, of course, good food. Capella Auxiliary is again sponsoring its country fair ben-efit September 21, 22, and 23, and I hope you will attend.

If you can't attend, you can still help. This year's grand prize is a new Mercury. This car, donated by a generous friend, could be yours simply by filling out the enclosed ticket stubs and mailing them with your donation of $5, $10, $20, or whatever you can. Your ticket might win you a new car.

Your donation will help make it possible for us to receive important vocational, recreational, and daily living training. Although no contribution is required to win the car, please remember your dollars do make a difference.

We are looking forward to your coming to Carrousel Capers, but if you can't, won't you still help by sending your check today?

Sincerely,

P.S. This unique Center is one of the oldest health agencies in the United States serving the cerebral palsied and others with developmental disabilities. It is independent of any other organization. Please make your checks payable to Cerebral Palsy Center for the Bay Area. Your contribution is tax-deductible.

The following letter to Dear Fellow Employee takes advantage of a specific situation to make an appeal for the United Way Campaign. The specific situation is a labor dispute during which office employees are doing manual work normally done by "blue collar" employees. The third paragraph is a transition from the labor dispute to the request for a contribution.

United Way

Dear Fellow Employee,

I recently read a publication that stated "Colfax people are pretty special." Never has this been any more evident than during our current labor dispute when almost everyone has had the opportunity of learning more about how our plants operate and of becoming more physically involved in the actual operation.

We've all discovered new uses for our eyes, arms, and muscles in our dedication to keep the plant going. It is hoped that most of the original aches and pains have disappeared and our muscles and senses are toned up, putting many in the best physical condition they have experienced in recent years. This is one of the fortunate aspects of the labor dispute in addition to our need to help one another.

Some of the local residents do not have the eyesight to learn as we do. Some do not have the muscle control to wrap a carton, push a broom or even push a button. Most of these good people, and I've personally seen many of them recently as they attempted to contribute to a working society, would give a fortune to walk, run, talk, write, or see as you and I do each living day. We can help them and others feel that they have a place in the sun, a place to meet and work and earn, and offer them some means of upholding their dignity.

One of the unfortunate aspects of the labor dispute is that it prevented us from early participation in the United Way Campaign, which enables us to help our neighbors and local communities. I now plead with you to help our plant contribute 100 percent to this cause by whatever monetary means you feel is fair. By single payment or regular payroll deduction beginning in 19__, you can support the local agencies through United Way. If you wish, you can designate the agency to which your tax-deductible donation is given. This is a new option, so feel free to make your choice on the enclosed card.

Thank you for taking the time to consider this.

> With appreciation,

The first CARE letter is directed to a wide, general audience. Numerous programs and ways of helping the underprivileged are mentioned or briefly described. The intent is that at least one of these programs will appeal to the reader. The second CARE letter is for the same audience, but the pleading technique is a story of success accomplished against great odds.

CARE

Dear Friend:

This coming holiday season, CARE will feed and help more than 25,000,000 men, women, and children in Asia, Africa, Latin America and the Middle East.

But there are still *others* in grave need. What of millions of children untouched by CARE? Those who wait for help but cannot get it because of a lack of funds? What is in store for them? Poor nourishment! Inadequate food! Too few jobs! Little education! A lack of clean water! Untreated sickness!

Without your contribution, their hopes for a better life shrivel and grow dim. Won't you help them see a better tomorrow?

CARE's nutrition programs are the *first* step in aiding the destitute. They are directed to the most vulnerable groups: infants, young children, pregnant and nursing mothers. Without proper nourishment, these helpless ones fall prey to disease and fail to develop. Weakened, they cannot help themselves.

MEDICO, CARE's medical arm, provides nations with a practical way to meet their own needs. An example is the 68 auxiliary public health nurses who were trained by MEDICO in Honduras in a recent year. The following year, they were healing and training their own people.

And when catastrophes such as floods, drought, and earthquakes strike, CARE is there.

Initially we care for the victims' immediate needs: food, blankets, shelter, and cooking utensils. Then reconstruction starts. We help villagers build simple, low-cost dwellings to replace those destroyed or damaged by floods or earthquakes, and assist farmers in restoring the fertility of their land. We help repair damaged schools and water systems. In short, we provide a wide range of services to victims wiped out by disaster.

Please join CARE's 19__ Holiday Food Crusade today and start the *first* phase of helping people to help themselves! For example:

$25 will train a village leader to teach other farmers how to grow more food, or

$250 will provide a core medical library for medical training purposes, or

$1,000 builds a day care and feeding center for preschool children.

All you have to do is include your tax-deductible Holiday contribution with the special contribution form in the enclosed, postage-paid envelope and return it to us today. There is no doubt, I'm sure, that you will always be glad you cared enough to share.

May peace and happiness surround you and yours in this holiday season.

                                        Sincerely,

Dear Friends,

CARE hasn't shipped a food package in twenty-five years.

We ship more now, however, than we ever did. It is just that the small package is not an efficient way of distributing food. Our emphasis now is on the Food-for-Work program. In Bangladesh in a recent year, 600 villages participated in earthwork projects and workers were paid more than 55,000 tons of wheat. One example:

The drenching, summer monsoons sweep the Indian subcontinent. The villagers of Harta, a small community in southern Bangladesh, anxiously watch as flood waters swell across their rice fields. Too much water now means disaster. Twice each day, the tidal surge from the Bay of Bengal pushes upstream, overflowing the banks of the Juffura River and inundating the fields. The slender rice stems break and the unripened heads rot.

Village chairman Kashiwer Roy submits a proposal for a protective earthwork embankment via CARE's Food-for-Work program. Only a few of these many proposals can be acted upon each year, but this year Harta is fortunate. With winter the rains have stopped. More than a thousand unemployed workers converge on the banks of the now quiet Juffura River. Digging the hard earth with hand tools and carrying their filled baskets on their heads, the dike begins to rise. Over three million cubic feet of earth are moved. For each 70 cubic feet of earth put into the project, a worker is paid 6 pounds of wheat.

In only 18 weeks, the new protective embankment is complete: 6 feet tall, 26 feet at the base, 8 feet at the top, and 6 miles long.

The following May the monsoons return, moisture-laden clouds move up from the Bay, the river rises, the tides come and go, but the embankment holds. By August, rice seedlings have been transplanted and stalks bend as the heads grow plump.

This is the Food-for Work program helping others to help themselves. But they need a starter, someone to provide the wheat so they can work to help themselves. And it is only through your generous help that we can start these people on their way to self-sufficiency.

Your tax-deductible contribution in the enclosed, postage-paid envelope will give many people the *start* they need. I am sure you will be thankful you cared enough to share.

Sincerely,

Sponsor a Child

Dear Friend:

At last! Children International offers a $12 sponsorship program for Americans who are unable to spend $20 or more a month to help a needy child.

And yet, this is a full sponsorship program because for $12 a month you will receive:

— a 3-1/2" x 5" photograph of the child you are helping.
— two personal letters from your child each year.
— a complete Sponsorship Kit with your child's case history and a special report about the country where your child lives.
— issues of our newsletter, "Sponsorship News."

All this for only $12 a month? Yes—because Children International believes that many Americans would like to help a needy child. And so we searched for ways to reduce the cost—without reducing the help that goes to the child you sponsor.

For example, unlike some of the other organizations, your child does not write each month, but two letters a year from your child keep you in contact and, of course, you can write to the child as often as you wish.

Also, to keep down the administrative costs, we do not offer the so-called "trial child" that the other organizations mail to prospective sponsors before the sponsors send any money.

We do not feel it is fair to the child for a sponsor to decide whether or not to help a child based on a child's photograph or the case history.

Every child that comes to Children International for help is equally needy!

And to minimize overseas costs, our field workers are citizens of the countries where they serve. Many volunteer their time, working directly with families, orphanages and schools.

Will you sponsor a child? Your $12 a month will help provide so much:

— emergency food, clothing and medical care.
— a chance to attend school.
— help for the child's family and community, with counseling on housing, agriculture, nutrition, and other vital areas to help them become self-sufficient.

A child needs your love! Fill out the enclosed coupon today.

Then, in just a few days you will receive your child's name, photograph and case history.

May we hear from you? We believe that our sponsorship program protects the dignity of the child and the family and at the same time provides Americans with a positive and beautiful way to help a needy youngster.

Sincerely,

(From a magazine advertisement; used with permission)

Lung Disease

FIGHT LUNG DISEASE WITH CHRISTMAS SEALS®

For more than seventy years, people have used Christmas Seals® as festive additions to their holiday mail. But their real purpose goes far beyond decoration.

Your contribution means vital support of Christmas Seals programs against Emphysema, Bronchitis, Air Pollution, Smoking, TB, and Asthma.

Your gift will bring victories that will enable children to breathe better on long nights and develop into healthy grown-ups—victories that will help you, and millions of others, enjoy healthier lungs in later years.

Strengthen this work. Use Christmas Seals®.

It's a Matter of Life and Breath®.

Mail your contribution in the enclosed envelope.

Thank you for your gift in any amount. It is tax deductible.

Sincerely,

(Reprinted with permission from a 1979 brochure. Christmas Seals® is a registered trademark of the American Lung Association.)

LIBRARY

Often a series of letters will succeed better than one in raising funds. One letter might be discarded or put aside without further thought, but the second letter reminds the reader of the first, and the third of the first two.

A series like this one for libraries should be planned for mailings covering a full year. Send one each two months until a contribution is received. Watch two things: 1) send letter three, Thank You, only if contributions were received during the previous year, and 2) when money is received, cancel further mailings for the current year.

If the first letter doesn't open the reader's check book, a subsequent one may. Constancy in fund raising as well as in advertising produces results.

Letter One—**What We Offer You**

Dear Mrs. Roth:

The Meadowvale Library has much to offer you, even though it has been here only three years.

We have 40,000 books in a range wide enough to satisfy nearly every reader's interest: general fiction, detective, western, biography, history, hobbies, travel, health, arts, nutrition and a complete reference section on (your state). Large print and talking books are available for the vision impaired. A small selection of braille books is also available.

Several hundred records and cassettes have started fast-growing collections of music and topics of current interest.

New books and those in high demand may be rented for a small fee. An inter-library loan can get you practically any book in print.

Paperback books are available on an exchange basis operated on the honor system: you return the number of books you check out.

We have growing newspaper and periodical selections, and an extensive financial reference section.

To provide all this, and more to come, we need your help. We are NOT tax supported. We depend entirely upon your membership, your gifts, your memorials, your bequests by will, and your volunteer help. All financial donations are tax deductible.

We can serve you in proportion to the support we receive from you. The enclosed envelope is for your convenience.

Sincerely,

Letter Two—Seeking Memberships

Dear Mrs. Roth:

I am sure you join us here at the Meadowvale Library and your friends in the community in wanting a first class library.

We have made a good start. We have an excellent selection of fiction and non-fiction books, many current magazines and metropolitan newspapers, financial periodicals and advisory services, ample table space and comfortable chairs, an extensive cassette collection, and a willing and helpful group of volunteers. Other services are planned: a copy machine, weekly movies, book review discussion groups, lectures on current and historical subjects, and a genealogy section.

Because we are not supported by taxes or other public funds, we need your contributions to continue and to improve our services to you.

You can become an important part of the Meadowvale Library by joining our membership, helping us to expand and to become more responsive to your needs. The Library is yours. It can use your help.

A membership card is enclosed with suggested levels of membership. Select the one you feel comfortable with and return it with your tax-deductible contribution in the enclosed envelope.

Sincerely,

Letter Three—**Thank You**

Dear Mrs. Roth:

Thank you for the contribution you made to the Meadowvale Library last year. The response from the whole community was heart warming.

We are pleased that we nearly reached our goal for last year—but now it is this year—and a new goal of $55,000 has been set. It would be most thoughtful of you if you would continue to include the Meadowvale Library in your tax-deductible "giving" plans.

The value of your giving is returned to you in our many library services that benefit the total community: a wide selection of books, home town newspapers, cassettes, financial planning aids, plus plans for lectures, movies, a genealogy department and more in the future.

Thank you again for your helpful support in the past and for the support you will provide for this year. Every dollar counts.

Cordially,

Letter Four—**Magazine Campaign**

Dear Mrs. Roth:

The friends of the Meadowvale Library urge you, your business or your organization to join with us in donating money to the library's magazine campaign. Contributions make it possible for Meadowvale Library to maintain a broad range of magazines for the use of everyone in the community. During the campaign, the librarians also welcome suggestions from you or your group about any periodicals you would like to see included in the library's magazine collection.

We hope that you will contribute to the Meadowvale Library's 19__ magazine campaign and that your donation will be generous since subscription rates for most magazines have risen steadily over the last few years. Our campaign for donations will continue through September, 19__.

If you wish, your name or that of your organization will be displayed prominently in the library along with the name of other magazine campaign donors. Remember, your donation is tax deductible.

Please make your check payable to the MEADOWVALE LIBRARY MAGAZINE CAMPAIGN.

If you have any questions or suggestions, please call Jean or Barbara at 000-0000.

We know that caring people will give to the Meadowvale Library Magazine Campaign for 19 __ because they want to promote quality library service in our community.

Sincerely,

Letter Five—Need Volunteers

Dear Mrs. Roth:

This is an invitation to you and other area residents to participate in the continuing growth of Meadowvale Library. Our library is the information, research, and recreational reading center of Meadowvale. It is here for your use, and it needs your volunteer help.

Most of our staff are volunteers. Only the head librarian and two assistants are paid. Checking books in and out, reshelving returned books, handling the information desk, and even housekeeping is done by our dedicated volunteer staff. Most work one or two days a week, but even a half day a week is a big help to our growing number of book borrowers.

Volunteers alone, however, will not keep our library operating. We need money for the three salaries, for new books, for magazine and newspaper subscriptions, and even such mundane necessities as water, lights, and heat.

We urge everyone in the community and especially our library users to consider seriously our 19__ funds appeal and to become annual participants in an orderly expansion of library facilities. Any amount you can contribute will be most welcome.

Please use the enclosed envelope and the slip with its suggested giving levels to mail your 19__ tax-deductible donation. And, if you can donate some time, please call Roger Smith, our head librarian, at 000-0000.

Yours for a better library,

Letter Six—**Exceed Last Year**

Dear Mrs. Roth:

Our Meadowvale Library circulates approximately 12,000 books monthly from its 40,000 book collection. The library is expanding, the community is growing and our needs increase.

Last year's solicitation resulted in contributions of over $46,000. This year we hope to exceed that amount. We need $55,000 if we are to continue to serve our expanding population.

We are finding more and more people using the reference section and we hope to increase it to meet the needs of our library users. We pride ourselves on being able to answer so many questions, but continually find we lack this or that reference work.

An increase in your annual donation would go far toward improving our reference department. Please use the enclosed slip and envelope to mail your tax-deductible donation. You will benefit from your own gift.

Cordially,

CHURCHES

In addition to God's blessings, churches, to survive in our era, need cold cash. The most successful solicitation letters include a secular appeal. An appeal made strictly from a religious or Godly or loving or intangible basis will, however, bring forth gifts from certain donors. As with other solicitation letters, the use to which the money will be put should be spelled out. One church letter makes a request for two specific, tangible items: seats and an altar rail—both to improve the worship area.

Secular Appeal

Dear Mr. and Mrs. Helverson:

We don't like asking for money any more than you do. But when the cause is just and the Christian spirit is there, the asking is easier.

As we have mentioned in recent Sunday worship services, the Sommersville Community Church needs your help in making it a better place to serve you. In particular, we need new pews at the back of the sanctuary and a new altar rail. (It's the rail, not our faith, that has been wobbly.)

The members with whom I have talked agree that these worship area improvements are necessary. The amount needed is $6,500. This money can be raised quickly if each member family contributes $55.

Please join your fellow members in accepting this invitation to make our worship facilities more pleasant. Please use the enclosed envelope which you may mail or place in the collection plate on Sunday.

The entire congregation will appreciate your efforts to continue His work in Sommersville.

Sincerely,

P.S. We hope all contributions will be made within sixty days. Then the improvements will be completed for our Christmas services.

Preparation for Fund-Raising Campaign

Dear Members and Friends:

Is inflation a problem in your finances at home? *Well, of course it is!* And you can be sure it is a challenge to our finances at the Riverside Community Church. To meet this challenge, our church has proposed a 7 percent increase in next year's budget.

Perhaps inflation can provide an opportunity for ALL OF US to prove our loyalty and to demonstrate our devotion to Jesus Christ, Our Lord.

Today's inflation knows no favorites. We who have been charged with our financial planning have looked at the needs that exist and have developed a proposed budget of $138,000 to meet our church's needs for 19__.

We plead with you to give your church your sincere consideration. Help us make a *unified* effort to provide for the ministry of this church.

Here is how you can help:

Increase your giving to the church to the point of *tithing.*
If not a tithe, at least increase your giving in proportion to any gain in income received since last year.

Remember! If all of us maintain the same level of giving as last year, our church's program will suffer greatly.

Please keep in mind that it is only through your continued understanding and related financial support that your church will be able to effectively minister to you and your family and the family of God!

Sincerely,

Dear Mr. and Mrs. Evans,

You will agree, I am sure, that the enclosed Proposal for our church sets forth a program of which we can be proud. We believe we can do this job with the help of the other members and you. Note especially the new local Missions program and the expanded youth activities program.

The Finance Committee of our church, reflecting the mood of our church members and friends, is interested in making this one of our most significant years. Your giving will supply the tools for building the programs that will positively help our community.

A few homes will be visited during the week starting September 7, in advance of our general solicitation. I know you will be giving serious thought to your share in our enlarged program.

Your gift not only brings hope to many others at home and abroad, but it also enriches your own life.

Sincerely,

Dear Church Friend,

After a careful study by our church, we have undertaken a greatly increased program of service for the year ahead. Areas of emphasis will be a local Missions program and expanded youth activities.

We need to become stronger in our personal faith. We wish to make our Christian witness more effective. We desire more aggressive action against the conflicts in our country and in the world.

You can help us achieve our goal. It is our sincere hope that you will first pray and then give in proportion to the need and to your ability. Your gift will help us build a more vital program through Jesus Christ.

One of our members will visit each home soon to talk over the needs of our church with you.

For Christ,

P.S. We are asking that each person pledge to support the needy outside the church as well as to support our own church.

Every Member Canvass

Dear Mr. and Mrs. Elender,

On Sunday, September 16, our church will take an important step forward. In a spirit of consecration and worship we will dedicate ourselves to greater service for Christ during the coming year.

We hope that you will be present to join with us in the simple service. Although no financial commitments will be taken then, the occasion will start our Every Member Canvass. This year we have two obtainable goals:

1. Every member pledging to local expenses and to help for the less fortunate
2. Every pledge increased

We are enclosing a copy of the proposed budget. It shows you both needs and opportunities.

During the week starting September 16, church visitors will call on all members and friends to discuss our plans for the coming year. We invite you to consider with concerned prayers your part in our enlarged program. Let us face together the challenge that economic need has thrust upon our church.

Plan to be with us on Dedication Sunday, September 16.

Cordially,

Budget Can Be Met

YOU HAVE RESPONSE-ABILITY

To: Members and Friends of Riverside Community Church
From: Bob Barton, Chairman of the Finance Committee

With the knowledge that the work of the church *will* be done and with the knowledge that an informed congregation *will* respond, the financial condition of your church is presented below:

Our budgeted income through 10-31-__	$99,590
Our actual income through 10-31-__	90,746
We are short of our goal by	$ 8,844

At least $7,500 of this shortfall must be collected. Each member MUST prayerfully consider his or her individual responsibility in this crisis situation and respond accordingly.

If 250 members and friends give an extra $30 during the month of December, 19__, the $7,500 will be raised.

With the knowledge that this request IS possible, we can move on into 19__ with a far greater hope and assurance that God's work—here and in the larger world—*will* be done.

We appreciate the concern and RESPONSE-ABILITY we know you will share with YOUR church at this time!

Sincerely,

The following letter is a lighthearted reminder to fulfill a pledge to the church. The layout is intended to attract attention and to lead the reader pleasantly to the realization that a pledge is a promise that must be kept.

Delinquent Pledge

Once upon a pledge card . . .Mrs. Arronson,
You promised your support to the Riverside Community Church Youth Building.
And then, the architects were called in
    and a contractor found (we signed);
    the cement arrived one sunny day,
    the foundation was laid, solid and square.
The passers-by observed:
    the floor that was poured
    and troweled so smooth,
    a two-by-four here,
    a rafter truss there:
    the roof was on.
Let's move in!
    an office desk in that corner,
    a class held here,
    a meeting there;
    a pot-luck supper is planned.
And then it happened—
    we found that you were behind
    in meeting your pledge—made
    once upon a pledge card.
Now, what do you think we should do about that?

(Signed by the minister)

Appeal to Faith

Dear Church Friend,

You and I—and the rest of our church members—are joined in a wonderful fellowship. We have the privilege of worshiping God together, of supporting one another in sorrow and trial, and of aiding others in our community. To a world enmeshed in conflicts and fears of war, we present the only hope for peace. An opportunity as well as a privilege is ours as church members.

We are now facing the future. Being dissatisfied with the past, we are determined to go out into larger fields of service. With your help—and the help of other members—we can realize our proposed programs. Your time, your prayers, and your gifts are all essential.

I pray that you may give in proportion to the great need and your ability. Our church aspires to strengthen our witness for Christ in our community. It all depends upon *your* help.

> In His name,

Love is a Reason for Giving

Dear Church Friend:

> Loving, Sharing
> Giving, Caring,
> This is what the Lord
> Meant Christians to be.

Have you ever given love and not had it returned? Then you know how God must feel much of the time. Love is sharing. Think of the happiest moments of love—moments with your children, with your spouse, with God, at Christmas time—and you realize that giving stands out. God's love was demonstrated by the ultimate gift, "For God so loved the World that he gave his only begotten Son."

Love is sharing.

You have an opportunity now to share your love with your Church. As we enter the period of stewardship emphasis, I appeal to you to show your love by making a financial commitment to God's work for the coming year.

> Care deeply for
> Christ our Saviour.
> Care for the Church as
> The Lord cares for you.

> Sincerely,

HOSPITALS

Both public and private hospitals feel the need to solicit the public for funds—funds that it is hoped will approach the need. The basic appeal is to the satisfaction that the giver receives from helping someone in need. A secondary appeal is the selfish one of helping oneself by giving to a hospital in which one has been or may become a patient.

The first letter from Mount Zion Health Systems, Inc., San Francisco, is to a prospective donor. The uses to which the donor's money will be put are listed and explained. The last paragraph suggests how much to give and mentions the convenient mailing envelope. A suggested amount and a return envelope are standard techniques—and they are effective; they should be included in all solicitation letters.

Updating Facilities

Dear Friend:

If you made an inspection tour of Mount Zion today, you would see the activity that has already taken place or is getting underway in the hospital's second year program of updating facilities and equipment. For example:

— Renovation of patient rooms.
— Moving of fifty patient beds from "C" Building (which can no longer house patient care facilities because of new earthquake requirements) to the new 7th floor of "A" Building.
— New Courtyard Building under construction to house new lobby, Admitting Office, Dispensing Pharmacy and kitchen.
— Construction of new quarters for Geriatric Day Care.
— Completion of four floors of the Mount Zion Pavilion for the Prenatal Center, including Obstetrics, Intensive Care Nursery, Regular Nursery and Alternative Birth Center.

All this work and much more has to be done to modernize and renovate our hospital. Space that is today handling a greatly increased volume of patient care programs with new lifesaving technology has not been changed in fifteen years and must be expanded.

We are not adding any new beds, but are seeking to preserve the quality of medical care for which Mount Zion Pioneer, a core group of supporters, has contributed in the historic first two years of our Annual Campaign.

A reply envelope is enclosed for your convenience. I hope to hear from you at an early date and to welcome you as a member of the Pioneers. A gift of $100 would be most appropriate—$1 for each of the hundred years Mount Zion has been serving the community.

Sincerely,

The second letter is to former patients who may appreciate their hospital care enough to contribute to the care of others. The persuasive technique is the use of success stories.

Success Story

Dear Friend:

Do you like success stories? We hope that your stay at Mount Zion was one, and we would like to share with you just two of the many at Mount Zion's Senior Day Health Center:

Mrs. W.S.

> 65-year-old widow. Residing with employed daughter since husband's death. Adjustment to this living arrangement complicated by a physical condition which worsened, severely limiting mobility and increasing dependency. Since becoming Center patient, occupational therapy with use of adaptive equipment has decreased dependency greatly. Able to assist daughter in meal preparation. Has developed many new interests. Contributes regularly to Center Newsletter. Involved in writing life history and recently has been learning to weave. Only complaint is that days are not long enough.

Mr. C.H.

> 75-year-old married man. Confined to wheelchair following stroke three years ago. Referred to Center by his disabled wife to whom he has been married 55 years. She attempted to care for him at home but even with maximum allowable homemaker assistance was unable to do so and

he had to be admitted to nursing home. Lost interest in life; both he and wife finding separation extremely stressful. Based on availability of Day Health Center services, discharged from nursing home. Motivation increased immediately. Now ambulates short distances with supervision. Enjoys copper enameling and has delighted wife with gifts made for her at Center. Couple now able to give each other emotional support that was integral part of their lives for 55 years.

The Center changes the lives of its patients from hopelessness and despair to happy, fulfilling days of newfound physical activity, new interests and new friends and sociability. This is why we are so anxious to make its new home, about which we told you in my preceding letter, comfortable, cheerful and suited to the needs of its patients. Won't you please help us furnish and equip it by making your gift to the 19__ Annual Campaign today? An envelope is enclosed for your convenience. We suggest $101—$1 for each year Mount Zion has been serving the community—but any amount is most welcome.

Sincerely,

This next letter is to a previous donor and reminds the reader of the tax-deductibility of the gift. Some uses of the gift are explained.

Equipment for Senior Patients

Dear Friend:

This time of year many people find that they are able to make an end-of-the-year charitable donation. If you are in this position, we hope that you will direct it to our 19__ Annual Campaign.

As you know, gifts to this year's campaign will be used to furnish and equip the new home of the Senior Day Health Center, the Mount Zion Facility where senior citizens find a new lease on life through new friends, new interests and new physical capabilities.

The average age of patients is 75—the range goes from 52 to 98. Whatever their age, sex, financial ability or living circumstances, they all need the wide range of services the Center provides. Their improvement in physical capabilities and morale, development of new interests or activated pursuit of old ones, enjoyment of newfound friends and response to individual care are a source of daily inspiration to the dedicated, hard working staff.

Please help us provide the Center with a bright, cheerful new home, equipped to take care of the needs of its patients.

A return envelope is enclosed for your convenience in sending us your tax-deductible 19__ gift today. Whatever the amount, it will be most welcome.

Sincerely,

The tone of the next letter is direct and positive. This candid approach will appeal to many, but the recipients of this frank letter must be carefully chosen.

Need for Continuing Support

Dear Mr. and Mrs. Haliburton,

Clayton Hospital spends a lot of money. For this we are often criticized. But this doesn't bother us because the money is spent to provide the best health care available with the money we have.

Last year, for example, we opened our new Intensive Care Unit to help the critically ill, and modernized our Pediatric floor. The value of lives saved is not measurable but the cost exceeded $3 million. And now a Cardiac Care Unit for patients with heart trouble is being planned, and will be built over the next two years.

Last year we received $500,000 in gifts from our many thoughtful donors. The result of these gifts is better medical care for you. To perpetuate this care, we must be assured of continuous giving.

The money comes from you! And we are asking for more. We need community support, and we need your support. We are asking that you please add Clayton Hospital to your list of tax-deductible annual contributions. A postage-paid envelope is enclosed for your convenience.

Your interest is sincerely appreciated by the staff and especially the patients.

Most sincerely,

The letter to Mr. and Mrs. Halstrom is similar to the one above and, like it, is straightforward. It is only slightly shorter, but the shorter paragraphs give it a crisper appearance and tone.

Expansion Costs

Dear Mr. and Mrs. Halstrom,

The hospital staff wants to help you!

To provide medical help they must have adequate facilities. Clayton Hospital is expanding to provide you and those you love with better medical care.

Our recent expansion includes a new Intensive Care Unit for the critically ill and a modernized Pediatric floor. During the next two years, a Cardiac Care Unit for patients with heart trouble will be built.

The value of lives saved cannot be measured but the cost will exceed $6 million. Much of this money must come from the community and donors like you.

How much should you give? That, of course, is up to you, but we suggest a tax-deductible minimum of $25.

This is an opportunity I hope you will take to invest in medical help for your community and for you.

Please send your contribution soon in the enclosed postage-paid envelope.

Sincerely,

P.S. The staff and patients, present and future, are looking forward to the help your donation will provide.

Maintain Quality Service

Dear Mrs. Jamieson:

Our new Medical Center is now open, and with pride we invite you to take a tour. Just stop by the Pink Lady desk in the lobby.

A large number of people have been pleased with two concepts we have adopted: mostly single rooms and ramps instead of stairs for emergency exits.

The use of single occupancy rooms has proved quite successful, and arrangements have been made with health insurance carriers to cover patients in single rooms.

The Pacific Northwest Medical Center was built with the support of numerous private citizens who recognized the need for a modern medical facility. The Center belongs to all of us, and the Annual Center Campaign requires our dedicated support. Will you do your part by contributing what you can? The purpose of the Campaign is to maintain the high quality of medical service we have attained. And don't we all have a personal interest in that?

Sincerely,

P.S. The enclosed postage-paid envelope is for your convenience in mailing your tax-deductible gift.

The three following letters are a series mailed to doctors who work at the hospital that is making the request for contributions. The mailings were approximately one month apart. The first letter appeals to our human need to be part of a group: "because you belong to the hospital family." The second letter appeals to the doctor's business experience (rare is the doctor who is not well versed in the business aspects of medicine). The third letter is a short review of the first two. The statement in the first sentence that this is the "last invitation" is both an appeal to give *now* and a relief to the doctor that no more solicitations will be received.

Doctors Join in Giving

Dear Doctor:

As a member of the Mount Zion family, you benefit from the contributions which the hospital receives in terms of improved facilities for the care of your patients. Therefore, I am sorry that up until now I have not had the opportunity to share with you what happened last year in one area of support.

For the first time in its history, friends of Mount Zion were asked to participate in an Annual Giving Campaign. Annual campaigns have long been a tradition in many hospitals throughout the country, and they provide a dependable source of support for current pressing needs.

By contributing $1 for each of the 99 years we had been serving the community, a donor could become a Mount Zion Pioneer. The response was so gratifying that we decided to reopen the ranks for the second year. After this, they will be closed.

You were not asked to participate last year, but because you belong to the hospital family I thought that you too might welcome the opportunity to join the Pioneers.

This is my invitation to you to become one by contributing $100 to the 19_ Annual Giving Campaign—$1 for each of the years we have served the community. I hope you will accept. Your support will help your hospital serve you better.

Sincerely,

Doctors as Business Persons

Dear Doctor:

I am writing again to invite you to join the Mount Zion Pioneers by contributing $100 to the Second Annual Giving Campaign— $1 for each of the 100 years the hospital has served the community.

In some ways a hospital is like a business—its facilities and equipment must be improved constantly. As you know, many of Mount Zion's facilities have not been changed in 15 years but are today handling a greatly increased volume of patient care programs with new lifesaving technology. They must be modernized.

The recent Capital Funds Campaign raised a substantial amount to assist with renovation and new equipment, but campaign goals are seldom realized and this one was no exception. Rising costs are another problem.

Notwithstanding, the work in progress must be completed as soon as possible and other phases of modernization gotten under way (see the enclosed Fact Sheet).

The real business of Mount Zion is LIFE—helping it to be born; strengthening it; saving it. Please help us provide you with the most effective medical facility possible in which to do it. Send your gift today and become a Mount Zion Pioneer.

Sincerely,

Last Appeal to Doctors

Dear Doctor:

This is your last invitation to become a Mount Zion Pioneer. The 19__ Annual Giving Campaign is ending soon, and I hope that when it is over your name will be on this year's list of contributors.

Mount Zion is your hospital and it needs your support in keeping abreast of advances in medical research and technology.

As you know, your gift will help provide optimum facilities for the care of your patients, and it is urgently needed to carry on the modernization and renovation program now underway.

As a member of the Mount Zion family, please do become a Mount Zion Pioneer; give $1 for each of the 100 years this hospital has served the community, and mail your check in the enclosed envelope today.

Sincerely,

Using a Specific Example

Dear Friend:

A broken arm . . . severed above the elbow in an automobile accident . . . a small incident in our troubled world—but of more than small importance to Janet Collins.

Two years later she has nearly full use of her arm and hand, thanks to the expertise of the microsurgery team at Cantebury Hospital.

Janet's severed left arm was picked up by a police officer at the scene of an accident and packed in ice from a nearby restaurant. The police sped her to the nearest emergency medical station from which she was rushed by helicopter to the downtown heliport, then by ambulance to Cantebury Hospital. The microsurgery team spent fourteen feverish hours reattaching Janet's arm.

The microsurgery team inserted a steel rod at the elbow, then brought the rod out of the cut and into the upper part of the arm. Then an artery and three veins were connected. Major nerves were tied, and finally the skin was sewn.

Nearly two years were required to get full feeling into the fingers. Therapy and slow progress are Janet's future, but she is happy to have the use of her arm again.

Cantebury Hospital is doing its small part to serve this troubled world. Will you share in the Hospital's efforts? The enclosed envelope is for your convenience in making a gift to Cantebury Hospital. You will receive the gratitude of our many patients.

Sincerely,

Replace Equipment

Dear Friend:

Our medical equipment does not belong in an antique shop—it merely seems that old. The rapid advance of medical technology is the reason for the early obsolescence of much of our medical equipment.

On the other hand, many of our beds have wobbly wheels, and some will crank only halfway up. The floor covering in three rooms is worn through.

Ordinary equipment does wear out, and lives depend on having the latest diagnostic equipment available when needed—when *you* may be the one in need.

Obsolete medical equipment must constantly be replaced, and that is why we appeal to you each year to do what you can to aid the community and yourself through a donation to West Center Hospital.

Contributions last year were generous, and we anticipate that they will be even more generous this year. The enclosed envelope is for your convenience. Whatever you give will be deeply appreciated and will ensure continued medical care for all of us.

Sincerely,

Appeal to the Ego

Dear Mrs. Elder:

We recently received a donation of $50,000 toward the purchase of a head scanner for Pleasant Hill Medical Center.

Donations of this size are both encouraging and necessary if we are to continue serving our community with the best medical care possible. The diagnosis of medical problems has advanced remarkably in recent years, and this requires sophisticated—and thus expensive—equipment.

Pleasant Hill Medical Center has doubled the number of beds in the past five years, and it will continue to improve its services with your contributions.

It is heartening to know that there are people sincere enough about helping their community to contribute substantial sums to back up their feelings. But even if you haven't $50,000 to contribute, we will appreciate your gift. Please give enough to make yourself feel good.

We have patients waiting.

Sincerely,

Join Hospital Foundation

Dear Friend:

Everything in the health care profession is changing—except the need for funds to meet today's demands and be ready for tomorrow's needs.

Today's health care institutions face unprecedented changes. These changes involve new concepts in medical care and treatment, increasing specialization in services and equipment, development of service training programs, government partnership in medical insurances programs, population growth, and changing sociological patterns. A program to develop critically needed supplemental income for our health care institutions is imperative.

The Foundation, an agency through which such a program is to be projected, has been created. The Wheeler Hospital Foundation is a completely autonomous, nonprofit, nongovernmental organization established to support Wheeler Hospital. The Foundation would afford a means for accepting in a legal, orderly manner, the philanthropy of donors who have the spirit and will to give.

Through a permanent Foundation, the independent financial security of the Wheeler Hospital may be achieved.

Through this Foundation, a fund will be built up year by year that will be available continuously for essential capital and supplemental operational needs. This Foundation, as the responsible agency for a continuing financial program, will embark upon programs that may extend far beyond the life span of any one individual.

The Foundation will involve many influential persons from all walks of life.

The Board of Trustees, consisting of 48 representative citizens of the area who volunteer their time and talents, invites you to regard the Foundation as one of highest priority. It will be both life-giving and lifesaving.

When you join with other leading citizens of this area as a member of this new nonprofit corporation, you will be part of a team dedicated to the development of the finest health care facilities possible. What could be more worthy of your whole-hearted support?

Sincerely,

P.S. The enclosed card and envelope are for your convenience in requesting more information about ways you can help.

SCHOOLS

The "old college spirit" often leaves the campus right along with the sheepskin. In an attempt to recapture that spirit, colleges write to alumni with requests for donations to the "dear old alma mater." To be successful, a request for a contribution must be for a specific project or purpose. The first letter requests increased giving to combat inflation and attract a more competent faculty. The main appeal is to pride.

Give More Than Last Year

Dear Mr. Warner,

Difficult choices must be made during difficult times. Increasing inflation rates coupled with reduced tax revenues make the choices of where and how much to give truly difficult. It is especially difficult for those of us who care deeply about Harcourt College and its 140-year tradition of excellence.

This year you are being asked to increase your annual gift by 20 percent. Last year's gift of $100 was encouraging—and we did manage to balance the budget. But, with __ percent inflation, we need more than that even to think about strengthening our traditional standards of academic excellence, community service, and social responsibility.

Our tradition of excellence and responsibility is ours to improve upon or to let fade away. As president of Harcourt College, I feel a special and personal responsibility to future generations of students. It is through past and continuing efforts of men like you that we can meet the expectations of future students. They too will want to experience the basic qualities of Harcourt College: a sense of honor and decency, a pride in academic proficiency, a feeling of joy and pleasure in both work and play, a love of growing and learning together, and the acceptance by our community. These qualities, although partially intangible, can be realized only in a climate of financial security.

Our strength has been the ability to attract students and faculty of the highest competence. This we must continue if we are to keep Harcourt College what it is today; but the cost will be greater tomorrow.

Viewed this way, perhaps our choices for giving are not too difficult. An increase of 20 percent in annual giving will maintain our tradition of excellence and assure its continuation for the benefit of our students, faculty, and community.

                                                    Sincerely,

Dear Miss Lipsky:

How can a private school continue without charging tuition?

Wellington College has done this for 107 years. Our specialized programs require students to work during alternate semesters. This has been done successfully for 107 years.

Yes, there is a secret to our accomplishments. We have succeeded in convincing a growing number of generous friends that our specialized school fits the educational needs of many of our young people—those who learn best by combining academic study with practical experience. Over the years, our friends have been willing to support their beliefs with their gifts.

This year we are asking for a little more: an increase of 10 percent over last year's gifts. We hope many of you can provide the extra dollars needed to balance our budget.

I am confident that we can meet the needs of the students who need Wellington College.

                                                    Sincerely,

The next two letters are similar except that the second is shorter and in outline form. This attracts attention and makes the style more snappy. The appeal is to the satisfaction of helping others. In addition, the postscript offers an ego-boosting suggestion.

Library Needs

Dear Graduate:

Quality in a university depends to a great extent upon the information available to its students in its libraries. We, as well as you, Mr. Garcia, are aware of how rapidly new information is discovered and published. Budget restrictions and inflation are putting a squeeze on available library funds, but we strive hard to buy the current publications required by our serious students. The quality of Riverside University is dependent upon our having access to the latest knowledge. Help from you and other graduates is essential.

Enclosed is a brochure describing our library, the study facilities, the friendly assistants, the quick service, the special department libraries, the areas in immediate need of funding, the plan for future growth, and items of particular interest to library users.

Your gift, Mr. Garcia, whatever its size, will improve the educational quality of the Riverside University Library. Please mail your tax deductible donation in the enclosed envelope today.

Sincerely,

P.S. Don't forget, for a donation of $30 or more we will send you a copy, upon request, of the book plate showing your name that will be placed in a book purchased with your gift.

Dear Mr. Garcia,

As a recent graduate, I believe you would gain much personal satisfaction from strengthening the Riverside University Library by making a donation *this* year.

Because:

— You learned the importance of *current* library resources during your school years.
— You are aware of spiraling inflation and recent budget cuts.

— A strong library benefits students, the library staff, faculty, alumni, Annual Fund donors, and state residents who use the library.

Please send your gift in the enclosed envelope today.

Sincerely,

P.S. Remember, with a gift of $30 or more, a bookplate showing your name and the name remembered, upon request, will be placed in a book purchased with your gift.

Alumni Solicitation

Dear Alumnus:

YOU make the difference between mediocrity and excellence.

Think about it.

Your considered gift to the Dartmouth Alumni Fund supports the Campaign for Dartmouth.

Sincerely,

Haven't Given Yet

Dear Fellow Alum:

The Texon University 19__ annual giving campaign ends April 30. Just noticed that your name is missing from the list of this year's donors.

To date, 30,000 alumni and friends have donated nearly $6 million. A gift of only $25 from those who haven't given would add at least $500,000 to this year's total, further enhancing Texon University's position as one of America's leading centers of higher education.

Please mail your check in the postpaid envelope, now! The students will appreciate your help.

Sincerely,

Dear Alumnus:

Have you given your share to Wadsworth University this year? If yes, a hearty thanks, and you deserve the University's congratulations.

The alumni and faculty have consistently led all givers in meeting their goals. Being so close to the University, what else could be expected?

We find, however, that some of you have apparently delayed making your contribution.

The faculty and alumni goal this year is $400,000. I am sure you will help us exceed that amount. We have enclosed a pledge card and a postage-paid envelope for your convenience.

Give as much as you can, and whatever your gift, it will strengthen Wadsworth University and ensure an even better education for the students and leaders of the near future.

Sincerely yours,

Dear Ms. Hasland:

I am happy to have been asked to get in touch with you classmates who have not yet responded to the 19__ campaign. Too few of us have given. The Fund this year will provide capital improvements to the Johnson and Guthrie Halls.

In recent years, the prestige of Cleveland Dental School has risen substantially. One indication is the number of articles published in medical and dental journals that are written by our faculty and former students. Another is the increasing number of highly qualified applicants for admission. Also, the number of graduate students choosing Cleveland Dental for research has shown a steady increase in recent years. Your prestige improves right along with that of the School.

Considering your interest in your profession and in your school, I am hopeful that you will use the enclosed card to pledge your support. Several convenient giving programs are suggested on the card. The enclosed envelope is for your convenience.

Working together, we can meet the capital improvement goal and enable Cleveland Dental School to continue its growth in education, service, and prestige.

Sincerely,

Dear Mr. Albert:

I believe you will want to join those who have already contributed to the Granger Graduate School Campaign this year because:

— You have contributed in the past.
— You feel responsible for the continued improvement of your school.
— You have received and continue to receive lifelong benefits from the School and the Alumni Association's work.

Your sincere and immediate consideration will be truly appreciated.

Sincerely,

Minorities Program

Dear Friend:

Today you can take your own giant step for mankind. Let us discuss for a moment how you can do it.

Olin College has a strong program to help Mexican-Americans . . . to give them hope and to break the pattern of impoverishment and hopelessness.

The College is using everything from private consultants to county farm agents.

The Minorities Department is giving assistance to 300 Mexican-American students in Practical English, Everyday Mathematics, and Farming. Other campus programs are helping these minorities in agriculture, drug education, and small business practice. The College is currently looking at other beneficial programs.

As you are well aware, the need is great and it is real. Better education makes better citizens, and better citizens make a better country in which to live.

Your financial help will benefit all of us in the near future.

Sincerely,

P.S. For making your tax-deductible contribution right now; we have enclosed a postpaid envelope.

Operational Funds

Dear Mr. Mann:

You have kept us going! While many colleges in recent years have been closing, Whittington College has remained open with generous contributions from alumni.

But the crisis of inflationary costs coupled with a declining enrollment has not bypassed Whittington. We have fought the financial crisis by delaying faculty salary increases, reducing service personnel, and putting off needed maintenance

These can only be temporary solutions. We need your contributions now to keep Whittington from joining the growing number of closed colleges.

Please use the enclosed postage-paid envelope to mail your gift, perhaps larger than the one you gave last year. But gifts of all sizes are needed and appreciated.

Sincerely,

Building Fund

Dear Mr. Cross:

Your gifts to the Computer Science Building Fund of Norfork University are now showing on campus in the form of a new building. We have reached 80 percent of our goal, with contributions coming in daily.

A visit to the building site will let you experience the excitement of dollars being turned into a facility for the advancement of computer knowledge.

We thank you for the gifts that are making the long-time dream of a computer science building an accomplished fact.

Sincerely,

Student Union Building

Dear Humboldt Parent:

As the parent of a student living away at college, how often do you get a phone call from your son or daughter that is for the sole purpose of exchanging pleasantries? Occasionally, we hope. Usually the call is for a little extra cash or transportation home.

This week, however, you will get a phone call from one of our students who is not your son or daughter. Humboldt students will phone each parent, asking for a donation for furnishings for the Student Union Building. The goal is $40,000 to complete the building for use next year.

A Student Union Building can contribute so much to the education of a student. A college education is not limited to classroom academics. Making new friends, sharing new experiences with old friends, trying a new hobby or activity, a lively discussion with one's peers—these are all a vital part of the college experience. A center for social activities encourages participation in this part of college life. A Student Union, run by and for students is an ideal center for college social activities.

When you receive your call from a Humboldt student this week, please respond favorably. It is your son or daughter who will benefit.

Sincerely,

Religious Appeal

Dear Mr. and Mrs. Winton:

Does God love some people more than others? We are taught that this is not true. We are also taught that those who receive more from God should share more of those receipts—be they blessings or money.

If "God so loved the world that he gave his only begotten Son," surely a small financial sacrifice should not be too much for you.

Buchanan University, a private school of higher learning for over 110 years, is one university that emphasizes the human side of learning. Buchanan has schools of Religion, Medicine, Dentistry, Nursing, Law, and Liberal Arts.

The heart, as well as the mind, is nourished here, and this has been going on generation after generation.

We ask for your financial support for the present and future generations at Buchanan, that they in turn may be able to help others.

Most Sincerely,

Financially Disadvantaged Students

Dear Mr. Stone:

This appeal is on behalf of the students of Webster Technical Institute who might not be able to complete their technical training without additional financial aid. Many of our 21,000 students support themselves and members of their families with part-time and temporary jobs. When any emergency occurs, a family illness, a job layoff, or a medical bill—there is no way for them to cope without temporary financial aid.

Many students enter Webster Tech directly from high school and lack the necessary skill for jobs that are available. But they too must buy books and school supplies. We find that many of these students run out of money before the school term ends. Often, $200 or $300 is all it takes to keep a student in school through the end of the year.

We do have a Student Fund Program, supported by donations from concerned groups and individuals. Your help is needed: our Fund is running low, and we don't expect all the money to be returned. All requests for money are thoroughly investigated, and no money is lent or given unless the need is real.

Your contribution is, of course, tax deductible. Please use the enclosed envelope. We appreciate your consideration of our many needy students as they struggle to learn a trade so that they can make their own way in this world.

                                        Sincerely,

Each of the following four letters opens with an interest-arousing sentence. These are good, but the writer must take care not to overdo a good thing and let the sentences get cute.

Every Little Bit Helps

Dear Mr. Allen:

Some alumni have never given to the University of Oregon! Their explanations go something like this:

> "Well, I never contributed because, well, because I didn't think my few dollars would be noticed."

I want you to know that the University of Oregon needs *your* financial support, however little. Small gifts have a way of adding up to large sums.

Our immediate needs are two endowed professorial chairs in the social science field and scholarships for Oregon residents.

Please take this opportunity to continue the improvement of your university and your state. Many others are giving. I hope you will too.

Sincerely,

Pledge Not Received

Yes—we are concerned, Mr. Hampton.

We have not recorded your pledged contribution to Ellsworth College. Time is short. The Anniversary Fund closes October 31. The Fund this year will provide new seats for Landon Hall. The need has long been obvious to us and to those attending public performances.

I hope you know that we need *your* help. All donations are needed—and appreciated—however small or large. We depend primarily on gifts from individuals: from you.

Please take a moment now—right now—to send your pledged contribution.

Your consideration and thoughtfulness is appreciated by the Fund committee, the students, the faculty, and the community.

Sincerely,

Request for Small Gift

Dear Barrows Alumnus:

Just a moment of your time, if you can, to talk about a $5 bill. True, it won't buy much today, but we are still interested.

Multiply that $5 by our over 50,000 active alumni and you have $250,000—not small at all.

We are asking for your $5 to establish an endowment for the science library as part of our struggle to keep it current; not an easy task when new discoveries occur so rapidly.

We will be grateful for your contribution, and I am sure you will feel good about giving. Your check in the enclosed envelope will be greatly appreciated.

Sincerely,

Worthy Projects

Dear Mr. Bronson:

We really don't mind asking for money—when the project is worthy.

At Cornwall College, all projects are worthy—or they don't get started. And we feel this one merits your special attention. A fine arts performing center will bring together our scattered fine arts department. The stage and auditorium will be available to the public, so that they as well as our students will benefit. Our goal is $800,000 to be raised through donations from foundations and the public. This center has long been needed by both our college and our community.

Please take a moment to consider this. Then use the enclosed reply card to make your pledge or contribution.

I know you'll feel glad about helping.

Sincerely,

Chapter 5

COLLECTION

The primary function of a collection letter is to collect money. To accomplish this, the writer must retain the goodwill of the debtor. This is especially true of personal collection efforts, directed toward individuals or businesses managed by one or two persons. A collection letter to a large business firm, however, need not put as much emphasis on empathy with the reader.

For purposes of comparison, let us for a moment explore the essentials of a business collection letter. The most important thing is to identify exactly what is delinquent. The letter should include:

> the delinquent customer's order number and date,
> the items purchased,
> the seller's invoice number and date,
> the dollar amount that is past due,
> the original due date.

These items are essential to the reader in identifying the delinquent invoice. The letter below was written by a collection agency to a company that receives over a dozen freight bills daily. The bill referred to could be one of several hundred, either paid or unpaid. Imagine the difficulty of tracing this particular bill:

> Your past due account in the amount of $22.06 has been brought to our attention by Freight Agencies.

> Please mail your check for this amount to Freight Agencies by May 5 so that no future action will be necessary.

The tone of a business collection letter takes second place to the identity of the delinquent item. This is true because in a large business organization a collection letter is delegated to the lowest ranking clerk capable of searching for the bill and determining if and when it was paid. The following letter displays an overly aggressive tone for a first reminder, but the research clerk ignored the letter's harshness and checked the facts stated in the letter.

Gentlemen:

In reviewing our records again, I find that your account is more than forty-five (45) days past due in the amount of $162.94 for statement dated 7/7/__.
OUR TERMS! ALL ACCOUNTS ARE DUE AND PAYABLE UPON RECEIPT OF OUR STATEMENT.
Please forward payment immediately.

Thank you,

(signed)

Credit Manager

ALL ACCOUNTS ARE DUE AND PAYABLE UPON RECEIPT OF STATEMENT

For the first three notices to a large business organization, a copy of the delinquent bill or a short reminder is as effective as a letter of persuasion. For the fourth notice, a letter explaining the delinquency, with a copy of the overdue invoice enclosed, will be helpful.

Do not, however, construe this functional approach to business-to-business collection letters to mean that politeness, fairness, and consideration for the reader can be ignored. The primary difference is that a business collection letter must contain more technical identification of the delinquent items than is usually necessary in a personal collection letter.

The last example above would never do as a personal collection letter, in which the reader's goodwill is of paramount importance. The personal collection letter should excuse the debtor while requesting payment. The delinquent person may have merely overlooked the due date, may be in temporary financial difficulties, or may even be a "professional procrastinator" (one who operates his or her business on money that should have been used to pay the bills). Whatever the reason, let the debtor save face and assume that the delay has not been spiteful.

Continue thinking well of the customer and omit any harsh and abusive language. In addition, omit words and phrases of this nature:

cannot understand   delinquent
remit promptly   ignore

failure on your part   require
we insist   compelled
our demand   wrong
unsatisfactory   cancel

Positive words sound better and bring you more favorable results:

respond   your payment
fairness   your check
you   mail today
your credit   please

A personal collection letter must be considerate of the reader. Therefore, give him or her a reason for paying promptly. Rather than saying, "We would appreciate prompt payment so we can clear our books," apply the "you" attitude and write, "Your prompt payment will keep your good credit rating intact," or "Your paying early enough to take the discount will allow us to continue our low prices for you."

Collection letters are a standard part of the collection process. The first notice to the delinquent is usually a copy of the bill with or without a sticker or rubber stamp impression stating "past due" or "have you forgotten" or "second notice." Following this are short and gentle letters, each one successively insistent upon a payment. Phone calls may be interspersed with the letters. The third or fourth letter is often long, making a sincere appeal to sympathy, pride, justice, fairness, or self-interest. The final step is turning the account over to a collection agency or to an attorney for legal action.

How to Receive a Prompt Reply

The surest way to receive a prompt reply is to enclose a post-paid, self-addressed envelope. Mention in the letter that one is enclosed.

An additional device for making the reply easy for the reader is to include a card or note showing the amount and date of the next payment. Leave a space for comments. This will be returned to the writer and will save the reader the trouble of writing a letter.

A third technique is to enclose a phone number with the name of a person who can be called.

How to Do It

1. State the purpose of the letter clearly and in an interesting way.

2. Include data relevant to the situation: what the writer is asking for, how the reader can be helped, and reasons for paying now.
3. Restate the request for payment.

Collection letters are a necessary part of managing a business. When asking for a payment, neither apologize nor beg.

Attention-Getting Openings—Humorous

The opening of a collection letter must attract the attention and arouse the interest of the reader. The techniques for doing this are limited only by the imagination and research efforts of the writer. Opening statements can vary from "Just a reminder that we have not received your last payment" to slapstick comedy in personal letters:

Dear Mr. Wilson:

"Hey, look at this, Bud!"

"Bad news, Joe?"

"Yeah, this guy wants my autograph."

But, gosh, that's a compliment. Aren't you proud?"

"But this guy wants it on a check."

We, too, would like your autograph on a check—$45.60 for the toaster you bought on February 7th. Please use the enclosed postage-paid envelope.

Sincerely,

Other stories and fables like those listed below can be used as attention getters for readers who will respond favorably to the light hearted and humorous.

An official whose garage delivered his car every day received a card on his windshield one day. "Merry Christmas from the boys at the garage." Two days later he received another card, "Merry Christmas, second notice."

This is a second notice to you about your overdue payment of $99.80 . . .

One mathematician to another, "Now that you have invented *zero*, what do you have: nothing."

Nothing is what we have received from you for your purchase in June . . .

In a similar vein, here are three snappy collection letters:

- Are you holding on to that check for $29.70?
- Might makes right. Right for us is a payment of $52.50. Might for you is a good credit record.
- We think a collection letter should be short and successful. We hope you do too. $32.95.

Just what to include in a collection letter (to be added to or subtracted from the model letter chosen) will depend on various combinations of the following considerations:

— First delinquency
— Continuing delinquency
— New customer
— Long-time customer
— Small debt
— Large debt
— Urgency of need for cash flow
— Value of customer's future business
— Type of approach (humorous, serious, short, long, light, pleasant, or persistent) the writer believes the reader will respond to.

A Strong Close

The end of the letter is its most emphatic part; make the last statement or request strong and definite. Be specific about *what* you want, *when* you want it, and *how* you want it done. At the same time, keep in mind consideration for the reader: an offended reader pays slowly. Examples for specific purposes follow:

For Prompt Action

In order to open your account for further purchases, please let us hear from you today.

To avoid additional expenses and unpleasantness, we expect to hear from you within ten days—before August 12.

Because we are anxious to provide fast service, please let us hear from you promptly.

We can help you just as soon as we hear from you.

To Build Goodwill

We are glad to cooperate with you, and look forward to serving you for many more years.

Thank you for bringing the problem to our attention. We are always happy to help.

We appreciate your cooperation.

Thank you for letting us help.

To Soothe

The mistake was obviously ours. We misunderstood your complaint. We have taken steps to correct the situation and hope you will bear with us for a few days.

We cannot disagree with your feelings; we would have felt the same in your situation.

We are sorry we had to take the action we did, but under the circumstances we had no alternative. We hope you understand.

This action may seem unnecessary at this time, but later I am sure you will appreciate what we had to do under the circumstances.

We would sincerely like to grant your request, but we are unable to do so now. We are, however, looking forward to serving you in the near future.

To Apologize

We are sorry for the inconveniences we caused you, and you can be sure we will make every effort to prevent it from happening again.

We feel bad about the trouble we caused you and hope you will accept our sincere apologies.

Thank you for calling the error to our attention so we may correct it. We are sorry for causing you an inconvenience.

Your patience is appreciated, and we thank you for your consideration.

Please accept our apologies. We have corrected the cause of our mistake, and you can be assured it will not occur again.

To Reassure

We appreciate the business you have given us, and we trust you will understand that we cannot be of service to you at this particular time.

Of course we are sorry to have to turn down your request, but we do look forward to serving you in future months.

We dislike, as all business people do, turning away a sale, but I am sure you understand why we must at this time.

A lost sale leaves us with an empty feeling, but, as you know from the circumstances, it is not possible for us to help you at this time. The near future may look more promising.

To Repeat

Again, prompt payment will retain your good credit rating.

To repeat, the sooner we receive payment, the sooner we can help you again.

Which of these two suggestions appeals to you? Please let us hear from you right away.

To prevent these added expenses and the inconvenience to you, please let us hear from you within ten days.

This order cannot be released until we receive your financial statement, Please mail it today!

To forestall bothering you again about this overdue balance, please mail a payment today in the enclosed envelope.

Repeated reminders are a lot of trouble for us and a bother to you. Please help us both by mailing your payment today.

Briefly, a partial payment now will keep your account open.

To Promote the Future

Now that we have your financial data, it will be a pleasure to approve your future orders promptly.

We are available to serve you at any time, so please call at your convenience. We will work hard to make you a happy customer.

We appreciate your prompt payment for your recent order. We look forward to more years of serving your needs.

Now that your account is on a current basis, we look forward to approving your future orders promptly. A continuing business relationship will benefit both of us.

Series of Collection Letters

A delinquent customer or borrower often needs only a reminder that the last payment was not made. Because of this, many firms use a series of from three to six short collection letters. These can be form letters, typed each time as originals, or they can be preprinted—even in booklet form—with spaces for filling in the amount and due date. Each letter is more insistent than the previous one. When these will suffice, the time and cost required for composing personal letters can be saved.

Series One, Three Letters: Reminder

Letter One

Just a reminder . . .
of the amount written at the bottom of this note. It hasn't been paid. Will you mail your check today?
$72.90

Sincerely,

Letter Two

Has the mail been delayed again . . .
preventing your check from reaching us? Did you mail a payment on your account recently? If you did, please stop payment and send another check for $72.90. We are anxious to have your account on a current basis.

With hope,

Letter Three

There has to be a reason . . .
why we haven't heard from you after our previous reminders.
Will you let us know why? Or perhaps you would like to spread the balance over a longer period. Please let us know how we can help.
The amount due is $72.90.

Concerned,

Series Two, Three Letters: Business Charge Account

Letter One

Dear Mr. Lemke:

Our records show that the following purchases by you are past due:

April 29, 19__	$761.30
April 30, 19__	92.00
May 4, 19__	76.10

It is to your advantage as well as ours to keep your credit accounts current.

We would appreciate your paying these amounts today.

Sincerely,

Letter Two

Dear Mr. Lemke:

You did not respond to our first reminder of your overdue balance of $929.40. Could you have overlooked our terms of 1 percent 10 days, net 30 days? If there is a reason for the delay, please let us know. Otherwise, a prompt payment will be appreciated.

Sincerely.

Letter Three

Dear Mr. Lemke:

Once again, Mr. Lemke. we ask for your cooperation in paying your past due account.

A prompt receipt of $929.40 will keep your account open so we can be of help when you make future purchases.

Since we don't want to have to take any further action, we will expect a check dated today.

Sincerely,

Series Three, Three Letters: Past Due Freight Bill

Letter One

Gentlemen:

Attached are copies of our freight bills that are past due. Just a reminder that our policy requires payment within ten days.

We would appreciate prompt payment.

Sincerely,

Letter Two

Gentlemen:

Although we sent you past due reminder copies of the attached bills three weeks after our original billing date and again after five weeks, the charges remain unpaid and are now seriously past due.

Since we know you wish to pay your bills when due, we expect that these open items are just an oversight on your part.

As you know, our policy prohibits us from extending credit to customers who have past due charges outstanding, and we have no alternative but to withdraw credit privileges in such instances.

We would very much like to continue extending you credit, and you will enable us to do so by sending us your remittance now.

Sincerely,

Letter Three

Gentlemen:

Two weeks ago we wrote to you with copies of the above freight bill numbers advising you that they were seriously past due and in violation of our policy, even though we had sent you several past due reminder copies of the bills.

We assumed that failure to pay these open items was an oversight on your part and that our letter would bring a prompt response and enable us to continue extending credit. We regret to see that they are still unpaid and the delinquent status of your account leaves us no alternative but to remove your company from our list of credit customers. Our terminal manager has been instructed to rescind your credit privilege and transact future business on a cash basis.

If the outstanding balance is not paid in ten days, our Collection Department will take whatever action is necessary to accomplish collection.

Sincerely,

Series Four, Four Letters: Make Account Current

Letter One

Dear Mr. Stockton:

We hope that this year has been a pleasant and successful one for you—and that next year will be even better.

To end this year happily, we would like to see you clear your past due balance of $73.20. A check mailed to us today will start your new year with a current account.

An envelope is enclosed for your convenience.

Sincerely,

Letter Two

Dear Mr. Stockton:

I am sure we both agree that a good reputation is essential to a prospering business.

Your past due account, however, does not seem to support your good reputation. We feel it is important for you to get your account on a current basis.

Sincerely,

Letter Three

Dear Mr. Stockton:

Your account is nearly six months behind our terms of 30 days. I am sure it is not your intention to ignore past due notices at the expense of your credit standing.

We strongly suggest that you make a payment within the next few days.

We are expecting your check.

Sincerely,

Letter Four

Dear Mr. Stockton:

The small balance of $73.20 in your account does not warrant any more of our time and expense to collect. We also feel it should not be placed with a collection agency.

We can write it off as a bad account, but your credit reputation will suffer. Your credit standing can be maintained, however, by a prompt payment—made no later than the end of this month.

Sincerely,

Series Five, Four Letters: Loan Past Due

Letter One

Dear Mr. Ballard:

May we call your attention to your loan payment, that you have no doubt overlooked? It is 30 days past due. The amount is $950.44.

Sincerely,

Letter Two

Dear Mr. Ballard:

Your loan payment is now 45 days past due. Prompt payment of $950.44 will be appreciated.

Respectfully,

Letter Three

Dear Mr. Ballard:

Again we call your attention to your loan payment due March 15. If there is some reason for the delay, please let us know.

We would appreciate receiving your check for $950.44 immediately.

Very truly yours,

Letter Four

Dear Mr. Ballard:

It bothers us more than a little to say this, but we insist on your paying the $950.44 you owe us. If we don't receive your check by December 31, we will be forced to turn your account over to a collection agency. Please save yourself the embarrassment and loss of credit standing this will cause you. The enclosed envelope is for your convenience.

Yours truly,

Series Six, Four Letters: Charge Account

Letter One

Dear Mrs. Cato:

Just a reminder that your account is 15 days past due.

If you have already sent your check for $332.90, we thank you for doing so.

Cordially,

Letter Two

Dear Mrs. Cato:

Patience is a virtue. We may sometimes seem lacking because we get a little impatient, but we try to be considerate of our friends and customers. Therefore, please accept this letter in that spirit.

Your account has become long past due (since February 15). Please send your check for $332.90 today. We are expecting it.

Sincerely,

Letter Three

Dear Mrs. Cato,

You have been a customer of ours since 19__, a long time. I am sure the reason is not only because we carry merchandise you like but because of our helpful clerks, our easy-pay credit policy, our prompt delivery service (at no extra charge) and our long established reputation for quality.

We do all these things to please our customers and to co-operate with them. But cooperation is a two-way street. To provide for our customers' needs, we need the cooperation of our customers. By paying your bills on time, we have the funds to rebuild our supplies and to continue providing services for our customers.

Your account has remained unpaid for quite a while, since February 15. If you are unable to pay now please call or write so we can make other arrangements. Otherwise, could you please help us to continue helping you by mailing your check for $332.90 today? A postage-paid envelope is enclosed for your convenience.

Sincerely,

Letter Four

Dear Mrs. Cato:

Your response to our letters about your long overdue account has been completely negative: not one word from you.

We feel, therefore, that we must turn your account over to our attorney for collection. We dislike doing this, and in fairness to you we will postpone any action for ten days, giving you until July 26, 19__. Please send us your check for $332.90 before that date to avoid the embarrassment of legal action.

Sincerely yours,

Series Seven, Five Letters: Charge Account

Letter One

Dear Ms. Bronson:

No doubt you have overlooked payment of the enclosed statement. Your prompt remittance will be appreciated.

Account No.   _____
Date Due   _____
Payment Due   _____

            Sincerely,

Letter Two

Dear Ms. Bronson:

Your attention is again invited to your delinquent account. To avoid an unfavorable report of your credit records, we suggest an immediate payment of the amount due.

Account No.   _____
Date Due   _____
Payment Due   _____

            Sincerely,

Letter Three

Dear Ms. Bronson:

It is apparent that you have ignored our two previous reminders. Your account is now seriously delinquent.

We must insist that you pay this account immediately, or personally discuss this with us.

Account No.   _____
Date Due   _____
Payment Due   _____

            Very Sincerely Yours,

Letter Four

Dear Ms. Bronson:

There must be a reason for not paying your account. Whatever the reason, we would be happy to discuss it with you. We can make arrangements for smaller payments over a longer period of time if that would help you. We must hear from you or receive a check within the next 15 days.

Account No.   _____

Date Due   _____

Payment Due   _____

Sincerely yours,

Letter Five

Dear Ms. Bronson:

Since you have apparently made no effort to pay the amount due us, we have no alternative to taking legal action. You may prevent this, however, by making payment by August 15, 19__.

Account No.   _____

Date Due   _____

Payment Due   _____

Very truly yours,

Series Eight, Five Letters: Charge Account

Letter One

Dear Mrs. Watson:

We sincerely hope you have no objection to a reminder that there is a balance due of $999.52 on your monthly account.

If you haven't mailed your check, could you do it now? Then your account will be current.

Cordially,

Letter Two

Dear Mrs. Watson:

You did not respond to our first reminder of your overdue account, but we have confidence that you will send us a check for $999.52 to make your account current.

Please use the enclosed postage-paid envelope.

Sincerely,

Letter Three

Dear Mrs. Watson:

We are interested in our customers and are always looking for ways to improve our customer service. For this reason, we would like to know if there is a reason for your delay in paying your long overdue account. If there is some way we can help—by making your payments smaller or extending our terms or by recommending a loan company—please let us know today.

We would appreciate a word from you—preferably a check.

Sincerely,

Letter Four

Dear Mrs. Watson:

Several times by letter and phone, we have discussed arrangements for the payment of your account. The following items are still delinquent:

No. 1527	5-4-_	$229.70
No. 1574	6-4-_	320.00
No. 1622	6-7-_	449.82

So far we have no indication of your cooperation. Thus at this time we must insist on immediate payment. Please use the enclosed postpaid envelope.

Sincerely,

Letter Five

Dear Mrs. Watson:

Is there anything we can do to persuade you to pay your seriously delinquent account? We have tried many friendly suggestions for extending the payment period, for making small monthly payments, for seeking help from lenders, and for at least discussing this matter with us.

We can't give up, but we have about exhausted our own resources. Therefore, we propose to seek aid from outside our own company. Our attorney has been consulted, and he reports that various legal avenues are available for collecting our money.

We dislike the thought of going to court, and have decided to extend your credit for two weeks—only 14 days. To avoid legal action, we must have your check for $999.52 on or before August 16.

Sincerely,

Series Nine, Six Letters: Slow Pay Business Account

Letter One

Hello Mr. Daws:

Why not start right now to check these invoices that are past due?

No. 1527	5-4-_	$229.80
No. 1574	6-4-_	3320.00
No. 1622	6-7-_	429.82

By paying them now, you save the trouble of having to check them again. If there is a reason for their not being paid, please let us know.

Sincerely,

Letter Two

Hello Mr. Daws:

If at first you don't succeed . . . Here is your second opportunity to pay these past due invoices:

No. 1527	5-4-_	$229.70
No. 1574	6-4-_	3320.00
No. 1622	6-7-_	429.82

We know you intend to pay them, so why delay? If you have a reason for not paying now, please mail us an explanation or phone us at 000-000-0000.

Sincerely,

Letter Three

Hello Again, Mr. Daws:

Why haven't you paid?
Why haven't you written?
Why haven't you phoned?
Do you intend to ignore your bills?
Surely not, so please mail you check today for $3979.62 covering our invoices 1527,1574, and 1622.

Sincerely,

Letter Four

Dear Mr. Daws:

With reluctance but apparent necessity, we remind you once more of your open account that is now 60 days beyond our 30-day terms.

Our previous reminders have apparently been ignored, but you can no longer delay payment if you wish to keep your account open.

Please call us now to discuss ways that we can work together to reduce your open balance. We will do what we can to help you.

Don't fail us and your company at this time. At the very least, send us an explanation for your delay. A check sent today will keep your account open.

Sincerely,

Letter Five

Dear Mr. Daws:

Any further delay in paying your balance due cannot be accepted. Your apparent desire to reject our suggestions of working together on getting your account current is having a bad effect on your credit record. We must have a payment at once.

If you cannot send at least a partial payment right now, call us so we can arrive at some workable agreement.

Please respond today!

Sincerely,

Letter Six

Dear Mr. Daws:

Ten days, ten short days, is the amount of time our legal department suggest we extend your open account. After that time—April 28—our legal staff will take action to collect your overdue account.

This decision should not seem blunt or surprising. We have repeatedly written and phoned your office asking for payment. Your response has been negative. We can no longer be sympathetic. As a businessman yourself, you can understand why we must have your cooperation.

We will expect a payment from you on or before April 28.

Sincerely,

Series Ten, Six Letters: Business Account Delinquent

Letter One

Dear Ms. Bowen:

We all appreciate an occasional reminder of a forgotten invoice. Perhaps you have mislaid the one of February 3. We have enclosed a copy.

Won't you write a check and mail it in the enclosed envelope—today please.

Sincerely,

Letter Two

Dear Ms. Bowen:

We are enclosing another statement of your balance of $9,401.

Since this amount has remained long past our 30-day terms, we feel an immediate payment should be considered by you.

Sincerely,

Letter Three

Dear Ms. Bowen:

Your account balance of $9,401 is still unpaid.

Not having heard a word from you, we assume you do not question the amount you owe us.

Now we must ask that you pay without delay.

Sincerely,

Letter Four

Dear Ms. Bowen:

You have received monthly statements from us for February, March, April, and May. You have received phone calls from us March 28, April 29, and May 30.

The result: no response.

It is our policy to help our customers as much as possible because we appreciate their business. If you have a problem with the merchandise or with your finances, please let us know what it is so we can help. We must hear from you to understand what the problem is.

Please phone or write today. That will help us both.

Sincerely,

Letter Five

Dear Ms. Bowen:

Should we take drastic action to collect the balance you owe us? Is drastic action necessary?

We hope not, but our letters have been unanswered and our phone calls ignored. A payment by you can no longer be put off. Please send at least a partial payment with a word of explanation about future payments.

We must have your cooperation if we are about to work with you in getting your account on a current basis.

Action is required now.

Sincerely,

Letter Six

Dear Ms. Bowen:

Your account is still unpaid in spite of our continual and friendly reminders asking for payment or an explanation for your delay.

It seems that our only recourse now is to take strong measures to collect from you. We will, however, be patient for another 10 days before taking legal action.

To forestall our taking legal action, mail your check for $9,401 today.

Sincerely,

The First Collection Letter Is a Reminder

Because the first collection letter is simply a reminder, it should be gentle. The purpose of the letter, however, should be presented in a positive and straightforward way. The reader should have no doubt, after reading the first sentence, that he or she is late in making a payment. A little sales pitch and an offer to discuss extended payments may be included. An enclosed envelope for customer convenience is recommended.

Dear Ms. Orley:

Have you forgotten the last payment on your loan?

The final payment is $65.20. Because your other payments were on time, I thought you would appreciate this reminder. Please use the enclosed envelope to send in your check for $65.20. May we have it today?

Sincerely,

Just a REMINDER, Mr. Egbert,

that you may have overlooked making the last payment on your account. A copy of our bill for $37.98 is enclosed along with an envelope for your convenience.

Regards,

Dear Mr. Moore:

Your check for $54.80 has not arrived.

This may be a small amount, but when multiplied by our several thousand credit customers, the total is a whopper.

Won't you please help out by mailing your check for $54.80?

Cordially,

Dear Mr. Eden:

Just a friendly note to let you know we are still waiting for the next payment on your account. An envelope is enclosed for your convenience.

Remember, too, our new, wide selection of Stanley power tools, designed especially for home workshops.

Cordially yours,

Amount Due: $227.55
Date Due: November 30, 19__

Dear Mr. Hudson:

I am sure there is a reason why you haven't paid your bill for $43.50 at Alex's Men's Wear. It is now 30 days past due.

If you have been ill or out of work or otherwise unable to pay, we are understanding. We can extend your payments. We would, however, appreciate hearing from you so we can work out a mutually agreeable payment schedule.

Please use the enclosed envelope or call us at 000-000-0000.

Cordially,

Gentlemen:

A routine review of your account reveals the following past due balance:

ITEM NUMBER	DATE	AMOUNT	DUE DATE
30.2233	2-4-__	$4355.90	3-4-__

If your remittance is not already en route, your assistance in expediting payment would be truly appreciated.

Sincerely,

Dear Mr. Davis:

As you requested, we have enclosed a copy of the item listed below that remains open on your account:

Item Number	Date	Amount
33-6632	11/29/__	$411.10

We believe this will enable you to place the above in line for prompt payment. If additional information is needed, please let us hear from you.

Sincerely,

Attn: Accounts Payable Bookkeeper
Re: No. 14-4438 10/12/__ $914.45

Gentlemen:

Enclosed is a duplicate copy of the above invoice.

We issued credit memo No. 1854 to cancel this invoice. You apparently used the credit to cancel the invoice and also to reduce the amount paid on one of our later invoices.

It would be greatly appreciated if you could review your records and, if they are in agreement, process the invoice for payment.

Please call us if we can provide additional assistance.

Very truly yours,

Dear Ms. Trimble:

Re: Invoice No. 99-4568 6/22/__ $3855.70

According to our investigation, this invoice represents a shipment of canvas made against your purchase order No. U-51786 dated 1/4/__.

As we discussed on May 6, we would appreciate your approving it for payment.

Sincerely,

Dear Mr. Oxford:

As one of our good customers, there must be a reason why your payments have gotten a little behind.

Is there anything we can do to help or something we should correct? Please let us hear from you.

Sincerely,

Dear Ms. Penderson:

19__ is almost over; time seems to fly by unnoticed. Perhaps that is why you have not yet paid the $49.99 for your last purchase at Ender's.

Now that you have been reminded, please mail your check right away.

Sincerely,

Dear Mr. Ashworth:

Your terms, as you know, are net the 10th of the following month.

Right now $239.90 is past due.

We would appreciate a prompt payment.

Sincerely,

Dear Mr. Maynard:

As I am sure you are aware, the balance due on your account is $329.44. This amount should have been paid by April 23, so you can see it is quite old.

Please let us know when you will pay or at least start by making partial payments. The enclosed envelope requires no postage.

Sincerely,

Gentlemen:

Just a friendly reminder that your account has gone past the discount period and is now past due.

If your check is in the mail, we say "Thank you." If not, won't you please give this your prompt attention.

Sincerely,

Dear Ms. Watson:

Your attention is directed to the attached list of freight bills, which our records indicate are unpaid beyond the credit period permitted by our written agreement.

You may have already made the payment and it has not reached our accounting department. If these bills have not been paid, however, a prompt remittance will be appreciated. Please mail your check to West Transportation Co., P.O. Box 0000 Arlington, VA 00000.

Sincerely,

Credit Union Loan

Dear Al Sanchez:

We would like to clear up an apparent misunderstanding about your payroll deductions to pay back two Credit Union auto loans.

You signed payroll deduction authorizations for loan No. 05-902, $70 and loan No. 05-993, $55, from each biweekly paycheck.

It is approved procedure and standard practice throughout the Corporation to make these deductions mandatory after deductions for payroll taxes, Worker's Compensation, and Union dues. If this leaves you with a negative paycheck, Form A425 can be signed by the plant payroll clerk as explanation for a smaller Credit Union deduction.

We must insist that payroll deductions be started again because your loan payments are now *seriously delinquent.*

Sincerely,

Middle Stages of Collection Letters

Second letters should still be reminders. They need be only variations from first letters, or slightly more irritating first letters.

Third or fourth letters become longer and more persuasive. The delinquent payer has ignored or given little importance to the short early letters, and now a change in tactics is required. An appeal is made to one of several human feelings; for example:

Sympathy: Your small amount due is only one of many accounts.

Pride or Self-Respect: We appreciate your past promptness, but now you are behind.

Justice: We have carried your account too long; be fair and pay now.

Self-Interest: It is in your own best interest to have a good credit rating.

Give the debtor an out by suggesting a longer payment period or at least the opportunity to discuss future payment arrangements.

Dear Mr. Manor:

We expected at least an answer to the last of several letters we sent you. As you know, you still owe us $422.

Truly, we are disappointed. I am sure you are not intentionally trying to make our work difficult, but that's what it amounts to. Is there some reason you have not paid? some difficulty getting the money? too many other bills to pay? Let's make this easier for both of us. Call us, and we can solve any problems together.

We have been fair with you, and now we believe you will be fair with us.

Sincerely yours,

Dear Mr. Reid:

This is somewhat embarrassing—embarrassing to us because you are a good friend, and embarrassing to you because you owe this good friend some money—money that should have been repaid long before now.

Some time ago (April 16, 19__) you purchased a chair from us, and we were happy to accept your promise to pay within 30 days. You seemed pleased with the chair and I am confident it has given you many hours of comfort. Isn't it only fair that you live up to your part of the agreement we made?

Let us be fair with each other. You have a comfortable chair. We would like our money. Since your payment is long past due, please make out your check now for $225.75, and mail it today in the enclosed postpaid envelope.

Sincerely,

Dear Mr. Addams:

We have sent you numerous letters requesting payment of the $302 open on your account since February 23. We have heard nothing from you, not even an excuse, and our patience has just about run out.

We must insist upon prompt payment.

Very sincerely yours,

Dear Mr. Danfield:

You have not made a payment on your account during the last nine months. We realize that financial conditions in your area have not been good recently, and you have not been pressed for payment. By now, however, we feel you should be able to start paying again. We will be glad to work with you in making a reasonable payment arrangement.

Please call or write and let us discuss what can be done to get your payments started again.

Sincerely,

Dear Mrs. Edwards:

I am sure you are concerned about the $300 you still owe us on the bedroom furniture you purchased last February.

We can understand that problems do arise that prevent prompt payments and possibly that is why you have not kept up. If that is so, we can extend your payment if you will pay $50 before the end of each of the next six months.

We are sure this will be agreeable to you, and we are expecting a payment of $50 by June 30.

An envelope is enclosed for your convenience.

Sincerely,

Dear Mr. Nolan:

You have not answered my previous letters asking for payment on your $1324 purchase. I doubt that those letters have just been overlooked. More likely you were short of cash. But after so long a period of time—an entire year—we feel that we should be entitled to at least a small portion of the money you do have available.

Could you please make a payment on the $1324 you owe us? I am sure the fairness of this will make you feel good.

Sincerely,

Dear Mrs. Allison:

We have several times reminded you of your past due account of $224.76. It is 90 days past due. Why have you not answered?

Simply, we are disappointed that our confidence in you was misplaced.

Not paying your bills on time can hurt your credit standing in the community. You can make time payments if you wish, and we will gladly work with you on a payment schedule you can afford.

Please restore our confidence in you and maintain your good credit rating by sending us a check now—even a partial payment will help.

Respectfully,

Dear Mr. Coughlin:

We have sent you several reminders about the $92.20 you have owed us since March 1. That was nine months ago!

In consideration of your own credit rating in this city, I think you should pay this amount now. Certainly you want to be fair to yourself.

Your check can be mailed in the enclosed postage-paid envelope. Please use it today.

Sincerely,

Dear Ms. Morris:

Your prompt payments on your open account in the past are appreciated by us. We hold customers who maintain current accounts in high esteem.

Now, however, your payments are lagging. If there is some reason for this, please let us know so we can work together updating your account.

We are counting on hearing from you. The amount due is $699.18.

Sincerely,

Dear Mr. Durer:

Dillon Company hates to keep bothering you with delinquency notes and letters, but your long overdue account is damaging your credit record. This is costing both you and me money: you are incurring additional monthly service charges and we are losing interest on uncollected funds. You could help us both by writing your check for $72.99 right now and mailing it in the business reply envelope enclosed.

Sincerely,

Dear Mr. Renquist:

We hate to keep bugging you, but $80.50 on your charge account is still past due.

If you have a reason for not paying, please phone us or use the enclosed postage-paid envelope to explain why.

If you have been merely putting it off, please mail your check for $1421.20 today.

Sincerely,

Dear Mr. Sanderson:

You will recall the recent reminder we sent you on May 5 about your overdue account. Is a check on the way?

If not, we are counting on your cooperation in making a prompt payment.

Sincerely,

Gentlemen:

We again call your attention to the following invoices which, according to our records, are still unpaid well beyond our normal terms:

Date	Invoice No.	Amount
7-17-__	78-458	$1444.77
8-25-__	78-789	864.57
		$2309.34

We would greatly appreciate your early remittance or informing us of the reason for further delay.

Sincerely,

Dear Ms. Atherton:

We try hard to be equally fair with all our customers, and I am sure you wish to be fair with us. Your account now shows:

April 30	$ 32.90
May 31	93.40
June 30	56.60
	$182.90

Perhaps you have overlooked these past due amounts. It would be only fair to pay them now. The enclosed envelope is for your convenience.

                                        Sincerely,

Dear Mrs. Solomon:

We provide open accounts for the convenience of our customers—to make your shopping easier.

To continue these open accounts it is necessary that they be paid within 30 days as agreed when they are opened.

As mentioned in our previous letter, your account is long overdue. Prompt payment will be appreciated.

                                        Sincerely,

Dear Mr. Sewell:

Your open account still shows the overdue amount mentioned in our recent letter dated June 27.

Please send us the $99.90 today, or at least let us know your reason for the delay.

Your cooperation will truly be appreciated.

                                        Sincerely,

Dear Mr. Collins:

You have not responded to our previous notices about your open account.

Your balance of $429.90 is considerably past due, and we ask that you give this delinquent amount your immediate attention.

Your cooperation will be appreciated.

                                        Sincerely,

Slow Pay—Terms Explained

Dear Mr. Wharton:

Recent payments of our invoices have been received long after the due date. Invoices appear to be paid in batches rather than individually when due.

Perhaps our terms are not clear, and I would like to take this opportunity to explain them.

Your credit terms are "Net 30 days," meaning that payment is due *here* 30 days after the date of our invoice. If you prefer to pay our invoices several at a time, we can change our terms to "15 Prox.," in which case payment is due here on the 15th day of the month following the date of our invoice. However, if the total amount of these groups of invoices exceeds your credit terms, more frequent payments will be necessary.

If you have any questions about your terms, or wish to change them to "15 Prox.," please call me at 000-000-0000. I will be happy to discuss this with you.

Please remember that continued delays in paying our invoices will result in our suspending shipments to you. We presume this will not be necessary, and look forward to continued business with you.

Sincerely,

Final Collection Letters

The final collection letter is the last step prior to turning the account over to a collection agency (which normally takes up to 50 percent of anything collected) or to an attorney for whatever legal action he or she thinks will open the delinquent's pocket book.

However exasperated the creditor is, the goodwill of the debtor must be retained. Do not demean the delinquent payer or use any foul language. Care is required to avoid writing anything libelous or even halfway libelous. Tact must be the watchword.

Dear Mr. Evers:

I would like to talk to you in person about your delinquent account. Since this is not feasible, let me talk frankly in this letter.

Your payments were on time until the beginning of this year, but since then we have received no payments. During this time you have continued to buy from us. You have ignored our past reminders. Something is wrong. Can we help? Please phone or drop in to visit so we can get together on a payment plan.

At this time we must insist on hearing from you within the next ten days. After that, we will have no choice but to cancel your credit and turn your account over to a collection agency. We don't want to do this because it may harm your credit rating. We must hear from you by November 20.

Very truly yours,

Dear Mr. Goodwin:

Although we have sent you a statement, three reminders, and two letters about your unpaid balance of $628.84, we have not heard from you.

If there is a reason for not paying, please phone or write us immediately. After June 14, your account will be turned over to our legal staff for whatever action they believe appropriate. This inconvenience, however, can be avoided by sending us your check for $628.84 before June 14.

Sincerely.

Dear Mr. Danzig:

Do you like taking a beating without fighting back? We don't either. We don't want to fight or take a beating. But you seem to have forced us into a fight.

Your bill for $442.90 is still unpaid—after 12 months. We have tried all the persuasive techniques we know, and now we feel forced to fight for our money.

You will, however, have 10 days in which to pay your bill. If we have not received the money due us by March 20, we will be forced to seek legal advice.

Please let us hear from you before March 20.

Sincerely,

Dear Mr. Addams:

You have not responded in any way to our recent letters about your past due account. Since February 23 you have owed us $302. If you do not reply by December 10, enabling us to arrange for periodic payments, our next step will be to consult our attorney about further action.

Very truly yours,

Dear Mr. Smythe:

You have not responded at all to our attempts to collect the $492.25 you have owed us since December of 19__. This leaves us no alternative to seeking legal action.

This step requires unnecessary time and trouble for both of us. Therefore, we will delay any action for ten days from the date of this letter. If we receive your payment by then, we will be happy to continue our business relationship.

Please let us have your check for $495.25 by January 22.

Sincerely yours,

Dear Ms. Cavell:

We tried,

We are trying now,

We don't want to have to try again . . .

to collect the money you owe us. Your payments used to be prompt, but this last bill is over a year old. You have not responded to our earlier reminders, and now we must have payment by November 30, 19__. After that we will turn your account over to a collection agency. To avoid this inconvenience, and loss of credit rating, please mail your check today in the enclosed envelope. The amount due is $429.90.

Very truly yours,

Dear Mr. Atwood:

NOW is the time for action!

Your account is seriously delinquent!

You have not responded to repeated requests for a payment on your past due account. We can no longer stand by and wait. We must have action on your part.

Unless we receive a check from you within ten days—on or before June 17—we will start legal action to make the collection,

Sincerely,

Dear Mr. Mack:

Because of the extreme slowness of your payments over the past two years, we can no longer extend credit to you. We have discussed this time and time again, but to no avail. Starting today, all sales will be cash-with-order.

We will be happy to continue serving you under these conditions. You can expect the same quality of merchandise and the same fast service—and our super fast emergency service.

We do expect you to make regular payments on your present balance. Appropriate collection or legal action will be taken if your delinquency continues.

Sincerely,

Dear Mr. Edwards:

Our long-time efforts to convince you of the importance of paying your accounts have brought no favorable response. We have offered many varied suggestions to make your payments easier for you, but you have declined even to discuss these. The only course left to us is legal action.

This can be inconvenient and time-consuming for you. It can also jeopardize your credit standing.

If you will make a payment within ten days, we will forget the legal action and consider you a paid-up customer.

We expect a payment within ten days.

Sincerely,

Dear Mr. Wingate:

Because our many letters have remained unanswered, we get the impression that you do not intend to pay the $472 balance in your account.

Therefore, we have taken steps to turn your account over to a collection agency. To forestall this action and its effects on your credit standing in the community, won't you please write or call us this week?

Sincerely,

Dear Mr. Herbert:

You don't want us to call in an attorney to assist in collecting the $1,439.80 you have owed us since April 15, 19__. We don't want to do that either.

Why not keep both of us happy by settling your account this week? A check from you on or before next Thursday will save us a call to our attorney and you the trouble of defending legal action.

Sincerely,

Dear Mr. Edgeworth:

We have had no response from you in answer to our many phone calls and letters during the past twelve months. Our invoice No. 4447H of March 12, 19__ in the amount of 14,217.90 remains unpaid.

Our next step is to take legal action to collect the money due us. This is unpleasant for both of us and is damaging to your credit rating. However, you may avoid legal action by making payment within ten days: on or before March 30, 19__.

Whether or not we take legal action is now your decision.

Sincerely,

Dear Mr. Nichols:

Our credit department has recommended that your account be referred to our attorney for legal action. Our numerous attempts to collect from you during the past year and a half have been unsuccessful, but because of our long-term relationship, I am reluctant to accept that recommendation.

I will hold the credit department's suggestion in my desk for ten days in the hope that you will respond favorably by then.

Sincerely,

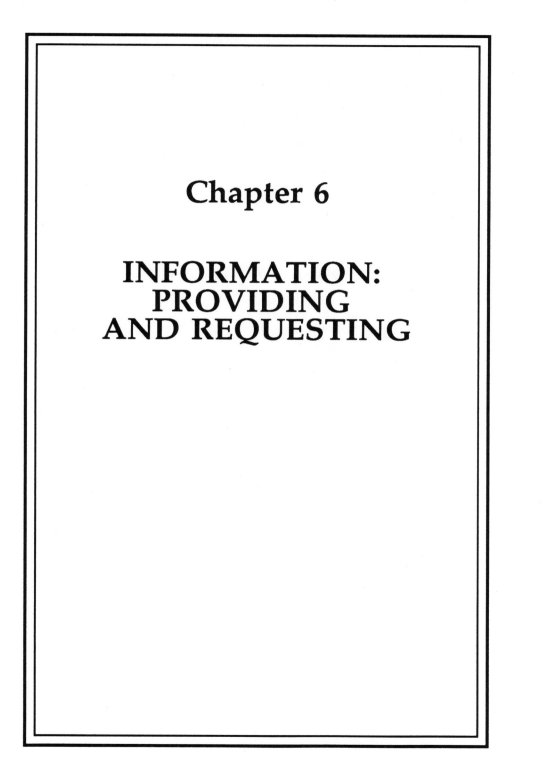

Chapter 6

INFORMATION:
PROVIDING
AND REQUESTING

PROVIDING INFORMATION

The basis of a successful letter providing information is clarity, and the key to clarity is brevity. Too often, adding supposedly clarifying details becomes a distraction to the reader. If you wish to say, "Starting in April, send the FICA report to J. C. Henning rather than to A. M. Mondale," an explanation of when Henning replaced Mondale, whether this is temporary or permanent, Henning's background and qualifications, whether Mondale has quit, retired, been promoted or shuffled sideways, and your regrets or congratulations are of no importance in getting the report rerouted.

Repetition should be eliminated. To write, "We would appreciate your taking the $188.50 credit we issued so that it can be cleared from our books and your account brought up to date," is stating the purpose twice. Eliminate either "it can be cleared from our books," or "your account brought up to date."

The second paragraph of the following informational letter illustrates the confusion resulting from disorganized thinking:

> General availability of railroad freight cars throughout the country improved slightly during the week as the weather moderated in the Northeast.
>
> We have shortages of high-roof box cars in the Northwest. In addition, the South Bend mill has been short of box cars throughout the week. We expect to clear up the South Bend shortage by Saturday, and we are using standard box cars in lieu of high-roof cars to avoid delays in customer shipments from the Northwest.

What the author has done is to organize the second paragraph this way:

Problem A, Problem B, Solution B, Solution A.

Going from solution B to solution A causes an awkward twist in the reader's thinking because he has to jump backward three steps to relate solution A to problem A.

The second paragraph should be reorganized as follows:

We have a shortage of high-roof box cars in the Northwest. We are replacing these with standard box cars to avoid delays in customer shipments. In addition, the South Bend mill has been short of box cars throughout the week. We expect to clear up this shortage by Saturday.

The rewritten paragraph is easier to follow and can be outlined as follows:

Problem A, Solution A, Problem B, Solution B.

How to Do It

1. Organize your thinking
2. Be brief.
3. Be clear.
4. Offer cooperation.

Because the ending of a letter is its most emphatic part, a courteous note that offers additional assistance is helpful in eliciting the reader's cooperation. Below are examples of simple but effective ending paragraphs:

If you have any questions about this subject, please let me know.
If you require additional information, please let me know.
Any questions should be addressed to me (to this department).
If you have any questions, please do not hesitate to call.
If you have any questions or comments, please let me know.
If you have any questions about this information, please do not hesitate to call me at 000-000-0000.
If you wish further details, please call me at 000-000-0000.
If you have any questions, please call me at 000-000-0000.
For further details, please contact me at 000-000-0000.
For further information, please call me at 000-000-0000.

Should you have any questions, or require additional information, please do not hesitate to contact me.

Please let me know if you need additional information.

Please call me if you have any questions.

If you have any questions, please call me.

Shipping Instructions

Dear Mr. Thomas:

When we place orders for aluminum wheels with you, either for our account or to be billed to one of our customers, please be sure they are shipped prepaid and the freight is included on your invoice to us.

We would appreciate your not making any collect shipments.

Sincerely,

Procedural Change

Dear Sales Manager:

Attached are three requests for credits from customers who state that they did not agree to pay for the molds used in making their aluminum castings. They understood that the mold cost was included in our sales price.

This has been a problem, and we will solve it.

We must have a clear understanding with our customers, and a definite commitment if our customer is to pay. The commitment must be obtained before we buy the molds. This is the responsibility of the sales representative.

Until further notice, all purchase orders for molds will be sent to me for approval. The purchase order must state whether we pay or the customer pays.

If you have any questions about this, please let me know.

Sincerely,

Price Increase

Dear Customer:

Due to the rapid rise in labor and operating costs, Ames Fast Maintenance finds it necessary to increase service charges on September 1, 19__.

Service charge increases will vary, depending upon the type of service your company uses: on call, when needed, or monthly preventative maintenance.

We appreciate your past business and look forward to a continuing friendly relationship.

Should you have any questions, Please call us at 000-000-0000.

Sincerely,

Dear Johnson Customer:

Due to an unexpected price increase from our manufacturing plant, the price of all colors of paint, excepting white and black, will increase 11 percent on March 1, 19__.

At present there is no increase on paint supplies and equipment, and our selection remains the best in this area.

We appreciate your being a customer and look forward to a continued association with you.

Sincerely,

Purchasing Policy

Dear Mr. Greene:

In order to do the best purchasing job possible, the responsibility for control of major raw materials, process chemicals, maintenance, and capital equipment is vested in the Headquarters Purchasing Department.

We are committed to a policy of buying materials and services at the Division, Mill, Plant, or Office closest to the point of ultimate use, commensurate with sound purchasing practice. This is a system of decentralized buying with centralized control.

Purchasing by Headquarters will be done only in two instances.

1. For those divisions that do not have a purchasing unit

2. In cases where such a procedure will save our company money.

Although the purchasing function is decentralized, the basic responsibility for policies and procedures remains the function of Headquarters Purchasing Department. Good two-way communication is essential.

Best regards,

Bid Price

Dear Mr. Crown:

This is to notify you that our bid price is $4,500 for each electric motor, to disassemble, replace worn parts, rewind, and reassemble. These are the six motors we discussed and looked at on April 7, 19__.

Sincerely,

Complying with Request

Dear Ms. Hollister:

Re: Invoice No. 0000, 12/22/__, $000.00
Enclosed is the copy of the invoice you requested.
Thank you for your cooperation.

Sincerely,

Data No Longer Required

Dear Miss Bell,

The monthly phone call analysis report, 247, and the stationery cost report, 477, are no longer required by this office.

Sincerely,

Dear Mr. Jose:

For the foreseeable future it will not be necessary to submit the quarterly tax information reports to Lawrence & Lawrence as you did in 19__ and 19__.

You should, however, continue to accumulate the data monthly so that your preparation of the annual tax reports can be done quickly.

Regards,

Lease Instructions

Dear Mr. and Mrs. McLennen:

Regarding the lease at 422 San Carlos Way, Mr. Wells has asked me to send you the enclosed new lease for your house. The lease is for a three-year term beginning the first of July,

19__, with monthly payment of $330 which should be mailed to Mr. Wells at this office.

If the terms are satisfactory to you, please sign both copies where indicated and return them to me with your check for $330, after which I will send you a copy signed by Mr. Wells.

A return envelope is enclosed for your convenience. If you have any questions, please call me.

Sincerely,

Action Taken

Dear Tom:

I received a copy of the letter sent to you by the chief accounting officer of the division of corporate finance of the SEC commenting on one of the financial items on the last 10-K report filed by Ace Manufacturing Co. This is not serious and I think it can be clarified by a short amendment to your 10-K report.

I am sending a copy of this letter to your accountants with a request that they prepare the amendment.

Sincerely,

Confirmation

Dear Mr. and Mrs. Homer:

This is to confirm the closing date of June 30 at 9:00 A.M. in our office.

Mr. Wilson has requested that you bring tax papers, fuel bills, insurance policies, and other papers you have that apply to the house when you come for the closing.

Sincerely yours,

Dear Mr. Dixon:

Confirming our telephone conversation of May 20, 19__, please cancel our purchase order number 000-0000.

Sincerely,

Payment Instructions

Dear Mr. Smith:

Due to our recent computer conversion, our accounts receivable system now requires that each customer location be identified by a customer number.

The customer number located on the above mailing label has been assigned to identify all invoices sent to this location. Your assistance in showing this customer number on all checks is requested.

Invoice numbers being paid must continue to be listed on your check.

This, together with your customer number, will permit us to promptly record the receipt of your payment.

Sincerely,

Continue Procedure

Dear Ms. Michales:

Over the past few months, significant progress has been made in controlling late payments. Your monthly report analyzing the late payments has brought much helpful attention to the problem.

Please continue sending this report to the headquarters Accounts Payable Department.

Sincerely,

Number Code Changes

Dear Mr. Chalbon:

In order to obtain more detailed information from our computer printouts, please make the following changes, effective May 1, 19__.

Old Number	New Number
8000-1200-1722-01	8000-1200-1721
8000-1200-1722-02	8000-1200-1722
8000-1200-1722-03	8000-1200-1723

Because of limited spacing in the computer program, the last two digits of the old number do not show on the printout.

We will appreciate your cooperation in making the changes.

Sincerely,

Repeated Instructions

Gentlemen:

As I have previously requested, all dividends and capital gains for my account should be in cash rather than in shares. I was surprised, therefore, to learn that the gains of December 1, 19_ were being held in shares.

Please forward the capital gain, in the amount of $492.10, in the form of a check.

Sincerely,

Distribution of Reports

Dear Mr. Greene:

The following will be mailed to you in several packages within the next few days for distribution to all salaried employees at your location:

1. A summary description of the new health benefit package and a cover letter from the Chairman of the Board (Please staple the cover letter to the description before distributing.)
2. A blue pamphlet describing medical benefits.
3. An orange pamphlet describing dental benefits.
4. A report and cover letter from Vice President A. B. Walker on Safety Performance by location for the year 19_ (Please attach the cover letter to the report.)

If any of these is not received by April 30, please call me at 000-0000.

Sincerely,

Claim Against City

Dear Mr. Martin:

It is a pleasure to assist you in your claim against Stewart City for the inadvertent damage to your property. The enclosed form is for your use in filing the claim. It is IMPORTANT that you read and follow the instructions on the back of the form.

My staff will be most willing to provide any assistance. Please feel free to call 000-0000 and ask for Claims Assistance. Your cooperation in returning the claim form as soon as possible will help us to complete the processing with a minimum of error and delay.

Before sealing the envelope, make sure you have filled in your CORRECT street address and phone number.

Sincerely,

Effect of Strike

Dear Customer:

Because of a failure to agree on terms, the Union has called a strike which may affect our operations. Despite this, our company intends to do everything possible to maintain normal shipping operations from our warehouse.

Our priority will be to minimize disruptions that might inconvenience our customers.

Your cooperation during this period is appreciated.

Sincerely,

Insurance Policy Transfer

Dear Mrs. Olsen:

Enclosed is your Original Insurance Policy No. 5107393 on property located in Hayward, California.

This policy should be cancelled as of 4/29/__, or transferred to your new residence.

Regards,

Layoff

Dear Joe Arvella:

This is to notify you that you are being laid off in compliance with Article XX, Section 3 of our current labor agreement. We hope you will be available for recall in the near future.

Please check with the Personnel Department to verify that your current address and phone number are on file.

Sincerely,

Statement of Future Occurrence

Dear Don:

As of March 15, 19__, the metal planer, operation No. 0330, will no longer be available in the Alderwild Machine Shop.

Please note this when scheduling work for this shop.

Sincerely,

Dear Mr. Atwood:

A new 1000 KVA Electric transformer will be installed in the Sitcom Plant during May 19__.

Preparatory to the installation, General Electric requires eight hours of downtime on all existing electrical systems.

The downtime has been scheduled for Saturday, March 13, 19__. There will be *no electrical power* in the Sitcom Plant on that day.

Sincerely,

Test Run Assigned

Dear Mr. Warring:

The test run of XY222 red die has been assigned to your plant. Please schedule the run as soon as possible after you receive the order, which we expect to get from Coddington within the next two weeks.

Please let me know when the test will be run and when it is shipped.

Sincerely,

Policy Change

Dear Mr. Rosen:

The Company announced in the news release on August 15 that certain Divisions will change their fiscal year-end from December 31 to September 30.

This will not change the monthly accounting procedures currently used by the Western manufacturing branches. Adjustments will be made at Headquarters.

Sincerely,

Change in Items Used

H. R. Baker:

As of April 1, 19__, we will discontinue using motor housing numbers 400-500 and use only the substitute numbers 800-900.

Please sell as scrap any remaining housings numbered 400-500.

Best regards,

Address Change

Dear Customer:

Our address for mailing payments is being changed to

_____
_____
_____
_____

This change is for invoice and statement payments only.

Other correspondence and purchase orders should still be sent to the address shown at the top of this letter.

Your cooperation in changing your records will be appreciated.

Sincerely,

Address Correction

RE: Riverside Corporation
AC: John A. Peale & Joanne Peale Jt Ten

Dear Shareholder:

We are enclosing stock certificates and accompanying documents for the above referenced security. Unfortunately, Alterwild Trust Company is not the transfer agent for this security. Please forward your securities to the below agent:

Wellington Bank, N.A.
Wellington Center
P. O. Box 0000
Detroit, Michigan 00000

Should you have any questions, please contact us at 000-000-0000.

Sincerely,

Will Contact You Again

Dear Mr. Franks:

We have received your claim forms for the transit damage sustained in your recent shipment form Watson, Co., San Diego.

One of our representatives will phone you within a few days to arrange an appointment to inspect the damage.

Sincerely yours,

Reason for Cooperation

To All Houseparents:

The daily Milk and Meal Sheets must be turned in to Jean Overland on the first working day of each month.

These sheets are part of a report that must be mailed to the State by the seventh day of each month.

A timely turn-in of the Meal Sheets is money in our pockets.

Sincerely,

REQUESTING INFORMATION

A request for information can be short and direct. For example:

Send me an analysis of steel tubing sales, by customer, for the month of October.

This is brief and functional, but the tone is unnecessarily commanding. The simple addition of the word *please* to start the request would increase the recipient's willingness to help. A word or two of explanation would also improve the reader's willingness by making him or her feel a part of the project. Two examples:

For our annual purchasing department study, please send me a list of the minority vendors from whom you made purchases during the last six months of 19__.

Mr. Holmes has asked that we provide him with an analysis of steel tubing sales, by customer, during October. Please send this data to my attention.

Long requests should be separated into items that can be listed and numbered. This clarifies the request and simplifies the answering. Here is an example:

Please send us quotes on the following:

1. 24,000 B22, 16 oz. cans

2. 5,000 A22, 1-gallon cans

3. 17,000 AA4B, size 14 plastic lids

How to Do It

1. Make the request specific.
2. State or imply a reason.
3. Show appreciation for the expected cooperation.

Because the ending of a letter is the part having strongest emphasis, the last paragraph should be a polite but persuasive punch line in your effort to obtain the information requested. The following are suggested ideas for the closing paragraph.

We look forward to receiving your reply.

Your cooperation will be appreciated.

Your cooperation will be truly (greatly) appreciated.

Your cooperation and understanding will be appreciated.

Your prompt reply will be appreciated.

We will appreciate receiving this information as soon as possible.

We will appreciate receiving this data by September 25.

A quote from you would be appreciated.

Thank you for your anticipated cooperation.

Your prompt attention will be appreciated.

Thank you. (This is a common ending for a letter either requesting or providing information. Some authorities object to a thank you in advance because it seemingly implies an end to communication on the subject.) An expression of appreciation is preferable.

A Report

Dear Mr. Willis:

Mr. Marquette asked me to inquire if you could please send him a copy of the report of the last meeting of the Cleveland Realty Board Committee. The subject of the report is Undeveloped Land Acquisitions.

He will appreciate your sending him a copy.

Sincerely yours,

Accounting System

Gentlemen:

Do you recommend a particular system or set of forms for bookkeeping for automotive shops? If you do, I would appreciate knowing what the system is and receiving a copy of the forms.

Also, many trade associations collect data related to production and financial activities from members, and summarize these. I would appreciate receiving your latest available data.

Sincerely,

Acknowledgment of Gift

Dear Ansel:

I know this is a busy season for you, but I wanted to ask if the parcel I mailed you on the 12th of last month has arrived. If it hasn't, I'll have the Post Office put a tracer on it.

The parcel is a leather portfolio case, and is a thank-you gift for the time you took from your busy schedule to show Harry Longworth some of the interesting parts of Denver. Both Harry and I appreciate your kind hospitality.

Sincerely,

City Information

Gentlemen:

Auburn, California is one of the locations my wife and I are considering for retirement, which will be in six years.

Please send us general information about Auburn, especially data that would be of interest to a retired couple. We may wish to buy residential property in Auburn before retirement.

Receiving this information would be greatly appreciated.

Sincerely,

Recent Sales Activity

Dear Mr. Rosen:

Once again we are at the time of the year when Mr. Keith Monte of Monte-Atlanta Corp. will wish to discuss can purchases for their Tampa Cannery.

Please let me know what their sales activity has been this past year and what you see for the coming year. This would include prices. quantities, delivery schedules, and other data you think pertinent.

It is Mr. Monte's plan to be in Miami Beach next month from the 15th through the 19th prior to calling on a supplier in Ohio. Could the company boat be available in Miami on the 19th, before his trip to Ohio?

May I hear from you soon?

Sincerely,

Strength Analysis

Dear Rod:

We are sending you samples of our AA21 boat cleats from our first trial run made 8/4/__. Please analyze them for strength under steady and alternating tension conditions.

Please send us a comparison of these test results with previous tests you've conducted for our St. Paul and Elkhart plants.

If you need additional information, please let me know.

Sincerely,

Data for Newsletter

Dear Mr. Robinson:

Our Personnel Manager has requested that we provide statistical data for the monthly Newsletter, as is done at other divisions.

Below is a suggested format. Please discuss it with your Division Manager and provide me with your suggested changes by May 1st.

	June This Year	June Last Year
Bbls produced		
Bbls shipped		
Production Efficiency %		

Your cooperation will be appreciated.

Sincerely,

Review of Claim

Dear Mr. Cote:

In late July, as you know, your Cincinnati Mill shipped a total of 100 three-inch finishing rollers to our Huntington plant against our order JU-0000, whereas the Huntington plant ordered only 10 rollers.

We were able to resolve the disposition problem by having Huntington accept 20, Lexington accept 20, and Charleston accept 20, with the remaining 40 being shipped to your Knoxville plant.

Attached are copies of your tally sheets, our Bill of Lading for the shipment to your Knoxville plant, and the freight bills for the shipments to our Lexington and Charleston plants to substantiate our claim. As outlined on the attached recap sheet, our claim amounts to $00,000, which includes the freight charges to Lexington ($000) and Charleston ($000).

We would appreciate your reviewing this and issuing your credit to our Huntington plant. If you require additional information, please let me know.

Sincerely,

Credit Information

Gentlemen:

We have the name of your organization as a credit reference for

_____

_____

It will be appreciated if you will give us the benefit of your credit experience with this company, as well as any other comments concerning its management and general reputation, which would assist us in extending an appropriate line of credit.

The information you share with us will be held in strict confidence and will be used for credit purposes only. We will welcome an opportunity to reciprocate at any time.

Year of First Sale_____

Highest Credit Last 12 Months_____

Amount Now Owing_____

Amount Past Due_____

Terms of Sale_____

Promptness of Payment_____

Special Comments_____

Enclosed for your convenience is a self-addressed return envelope. Your early reply will be appreciated.

Cordially yours,

Here is a short version of the above letter (it is advisable to enclose a postpaid envelope):

Would you please submit the following credit information on the above-named firm. We appreciate your cooperation and will gladly reciprocate at any time.

Then list the information required from the model letter above. Additional facts that could be requested include the following:

Date of last sale	Number of days slow
Average credit extended	Prompt in payment
Recent high extended	Unjust claims
Unearned cash discounts	Referred to collectors
Discount period	Written off to expense

Credit Card

Dear Mr. Henry:

Please arrange to secure a telephone credit card for John Hamilton who has transferred to our administrative staff. Please forward the credit card to my attention.

Sincerely,

Warranty Questions

Dear Mr. Donaldson:

We are delaying payment of the attached invoice for service work performed by you to make our second cooler operable.

Even though the cooler has been installed for several months, it was not operated until last month. The adjustments you made were adjustments I feel should be covered by the warranty. Additionally, I was under the impression that when you volunteered your help, it was covered by the warranty.

Please look into this, and let me know what will be done.

Cordially,

Making an Appointment

Dear Harry:

I have looked over the proposed agreement for the sale of your heavy equipment. It meets all the normal requirements, but I do have a few questions and want to go over the payment schedule.

We can discuss the questions over the phone or you can phone for an appointment before May 25, when it will be necessary to sign the final document.

Sincerely,

Dear Clyde:

I will be glad to talk with you concerning your contract with the publishing firm in San Francisco. If you would please call or write me at least two weeks before you plan to come to San Francisco, we can arrange an appointment.

Sincerely,

Old Equipment

Branch Managers:

The Johnson hoists at many branches have fallen into disrepair and many are no longer used for a variety of reasons.

I would like to evaluate the status of this equipment at each branch to determine the cost of repair, how much help you may need from Central Engineering, and what performance and saving opportunities are available.

By Monday, July 7, I would like replies to these questions from each of you:

1. Are the hoists operational? If not, why not?
2. When were attempts last made to repair them?
3. Describe the repair work necessary to make the hoists operational.
4. What savings are possible compared with your present hoisting system?

John Harvey is available at Central Engineering to help you answer the above questions. Feel free to call him at 000-0000.

Sincerely,

Pollution Check

Dear Mr. Watson:

On September 4, 19__, you took samples of our manufacturing plant's smoke stack emissions. Has any testing been done yet?

Our corporate office would like to know the requirements our emissions must meet now and five years from now. We need this data so capital budgeting can be planned if additional filtering or treatment is required.

What information can you give us now?

Sincerely,

Corporate Name

Gentlemen:

Please reserve the name B. C. Manufacturing, Inc. for a corporation that is being formed. The ten dollar reservation fee is enclosed.

Sincerely yours,

Dear Mr. Davidson:

I will proceed to clear the proposed name of your new corporation and arrange to set it up as soon as you notify me to go ahead. When you call me, I will also need the following information:

1. Names and addresses of directors to be elected at the first meeting
2. Names and addresses of officers of the corporation
3. The fiscal year to be selected by the corporation

I enjoyed meeting you yesterday and look forward to meeting the other principals as soon as they are all back in town.

Sincerely,

Please Investigate

Dear Josh:

Thank you for your letter of November 10 about Sanders Company complaints.

Although your letter refers to four complaints from them, we have received only two written complaints as of the first of November. As explained to you over the phone, the complaint on service did not exist. I wonder, therefore, who or what has caused the sudden rash of excuses to cease buying our belting.

I would be interested in hearing if you are able to determine who is really the culprit who is trying to instigate our removal as their supplier.

Sincerely,

Incomplete Files

Dear Ms. Pennington:

In reviewing our major construction project list, the item of sound enclosures for the hammer mill raised a question in my mind. Because of recent changes in office personnel, my files on the noise citation by the State are incomplete.

Would you please review your files and let us know when the sound enclosure should be scheduled for completion.

Sincerely,

Office Furniture

Gentlemen:

Please send us a catalog of your office furniture and supplies. We are planning to purchase new furniture and file cabinets.

Sincerely,

Life Insurance Questions

Dear Mr. Thomas:

Can you help me find the answers to a few questions about my life insurance policy No. 5320116? The questions are these:

1. What is the present death benefit?
2. What is the present cash value?
3. What is the current loan against the cash value?
4. What will the death benefits be at March 30, 19__?

Your reply will be appreciated.

Sincerely,

Correct an Error

Dear Ms. Caldwell:

Account No. 000-0000-00000
The enclosed check No. 0000 was included in our batch of checks paid per your bank statement dated December 30, 19__, copy enclosed.

This check belongs to our Watson Division at Salt Lake City. Please make the necessary corrections.

Sincerely,

Restricting Receiving Hours

Dear Mr. Carter:

In order to meet the shipping schedules required to fill our customer's demands, without increasing the personnel and equipment of our shipping and receiving department, we must restrict the receiving of raw materials to either the day or swing shift. Our primary supplier prefers the swing shift, but this may interfere with our secondary supplier with whom you deal directly.

Please investigate this from the secondary supplier's point of view and let me know your thoughts.

We must act on this soon.

Sincerely,

Using Credit Memo

Attn: Accounts Payable

Enclosed is a copy of our credit memo No. 1444 dated March 23, 19__ in the amount of $277.77.

This credit is open on your account, and we would like for you to deduct this amount when making your next payment. This will make your account current.

If you have any questions, please call me at 000-0000. Your cooperation is appreciated.

Sincerely,

Procedural Change

Gentlemen:

Your current practice of mailing two copies of your invoices to A. C. Corporation, Milwaukee branch—one marked *original*—and also mailing two copies of the same invoice to the A. C. Corporation headquarters office, Detroit—one marked *original*—is confusing. This has resulted in duplicate payments because two copies are marked *original*.

In the future, please mail your invoices, one *original* and three copies to A. C. Corporation, Milwaukee only.

Your cooperation is appreciated.

Sincerely,

Dear Mr. Hiller:

Last year we received a number of product complaints that could not be tied down to specific dates and crews. I would like to suggest that we stamp or print the factory job number on each item. This would also separate the jobs we have man-ufactured for us by outside firms.

I would appreciate your comments and any suggestions.

With regards,

Keep Records

Dear Bob:

Because of recent problems with the telephone switch-board, please have your people keep records of problems with incoming calls and complaints about phone service from our customers.

Let me have a report each Friday until the situation has been corrected.

Sincerely,

Reporting Period Changed

Dear Mr. Teller:

In my letter of February 14, 19__, you were requested to pre-pare Special Fund data as of the end of each quarter in 19__. Please refer to that letter and prepare the data requested for the six months ended June 30, 19__. Do not submit the infor-mation for the second quarter only. Please reply by July 22, 19__.

If you have any questions about this request, please call Hal Lorimore at this office.

Sincerely,

Personnel Evaluation

Dear Tom:

Please make a brief written evaluation of each of your fork truck drivers, covering the following points:

1. Description of duties
2. Performance rating for each of the duties

3. Outstanding weaknesses and strengths

Rank performance from a high of 4 to a low of 1. Number 4 is consistent performance above the position's requirements.

Please have these ready for my review by October 14. We will discuss the ratings on October 16, and set up a program for performance improvement.

Sincerely,

Safety News

Dear Martin,

Because of the recent increase in our accident frequency rate, our District Manager suggests a monthly bulletin to publicize our safety activities.

This will be posted on all bulletin boards and will increase safety awareness among our employees.

Let's get it started this month.

Regards,

Price Quote

Gentlemen:

As part of our program for developing vendor sources,[*] a quote from you on the items listed below would be appreciated.

_____

_____

_____

Please return your quote in the enclosed, postpaid envelope.

Sincerely,

[*]   The words *vendor sources* can be changed to *alternate suppliers* if applicable.

Where Is the Report?

Dear Al,

I am still looking for:

1. Supplies inventory changes you recommended
2. Purchase order study
3. Standard costs for ink usage

Please let me know when you expect to have these ready for my review.

Best regards,

Dear Bob,

What happened to the report comparing manufacturing and purchasing costs of tie-downs?

Sincerely,

Chemical Hazards

Dear Supplier:

In order to ensure the safety and health of all our employees, protect the environment, better serve our customers, and comply with current Government regulations, we must identify any hazards associated with the chemicals you supply us.

All of the questions on the enclosed SAFETY ADVICE are important. We would like a response that leaves no spaces blank. Answer each question as completely as possible.

Upon receipt of your response, it will be reviewed in light of our use of the chemical. If further information is required, we will phone or write for the specific data needed.

Any future changes in composition of the chemicals from that currently used should be reported promptly with a revised SAFETY ADVICE.

Your assistance is greatly appreciated, and we look forward to continuing our friendly relationship.

Sincerely,

Physical Inventory

Gentlemen:

We request that you take a physical inventory on September 30, 19__ of all merchandise held by you for the account of A. C. Corporation. This inventory is necessary due to our Fiscal Year Closing on December 31, 19__.

Please prepare your inventory report in triplicate and attach an Inventory Certificate to each copy of your report. Copies of Certificates are enclosed.

Please mail all three copies to my attention.

Please be certain that the cutoff is as of the end of business on September 30 and that all receipts and shipments or deliveries of merchandise up to the time of taking the physical count are properly recorded.

Sincerely,

Opinion Asked

Dear Fred,

Attached is Alex Smith's proposal to simplify our die usage calculations and make them more accurate. I feel that Alex did a fine job improving the procedure.

If you agree with the procedure, Alex will be available to run a short training seminar on the use of the revised system.

Let me know your feelings.

Sincerely,

Survey of Consumption

Gentlemen:

The State of California Department of Water Resources would like to ask your help in an important survey of industrial water use. Our objective is to obtain information on the specific nature, location, and amount of water use that will enable us to develop plans for effective water management and development. Your plant water data will help us estimate future water needs and the need for supplemental water supplies.

Our last survey, in 19__, revealed a total industrial water requirement of about 500,000 acre-feet, or about 20 percent of total urban use. We believe that percentage figure has changed because of increased awareness of the need for water conservation and because of the increased water recycling and reuse by industries such as yours. The 19__ drought emphasized the potential economic threat of a water shortage. Today's demands on our existing supplies emphasize that shortages could occur unless we plan for the future now.

We believe the information we need will be readily available from your 19__ year-end reports. We will of course treat your plant data as confidential, privileged information and will not publish individual plant data.

We would appreciate your returning the enclosed form by May 15, 19__. Please direct any calls you may wish to make regarding this survey to the nearest Department office as indicated on the back of the questionnaire.

Sincerely,

(With thanks to Superior Court Judge Ronald B. Robie, former Director, California Department of Water Resources.)

Claim Follow-Up

Dear Steve:

I am attaching copies of two letters dated January 27, 19__ to which we have had no reply.

The letters pertain to freight claims No. A477 and A479 on shipments to Grand Rapids.

We would appreciate your reviewing these claims and letting us know their current status. If you require copies of the backup material sent with the letters or any other information, please let me know.

Sincerely,

Suggestions

Gentlemen:

To help me update our commodity file index, I need your input in the form of suggestions for items that should be added to or deleted from the present index.

In order for your responses to be incorporated into the revised index, your input is needed by February 27, 19__. If no response is received by that date, I will assume that the present index is satisfactory.

Your suggestions will be appreciated.

Sincerely,

Record of Address Change

Dear Mr. and Mrs. Cox:

Please sign the enclosed change of address card for our records and return it in the enclosed, postpaid envelope at your earliest convenience.

Sincerely,

Claims Service Evaluation

Dear Mrs. Davis:

You recently contacted our claims office by phone. We are striving to provide our customers with timely and clearly explained replies.

To help us evaluate and improve our service, would you please take a moment to complete the enclosed, postpaid card and return it to us.

Your assistance is greatly appreciated.

Sincerely,

Medical Facility Evaluation

Dear Mr. Segal:

Regional Medical Center is conducting a survey of patients to determine their satisfaction with our service. The study seeks to determine how our system can provide better care to those who visit us.

The study includes a telephone survey of a number of patients to discuss their most recent clinic visit. An individual from the Medical Research Bureau, an opinion research firm, *may be* calling you soon regarding your participation. Your response will be strictly confidential.

  We sincerely hope that you would be willing to give us your valued thoughts. Please contact Andrea Wilson at 1-000-000-0000 before June 12 if you *do not* wish to be called.

  We appreciate your cooperation.

Sincerely,

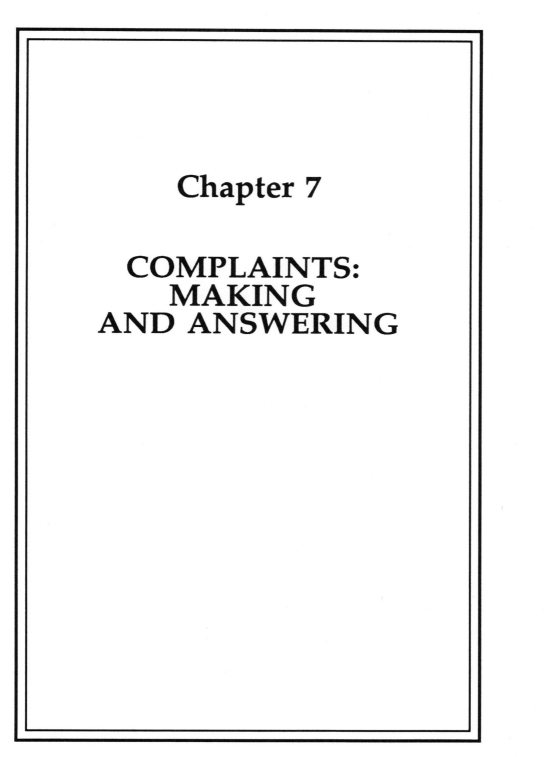

Chapter 7

COMPLAINTS: MAKING AND ANSWERING

MAKING COMPLAINTS

Some people love to complain. Most people don't, but at times writing a complaint letter is necessary. A consumer writing a long, rambling complaint about a product or service can expect a return letter outlining a method of correction that is more troublesome than helpful:

> Please fill in the enclosed form and mail it to us. Under separate cover send the clock to our Central Service Center. After we have received both, we will examine the clock and then send you an estimate of the repair cost if the damage is not covered by our limited warranty. If you accept our estimate, you can notify us by mail. We will then repair the clock, send you the bill, and return the clock when payment has been received.

Perhaps you will receive a form letter that hardly touches the issue:

> Please accept the four boxes of Super Soap we are sending you. Super Soap makes your clothes whiter and brighter.

To get a proper response, the complaint letter must be brief and clear. The items of complaint must be specified or listed. Acceptable solutions to the problem or the requested action must be spelled out or listed.

The complaint letter below is short, direct, positive, and insistent—but still polite. The politeness is emphasized by the use of the phrases "will you please" and "we would appreciate." The most derogatory statement is a mild "so far we have heard nothing from you." The insistence is shown by the phrases "it is imperative" and "your doing this immediately."

The situation has been made easy for the receiver of the letter by enclosing copies of the original request and the original inventory certificate. Both the purpose of the letter and the requested action are stated clearly.

Gentlemen:

On September 12, we mailed you a letter requesting that you take a physical inventory on September 30, 19__. A copy of this letter is enclosed.

So far we have heard nothing from you, and it is imperative that we receive the inventory certificate, copies of which are also enclosed.

Will you please follow through on this request and return the certificates to the locations shown in our letter. We would appreciate your doing this immediately.

Sincerely yours,

How to Do It

1. State specifically what is wrong.
2. Explain your viewpoint in a reasonable manner.
3. Suggest specific adjustments or corrections.

Transit Damage

Dear Mr. Baldwin:

Attached are some photos of a truck shipment of cereal boxes that arrived at Des Moines this morning on our order No. 7771.

As you can see in the pictures, there was a space of about three feet between the last stack of boxes and the truck door. This space was not braced or filled with dunnage, allowing the boxes in the rear of the truck to shift and fall over.

Please call this to the attention of those in charge of loading trucks. Reasonable effort must be made to minimize damage while in transit.

Sincerely,

Cost of Purchases

Dear Jim:

During recent months there has been a substantial increase in the dollar amount of rollers purchased rather than manufactured. This has led to a variety of problems. Internal paper work has left much to be desired. Our controller, working with the Sales Department, has this aspect of the problem under study.

Second, the effect of purchased rollers on profit forecasting has contributed to great variances in two of the last three months. This part of the problem will be brought under control through an improved flow of information from the Sales Department to the Administrative Department. Again, our controller will be calling on the Sales Department to assist him with this part of the problem.

In the future, before a commitment to purchase rollers is made, I want to review the cost, price, and profit relationships. It appears that in some cases we are not breaking even as planned, but are actually losing money.

My review will continue until I have satisfied myself that these outside purchases are contributing to our profits.

Sincerely,

Incorrect Mailings

Dear Ms. Gerald:

The Accounts Payable computer printouts are being processed and mailed on a timely basis. For the past several months, however, mailings have been to the wrong destinations. This delays our accounting closings.

Specifically, there is complete confusion between Portland and Vancouver, possibly because both are supervised by the same controller. But they are not one; they are not the same.

Please try to have the printouts mailed separately and to their separate destinations.

Sincerely,

Inadequate Explanation

Dear Don:

I cannot accept the answers you gave regarding the attached manufacturing complaints. The statement that the valves are not likely to leak does not answer the complaint that the rejected valves are leaking—especially when Ames is asking for a credit of $846.

Please provide a more acceptable answer to these complaints: which crews and persons are responsible; what will be done to prevent future complaints, or preferably, what you have already done.

Please return the complaints with your answers by April 20.

Respectfully,

Messy Work Area

Dear Ms. Warren:

I pointed out three weeks ago that the finish polishing area is a filthy mess. I expect immediate action from everyone to clear the area and to keep it clean on a daily basis.

This is one area that should be kept as clean as your kitchen.

Sincerely,

Low Sales

Dear Gordon:

As of your March 31 report to Tony Andrews of Willow Pass Co., we are running far behind last year's sales to them.

It was my understanding with our salesman, Bill Boyd, that he and Tony agreed on 4 to 5 million units per month this year. At the rate we are going, it looks like we will average only 3 million units per month.

Being Bill's sales manager, find out how he and Tony explain this.

Sincerely,

Sales Forecast

Dear Gordon:

After reviewing the sales forecast for the next four months, I can see trouble ahead. Each month our salesmen are forecasting a decrease in sales from our budget. When you had the opportunity to change the budget, you elected to stay with the one put together by our previous sales manager.

The real problem will be in March. The salesmen have forecast a reduction from the budget on 190M units, which is less than February, although March has three more working days.

Is your March forecast realistic? If it is, we must cut back from our normal two-shift operation.

Sincerely,

Manufacturing Errors

Dear Jim:

A. J. Token is one of our more profitable accounts. Until recently, we served them 100 percent. During our recent strike and immediately after when we were having printing problems, Token gave a trial order to our competitor, Smith Manufacturing. Now Smith has 30 percent of Token's can business.

Two problems are contributing to this:

1. While it is not economical to run volume orders to precise quantities, Token has repeatedly asked us *not* to underrun orders because they must fill specific orders with our cans. We are consistently shipping both under and overruns.
2. Token picks up most of their own cans from us. Too often they will make an appointment to pick up at a specific hour and then have to wait as long as four hours to be loaded. Idle driver time costs Token as much as on-the-road time.

Although these may seem like minor items, unless they are corrected, they will lose this business for us.

What can you do to correct these problems? What can I do to help you? I would like a reply by July 20.

Sincerely,

Dear Mr. Graham:

Attached is a sample of box board that your plant manufactured with metal particles embossed in the board. Your plant does not appear to be making progress on the elimination of scrap metal.

Metal of this nature, if found in a finished food box, could cause one big suit against our company.

Please let me know what action is being taken to remove this problem.

Sincerely,

Dear Mr. Glen:

The front trailer caps made for our last order, No. 78-0000, vary too much from the pattern we supplied you.

We can correct the caps we have, but we cannot tolerate such variances in the future.

Regards,

Manufacturing Problem

Dear Mr. Elkart:

We are having a problem with the Boro Air Hammer, manufactured by your company which has caused a drastic decline in our production rate.

Dust is being drawn into the lubricating system, activating the machine's emergency cutoff. After a great deal of investigation, we find that we can operate the hammer if the speed is reduced.

It appears that one of two steps could be taken to correct the problem:

1. Take measures to prevent dust from entering the lubricating system.
2. Install a filtering system sufficient to remove the dust.

I would appreciate having someone from your company take an in-depth look at this problem. May I hear from you soon?

Sincerely,

Shipping Errors

Dear Bob:

We are having a lot of problems with sales to Adam-Sloop Co., and these seem to stem from your shipping department. Here is a sampling:

1. On 11-12-__, our dray tag 3300 indicated Adam-Sloop's order 1221 "complete" with a quantity of 5000. Adam-Sloop recorded receipts of 15,000. There were probably three units per package, but the quantity should be stated correctly.
2. Dray tag 3322 of 11-15-__ indicated "various" for Adam-Sloop's purchase order number. They had to unravel which orders this shipment applied to.
3. On 12-18-__, a load was received on dray tag 4412, four weeks *after* they received our invoice.

Bob, these are only a few of the current problems. Adam-Sloop has about had it untangling our sloppy shipping procedures. We don't want to lose this customer.

Will you please check into this problem, and let me know if you need more information.

Sincerely,

Billing Error

Dear Mr. Danzig:

In reply to your letter of August 11, 19__, please, please, please! try to get your computer-billing and receivables departments together. We are developing a large correspondence file because of errors on your invoices.

The invoices mentioned in your letter, numbers 8-1-4949, 4950, and 4951, are internally inconsistent: they state "freight allowed" but do not allow the freight that should have been allowed because we paid the freight bills. (See paid copies attached.)

Please correct your records.

Sincerely yours,

Computer Error

Dear Mr. Lucas:

As you requested, this is why we had to rerun your branch's payroll for the week ending August 21.

The payroll card transmission from your terminal for August 19 was dated August 18. The error report we sent to your branch indicated the error, but it was apparently ignored. Thus, the computer automatically paid overtime rates for the hours worked on August 19 but reported as August 18.

We reran the weekly report correctly on August 24 for an additional cost to you of $840.

This situation points out the necessity of checking all input data and any error reports from our center.

If I can be of further help, please call me.

Sincerely,

Catalog Order

Gentlemen:

The enclosed dress was not what the catalog photo made it appear to be, so I am returning it.

Not only was the style different but the color sent to me was not the one I ordered.

I'm enclosing the catalog page. If you can send me the dress pictured in the proper color, please do. If this is not possible, I would like a refund.

Sincerely,

Labor Law Violation

To The Board of Directors:

This is a formal complaint concerning wages and hours.

I am in the process of filing a formal report to the Labor Commission under Section 3, paragraphs A and D, of the Industrial Welfare Commission Order No. 5-80. According to this code, my income is at least $200 per month under the allowed minimum wage and overtime amount.

The response of your manager, Mr. Williams, was, "Mentioning your action to anyone in this organization will result in your immediate termination."

I hope that your concern about this situation will make it possible for you to resolve it without any further action on my part.

Respectfully yours,

Misrepresentation

Dear Mr. Randall:

It isn't often that I become upset enough with sales personnel in a store to write a letter to the manager. However, a recent incident occurred in your sporting goods department that left me both angry and frustrated—and more than a little disappointed.

As a novice camper, I am far from knowledgeable about the types and quality of equipment required. Because of this, I relied upon your clerk, Harley Stolman, to provide me with accurate information when I needed a lantern. My original intention was to buy a Coleman, a well-known brand, even to me. The department clerk persuaded me that the store brand, on sale at the time, was a better buy in the long run and of equal quality to the Coleman. When I used the lantern this last week, it failed to provide adequate light and was difficult to operate. I am thoroughly dissatisfied with it. I realize now that I should have refused to give in to the clerk's persuasive tactics.

I would like to return the lantern and apply the price to the purchase of a Coleman lantern. The original receipts are enclosed, and the lantern is being returned by parcel post. Please let me know the additional amount of money required. Please ship it to the above address via UPS.

Sincerely,

Parking in Driveway

Dear John Stover:

Our neighborhood has really gotten crowded in the past few years and little space seems to be available. However, I'd like to ask you to no longer park in front of my driveway.

Not only is it illegal, but it has kept me from getting out of my garage on several occasions.

Perhaps you may find parking further down the block.

Sincerely,

Noisy Driver

Dear Mrs. Frames:

I don't like being a wet blanket, but I feel it is necessary to say something about the noise outside my window each morning at 4 a.m.

Everyone's schedule is different but, since I work and your son doesn't, I'm usually sound asleep when he zooms in from a party or whatever. The shouting and screeching of tires have left me bleary-eyed.

I would appreciate it if you would speak with him and ask him to be a little quieter at that hour of the morning. Some of us need our sleep.

Sincerely,

Meetings Out of Control

Dear Mr. Swanson:

The town meetings need to be better structured if any effective business is to be carried out.

Last week's meeting required over three hours to do what could have been completed in five minutes. Everyone in the audience seemed to be talking and the speakers went unheard.

Perhaps following *Robert's Rules of Orders* would help to organize future meetings better.

Sincerely,

Muddy Newspaper

Dear Mr. Bishop:

Jimmy W. is a good newspaper carrier in most respects, but I cannot convince him to place the paper on my front porch each morning.

He often throws it in the garden, or on the wet lawn, or in the mud, or most often leaves it at the end of the driveway. I like to enjoy my paper with my morning coffee.

Without reprimanding him, or making him uncomfortable, could you instruct him to put the paper on the porch?

Sincerely,

Delivery Person

Dear Ms. Bell:

Having a dry cleaner who still delivers is a luxury for which I am grateful. However, I've had several difficulties with your delivery man recently.

The deliveries sometimes arrive when I'm not home and I've come home to find my clothes hanging on the doorknob or piled carefully on the porch.

Would it be possible, so I can avoid possible loss, for you to notify me in advance approximately what time the clothing will be delivered?

Sincerely,

Barking Dog

Dear Mr. McDowell:

The barking of your dog all night has kept me from sleeping for the past week. I realize that in this part of town a dog is required for protection. However, he seems to be spending half the night howling to get in.

I don't mind when I don't have to work the next day, but getting up at 6 A.M. is hard after losing half a night's sleep.

Is the entrance where the dog scratches and barks to get in at the opposite side of the house from where you sleep, making it hard to hear him? If that's the case, would you mind if I would call you each night just as a reminder that he's out there? I'd appreciate it greatly.

Sincerely,

No Stop Light

Dear Council Members:

The lack of a stoplight or a sign at the corner of East St. and West St. has created a dangerous situation for both motorists and pedestrians.

In the past six months, seven accidents (two of them serious) have occurred. School children must cross East St. at that point to get to school and often have to dodge cars to do so.

In order to prevent further accidents and to save our children's lives, it is absolutely imperative to place a traffic control at that point.

Sincerely,

Gardening Problem

Dear Mr. Balenchine:

About the gardening here at the house we are renting from you: the tree near the driveway and the walk from the front porch had pale green leaves when we moved in, but now it appears to be dying, possibly from lack of water. The gardener has not been good about checking the sprinkler system coverage, and we haven't been able to figure out how it is controlled. We have discussed this situation with the gardener, but nothing has changed. Mr. Hayes spends under 10 minutes a week mowing the lawn, and does no more unless we are home to question him. This fall we plan to do quite a bit of traveling. We suggest you consider hiring a different gardener.

Sincerely,

ANSWERING COMPLAINTS

If we were all perfect, adjustment letters would be unnecessary. But such letters are necessary, and the writer answering a complaint can grasp this opportunity to write what is in reality a sales letter. The writer is selling goodwill.

Answer promptly or the goodwill will melt away as the complainer begins to boil. If no answer is possible immediately, at least let the complainer know you are working on the problem. The problem may seem a slight irritant to you, but to the complainer it is important or it would not have been mentioned. The complainer's viewpoint must be recognized because he or she is your customer or perhaps your neighbor. The friendship of neither should be jeopardized.

There are, however, times when the complainer is out-and-out wrong. Don't say that in your letter, but remain calm and polite and thank the writer for bringing the problem to your attention. Give convincing reasons for your position and, when possible, offer some help or an alternative. End on a friendly note.

Adjustment letters must use positive statements—positive from the complainer's point of view. For example:

Negative—We can't make the adjustment.

Positive—We suggest you talk to your local dealer.

Negative—Your complaint arrived today.

Positive—Thank you for bringing this problem to our attention.

Negative—We don't know what is wrong.

Positive—We are investigating the problem and will let you know as soon as possible.

Remember: you are selling goodwill.

How to Do It

1. Agree with the complainer on some point or thank him or her for bringing the problem to your attention.
2. Tell what action has been taken.
3. End with a goodwill-building statement.

Opening Sentences

Start with this thought in mind: *my customer is the one who keeps me in business.*

We are shipping you a new vase today to replace the broken one you received.

Thank you for your letter of May 23, pointing out a problem with your new washer.

We appreciate the concern you felt when your new vacuum cleaner began to smoke.

Your replacement motor will be shipped tomorrow.

Yes, we certainly will honor our guarantee.

You were absolutely right in feeling cheated.

Thank you for bringing our billing error to our attention.

Closing Sentences

The closing thought for a letter adjusting a complaint is this: *if I am going to keep this customer, I must keep his or her goodwill.*

We shall always appreciate your business and your confidence in us.

We appreciate your telling us this problem and giving us the opportunity to correct it.

We appreciate your business and will continue to do our best to earn your confidence.

We are always ready and willing to help a customer with a problem.

If you ever have problems again, please let us know. We are ready to help.

We service what we sell. Call us at any time.

We are sorry for the inconvenience we caused, and we will make every effort to prevent a recurrence.

Above all, we want our customers happy.

Disturbed Retail Customer

Dear Mrs. Lincoln:

Your letter of May 14 really took us down a few pegs. I will admit that we were partly to blame for the mix-up, but surely our whole organization can't be as bad as you picture it.

We are sorry for the confusion with your order, and we are sending you a new sofa with the pillows and seats upholstered as you requested. Please come in for a visit before deciding to quit us completely. We have served you well in the past and we know we can in the future.

Sincerely,

Our Mistake

Dear Mr. Evers:

You are absolutely right in not liking the way we handled your proposal for extending payments on your account.

Please accept my apologies for sending you a letter that should never have left our office. It was a form letter to delinquent customers, and was sent because somehow your letter proposing an extended payment plan did not reach our credit department when it should have. Communications between our own departments failed at a crucial time.

As we discussed on the phone, we are happy to cooperate in making your payments easier. If you will sign the enclosed agreement and mail it to us with your first payment, we will again be working together.

We are sorry for the inconvenience this has caused you, and if you wish to discuss any details further, please call me personally.

Sincerely,

Misunderstanding

Dear Barney,

I admit that my letter of April 7 must have confused you. It was dictated and sent to the steno pool before I learned from Mr. Thompson that the two of you had agreed our contract should be changed to include service to the hydro cooler. I agree that this change should be made.

Unfortunately, my original letter did get mailed. I am sorry for the confusion, but am glad that we now agree on all points.

Sincerely,

Incomplete Instructions

Dear Mrs. Wordsworth:

We agree that the blouse you returned shrunk in your washing machine. This particular blouse is not washable although some blouses of similar appearance are. Our sales staff has been instructed to make each customer aware of how each blouse must be cleaned. Sometimes a clerk will forget.

Whether or not this was the case, we are sorry, Mrs. Wordsworth, for the disappointment and inconvenience to you.

Please let me know if you wish a replacement of the blouse or a credit to your account. Above all, we want our customers happy.

Sincerely,

Misdirected Mail

Dear Mr. Fife:

The purpose of this letter is to follow up on our phone conversation of July 11, and your letter of June 28.

The problem referred to in your June 28 letter appears to have started earlier this year when some operations were discontinued at San Jose. At that time, we were requested to route *some* reports to San Mateo that previously had gone to San Jose. These instruction changes obviously did not result in proper routing of all reports affected.

We have issued report distribution instructions to correct the problem pointed out in your letter; we believe this will correct the mailing problem.

I would like to mention, however, that members of my group have found it extremely difficult to acquire and verify proper mailing instructions for reports. Letters such as the one you initiated on June 28 are helpful in assuring correct distribution and we appreciate your notification of the problem.

I encourage you to continue calling our attention to any problem of this nature. Please call Linda Arnette at 000-0000, extension 0000, to expedite the notification process.

I am sorry for the inconvenience caused by the erroneous mailing instructions.

Sincerely,

Late Delivery

Dear Mrs. Polk:

Your annoyance at not having received the engraved silver cups you ordered March 4 is understandable.

Orders requiring engraving work require from four to six weeks for delivery. Our salesperson apparently did not make that clear, and we are sorry for the misunderstanding.

Your order will be shipped on Tuesday of next week and should arrive within four days. Please forgive the delay. I am sure you will like the fine workmanship in the engraving.

Sincerely,

Shipping Error

Dear Mrs. Montez:

You are certainly justified in being angry about our blunder in returning the unordered merchandise you had returned to us. Please let me apologize. The error was ours, but it would help us when you return merchandise if you would enclose a note to me or our sales representative stating why it is being returned. This will ensure proper credit to you.

You will receive immediate credit for this returned merchandise and all shipping charges.

Again, I am sorry for the inconvenience to you. We do value your business and your friendship.

Cordially,

Delayed Order

Dear Mr. Olin:

We received your order No. 4270 for six dozen lamps No. 4477 on March 17.

We are sorry for the delay, but we no longer make this particular style and ordered it for you from Sunset Lamps. They promised delivery by April 15. If this is not satisfactory, please let us know.

Sincerely,

Delivery Method

Dear Mr. Bruno:

We shipped your order No. 84222 for three air valves air express, special delivery rather than parcel post because we assumed time was a critical factor.

Because our assumption was in error, we are mailing you a credit memo today for the difference in delivery rates.

Sincerely,

Damaged Merchandise

Gentlemen:

Thank you for your letter of July 17 describing damage to the coffee makers you received July 14.

A replacement order was shipped today.

We are sorry about the damage and the inconvenience it is causing you. We have installed a new conveyor loading system and although the product damage problem is nearly licked, we have an occasional setback. We will try harder next time.

Sincerely,

Dear Mr. Shawner:

This is to thank you for your letter of July 7, 19__ and the five dollars for handling expenses.

I am very sorry to learn that the Abrahm lamp shade we sent you arrived damaged.

I am sending you a new shade and am requesting our Accounting Department to issue a refund check for five dollars.

Thank you for bringing this to our attention. If we can be of help at any time, please do not hesitate to call us.

Sincerely,

Dear Mrs. Appleton:

We are sorry your table arrived damaged. A replacement will be delivered Thursday, and the driver will pick up the damaged one.

We thank you for your courteous letter explaining the damage. We hope the inconvenience to you was small and that you will enjoy your new table.

Sincerely,

Dear Mr. Guthrie:

We are sending our salesman, James Hatton, to look at the damaged boxes you received on September 27. He will be able to determine if it is a manufacturing error or shipping damage, and he will want to get a count of the damaged boxes. In either case, we will give you credit or rerun the order. Please discuss your preference with Mr. Hatton when he arrives Tuesday afternoon.

We are sorry for the inconvenience to you, but James Hatton will set things straight. We value your business and friendship.

Sincerely,

Merchandise Guarantee

Dear Mrs. Wells:

Yes, we certainly will honor our guarantee. If you wish, we will refund your money or send you a replacement for your new oven that does not heat properly.

We would like to suggest, however, that our serviceman for your area first check your oven. The problem may be small and could be fixed in your home. Our service representative, Mr. Harold Bentley, will phone you to make an appointment at your convenience.

We are sorry for the trouble the oven has caused you, but we are confident it can be fixed to your complete satisfaction.

Sincerely,

Wrong Style

Dear Mr. Elton:

Please return the lamps (your order No. P2233) to Sunset Lamps and they will replace them with the style you ordered.

We are sorry for the confusion and delays and will work harder in the future to have your orders filled correctly.

Sincerely,

Unsatisfactory Chair

Dear Mr. Brooks:

We were disturbed to learn that the chair you recently purchased from us did not hold up. We want our customers to be happy, and that is why we have a policy of guaranteed satisfaction.

There are three ways we can handle this situation: (1) we can replace the chair, (2) we can give you a full refund, or (3) you can apply the amount to any other merchandise in our store—you may decide that a different chair will suit you better.

Please indicate your preference on the enclosed postcard and also write in the date that we can pick up the chair. Pickups are made in the afternoons.

We are sorry for the inconvenience and do appreciate your calling the problem to our attention.

Sincerely,

Unsatisfactory Recorder

Dear Mr. Abbot:

Thanks for your letter of July 8 calling your dissatisfaction with our Nicord recorder to my attention.

I'm investigating the problem personally and hope to have an explanation for you shortly. I intend to straighten it out—we want our customers to be satisfied customers.

In the meantime, could you please send me a copy of the sales slip. This will help by giving me the model number, serial number, and date of purchase.

You will hear from me immediately after I receive the sales slip.

Sincerely,

Foreign Object in Food

Dear Mr. Dennison:

I was shocked to learn that you found a tack in one of our Krispy Kookies, but we are grateful that you suffered no injury. You can rest assured that we will take every step necessary to ensure that no similar incident will ever occur again.

We thank you for bringing this to our attention. Please accept our sincerest apologies for the concern this incident caused you.

Sincerely,

Declining Responsibility—Frozen Food

Dear Mr. Bishop:

We regret that our frozen dinner did not meet your expectations, but we doubt that the problem is in the processing. We carefully control the quality of our products up to the time they leave the processing plant. Sometimes, during their handling in the retail stores, they are allowed to thaw and are then refrozen. This may cause problems when customers prepare them.

Because we feel we cannot accept responsibility for handling damage after the product leaves our plant, we suggest you check with your local store for a possible refund.

We appreciate your interest in Jamieson's frozen foods.

Sincerely,

Pricing Error

Dear Mr. Helverson:

Your check for $12.50 is enclosed. You were right in discovering that our Arctic electric blanket was advertised at a price higher than in other stores in this area.

We have built a large volume business on the basis of quality at the lowest price. We are proud of our reputation.

Upon investigation, we found an error in the advertisement. We are happy to send you—and the others who bought a blanket in response to our ad—the difference between our advertised price and our competitor's price.

We are sorry for the inconvenience we caused you and look forward to serving you for many years to come.

Sincerely,

Billing Error

Dear Mr. Mapes:

You are correct. We did make an error on our invoice No. 42772 of January 10. You are entitled to the 7 percent discount that we unintentionally overlooked. We will mail you a corrected invoice today. I am sorry for the trouble this error caused you and thank you for calling it to our attention.

Sincerely,

Dear Mr. Watson:

We are sorry for our error that made it necessary for you to return our last bill.

You are correct that we omitted the normal 10 percent discount. The $32 freight charge, however, is for air express that you requested on the shipment of diaphragms from our Cleveland plant.

A corrected bill will be sent today.

We are sorry for the inconvenience to you and we assure you we will make a special effort to prevent future billing errors.

Sincerely,

Dear Mr. Harding:

Thank you for calling our attention to the error in Mrs. Harding's account. It has been corrected and a revised invoice will be mailed tomorrow.

Please extend our apologies to Mrs. Harding.

Sincerely,

Dear Ms. Casey,

It's easy enough to understand your disturbed frame of mind about Sport Center's repeatedly billing you for the baseball shoes you returned on May 29. Our billing department is certainly throwing you a curve. Please accept our apologies.

We finally got the data into our new computer correctly, and you will no longer be bothered with the erroneous charge.

Cordially,

Statement Error

Dear Mr. Mayer:

The error in your October statement showing a charge of $329.99 for a shipment of batteries was due to a billing error.

We are sorry for the inconvenience, and a credit memo to cancel the billing is enclosed.

Sincerely,

Dear Ms. Horner:

Thank you for bringing the errors in your December statement to our attention. The accounting department is now revising your statement, and it will be mailed today.

Thank you for your cooperation and understanding.

Sincerely,

Complaint Handling Procedure

Dear Mr. Kowalski:

In reply to your letter asking for our procedures for handling complaints, you must have had some problem with the plastic shrink wrap machine you purchased from us, or you suspect you may have problems in the future. Let me assure you that any problems occurring during our two-year warranty period will be resolved at our expense.

We do have a procedure we follow closely.

First, we ask you to have your own maintenance department try to locate and correct the problem. You may submit a schedule of labor hours and costs, parts replaced and their costs, and a short explanation of what was checked and what was changed. Our engineers will evaluate this data, and if it is reasonable, you will be reimbursed.

Second, if that procedure does not produce satisfactory results, we will send the nearest qualified mechanic to your plant to make the necessary repairs. This service is at no cost to you.

Third, if he cannot correct the defect, he will report his finding to us, and we will send a man or crew from our factory.

Fourth—and this should never occur—we will replace the machine.

We honor our two-year warranty, and we sincerely hope you will not have the opportunity to test us on this point.

I appreciate this occasion to explain our complaint procedure to you.

Sincerely,

Dear (Customer):

File No. #_____

Thank you for taking the time to contact Ford Motor Company to explain the concerns you are experiencing with your vehicle. We regret any inconvenience you have experienced and assure you that we are anxious to retain you as a satisfied customer.

A summary of your concern has been sent to your _____. Please contact the service manager at your dealership within three days after you receive this letter and provide him with the above file number.

If you need further assistance, you may recontact us at 1-800-392-3673. To help us serve you more quickly, any future contacts should reference the above file number.

Thank you for giving us the opportunity to assist you.

Sincerely,

Owner Relations Operations
Ford Customer Assistance Center

(With thanks to Ford Motor Company)

Dear Mr. Arlington:

As one of our new customers, you will be interested in our complaint procedure. We hope you never need this information—but just in case . . .

If one of our small tools or appliances should fail, please return it freight collect with the packing slip (don't forget this detail) and a short statement of the problem as you see it. We will check the tool or appliance and either repair or replace it. We will also honor your request for a refund, but we think our merchandise is too dependable for you to want that.

Customer satisfaction is FIRST. Only after that do we get on with our other business.

Best regards,

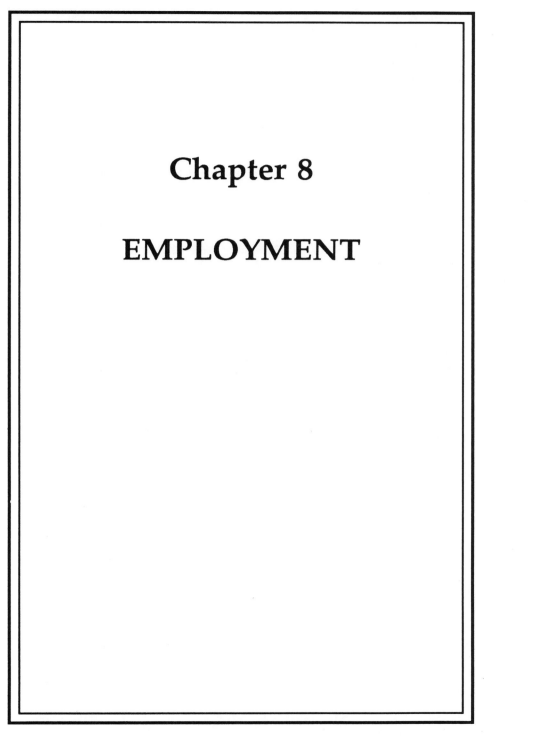

Chapter 8

EMPLOYMENT

Both employees and employers find matching the person to the job a difficult and frustrating experience. As an applicant, a good letter or résumé won't guarantee that you'll get the job, but they can help open the door. As an employer, you'll find yourself called upon to write a wide variety of letters ranging from rejections to acceptances, from references to reprimands, and how you do it reflects not only on you and your company, but may also have legal ramifications. In both cases, carefully written letters are essential.

Section I contains letters to be written by applicants; Section II, letters by employers; and Section III, letters by third parties. This series of letters does not comprise a job hunting or employee search program, but is an aid to these undertakings. It will be helpful to both employers and applicants.

SECTION I—LETTERS WRITTEN BY JOB APPLICANTS

Cover Letters for Résumés

Résumés and job application letters may be mailed to employers with or without a cover letter: opinions of human resources managers vary as to which is more effective. The key to a result-getting cover letter is brevity, because the purpose of the letter is to save the reader time. People reviewing résumés usually do this infrequently and are busy with their regular work.

Although the cover letter should be short, it must also be long enough to persuade the reader to turn to the résumé itself. Mention the job you are applying for and one or two of your strongest selling points.

How to Do It

1. Indicate what job your are applying for.
2. Provide one or two items of experience.
3. Mention that the résumé is enclosed.

Sales Representative

Dear Mr. Campbell: (To a corrugated box manufacturer)

In answer to your advertisement in the *Los Angeles Times* on February 26, 19__ for a sales representative, I have three years experience in sales with a corrugated box manufacturer, plus the background of two years in the plant and three years in the purchasing department.

I am prepared for the long hours and travel required of an effective salesperson.

My résumé is enclosed.

Sincerely,

Chief Accountant

Dear Mr. Scott: (To a truck manufacturer)

I am applying for a position as Chief Accountant. I am currently a plant accountant with full responsibility for the monthly profit and loss statement and the accompanying details and analyses.

The last fifteen of my twenty years of varied industrial accounting experience has been with a truck manufacturer.

My résumé is attached.

Sincerely,

Buyer Trainee

Dear Ms. Schweitzer: (To a department store)

This is an application for a position as a buyer trainee. I recently graduated from the University of Michigan with a degree in business.

Having worked for Frederick & Nelson during the past three summers and Christmas seasons, I am most interested in the department store field. I have experience in receiving, stocking, ordering and selling.

My résumé is enclosed. I will be glad to discuss my qualifications in an interview.

Sincerely,

Cover Letters for Job Applications

Job application cover letters are similar to résumé cover letters, but should be even briefer. Mention what job or position you seek, only one or two strong qualifications for the position and that your job application letter is enclosed. Your objective is to get the human resource manager to read your application letter immediately.

Use the same three-step How to Do It outline suggested for résumé cover letters.

Plant Accountant

Dear Mr. Franklin:

I have twenty-five years experience in all phases of plant accounting, including closing the accounting books, training personnel, making government reports, and signing checks up to $10,000.

The enclosed letter details these responsibilities and accomplishments.

Sincerely,

Secretary

Dear Mr. Finkelstein:

My eleven years as a private and legal secretary, added to two years of teaching office procedures, should meet the requirements for a private secretary in your busy office.

I am interested in such a position with your company.

The enclosed letter explains my qualifications further.

Sincerely,

Résumés

Résumés are a form of advertising. Their purpose is to get an employer to call you.

Because your résumé represents you, keep it neat, specific and accurate. Remember the old but true cliché, "You will never have a second chance to make a first impression."

The ideal length is open to question, but most agree that it should be no more than two pages. Emphasize your strengths, and omit your shortcomings rather than trying to explain them. Mention your education. The employer is interested in your highest level of schooling, and in any courses that are directly applicable to the job you are seeking.

Two styles of presentation are recommended. First, what might be called an "impersonal past tense," for example, supervised twenty-four clerks, designed machine tools, sold women's clothing. Second, the "impersonal present tense." For example, supervising twenty-fours clerks, designing machine tools, selling women's clothing.

Even if you don't send out your résumé—you may choose instead to write a Job Application letter—writing a résumé requires that you review your experience and organize it logically and clearly. You'll learn about yourself while going through this exercise, and be better prepared to make a good presentation at your interview.

Advertising Executive

JAMES BECKER
0000 Bedford Ave.
Brooklyn, NY 11226
(718)000-0000

OBJECTIVE: A position in advertising where I can maximize my advertising, supervisory, research, estimating, and buyer skills in both print and media.

SUMMARY: Offering over 15 years experience, an A.A. degree in Business, and a comprehensive background in all areas of advertising marketing: display, media, and out-door. Ability to thoroughly research, analyze situations, propose creative solutions, develop good rapport, and bring projects to completion under budget deadlines.

EMPLOYMENT HISTORY

Print Advertising/Sales Director
United Media, Phoenix, AZ 1989–Present
Responsible to publisher of Equal Opportunity Employment journal for selling and placing advertising in the *1990—Recruitment and Education Publication*, for equal opportunity employment.

- Brought in major new accounts, including American West Airlines, TRW, and Acme Printing Company.

- Won opportunity to attend California training seminar in telemarketing/ sales for being one of the two highest sales people.

HBE, Inc., Brooklyn, NY 1985–1989
Media Supervisor/Public Relations/Sales Supervisor
Responsible to manager for billing, account activities, office management, client entertainment, and advertising.

- Supervised production of eight sales representatives.

- Increased sales advertising of present accounts 30%.

- Computerized billing procedures from manual operation to IBM system.

Grey Advertising, Inc., New York, NY 1983–1985
Media & Print Estimator
Responsible to supervisor for invoices, estimates, media placement, and client/agency communications.

- Responsible for over two million dollars of account estimating.

- Responsible for print and media advertising for Revlon Cosmetics.

- Increased Revlon account 25%.

Media Corporation of America, New York, NY 1978–1983
Print Media Supervisor
Responsible to vice president for invoices, schedules, and coordination of client services.

- Instituted telemarketing program to determine placement of effective advertising.

- Managed research development projects.

- Increased sales production over 25%.

- Acted as trouble-shooter for major accounts.

Atwood Richards, Inc., New York, NY 1972–1977
Media Coordinator/Public Relations Administrator
Responsible to Account Executive for media layouts and client functions
on the Daily News (newspaper) account.

- Coordinated advertising promotions of barter products for TV shows.

- Managed marketing and sales of house accounts.

- As supervisor of out-door display advertising, increased sales 25%.

ADDITIONAL EMPLOYMENT

Time, Inc., New York, NY
Biller/Payer/Estimator
Responsible for invoices, schedules, and sales communications for public
accounts.
B.B.D.O. Advertising Agency, New York, NY
Media Print Biller/Estimator
Responsible for invoicing and payments for
Dodge Motors and General Foods accounts.

ADDITIONAL INFORMATION

Education
Associate Arts degree, Kingsborough Community College, Brooklyn, NY.
Continuing Education
Accounting, Brooklyn College; Sales/Marketing, Pace University.
Affiliations
Society of the Arts, Sales Professionals.

Senior Accountant

MARK W. SANDERS   19__
7122 Yorktown Lane
City, California 00000   000-000-0000
Education
University of Washington, Seattle, Washington.
B. A. degree in business.
Additional accounting courses.

Business Experience

Senior Accountant, Crown Zellerbach Corporation, manufacturer of forest products.

January 1967 to Present

<u>Accounting Responsibilities:</u>

Closing the accounting books monthly.

Completing monthly profit and loss statement and balance sheet.

Preparing journal entries and supervising preparation by others.

Making detailed analyses of General Ledger balances.

Preparing monthly cost statements for Materials, Labor, Plant Operations, Selling, Administrative, and selected cost centers.

Assembling detailed reports of costs and variances from the budget. Some examples:

Feedback report that compared actual and standard costs of products shipped.

Month-by-month comparison of fixed overhead costs by categories.

Status of construction projects in progress.

Detail of each element of cost of pallets used.

Travel and entertainment costs by categories and sales people.

Maintenance costs categorized by labor, material, and cost centers.

Calculating a mid-month estimate of profit for the current month.

Reconciling bank statements.

Preparing annual report of SEC data.

Preparing year-end tax data reports.

Completing Federal Census of Manufacturers report.

Making monthly and quarterly sales and use tax reports.

Writing workflow procedures: e.g., accounting for printing die costs; obtaining cost of raw materials used.

Approving vendor invoices for payment, with check signing authority of $10,000.

Training and supervising accounts payable clerks, billing clerks, and junior accountants.

Supervising statistical and production clerks.

Assisting in preparation of annual budget.

Controlling inventory by using card systems and usage reports to reconcile actual material usages to standards. Explaining variances.

Cost Accountant and Purchasing Agent for Reliance Trailer & Truck Company, San Francisco, manufacturer of trailers and truck bodies. January 1963 to November 1966.

Establishing procedures for analyzing project costs. Preparing cost estimates. Installing a card system for control of purchases and inventories.

Cost Accountant and Work Order Clerk for Fruehauf Trailer Company, San Francisco, manufacturer of truck trailers and truck bodies.
July 1961 to January 1963.
Having responsibility for job costs of manufactured truck bodies and repair work. Billing customers. Assisting with purchasing. Making card systems of inventory control operate effectively.

Further Experience
Preparing business and personal income taxes for two CPA firms. Doing the accounting and tax returns for a small corporate manufacturer.

Assistant Staff Manager

Patricia Wingate

0000 Jewel Drive

City, Colorado 00000

(303) 000-0000

WORK EXPERIENCE

1956–19__   MOUNTAIN BELL, Denver, Colorado

1985–19__ Assistant Staff Manager—Division of Revenue
* Managed and directed the development and completion of land and building investment studies, space analysis studies and operating rent studies for a seven-state area.
* Verified studies for accuracy and integrity to ensure correct revenue income from interstate toll within the Bell System.
* Negotiated with AT&T Long Lines to establish rental arrangements and originated new methods to expedite billing corrections.

1980–1985 Facilities Planner—Engineering
* Originated special studies for AT&T involving circuit analysis, video channels and embedded costs.
* Implemented a quality control system along with job aids for a staff of eight engaged in separation of interstate telephone toll revenues.
*Analyzed and compiled costs of outside facilities for sale to and purchase from independent telephone companies, the U. S. Government and other common carriers.

1979 Engineering Technician
* Analyzed and scheduled central office equipment installation.

1974–1979 Technical Assistant
* Coordinated pole attachment agreements with cable Antenna Television Companies and Power Companies.
* Conducted field audits and authorized billing.

1964–1974 Service Representative—Commercial
* Performed all customer contact functions in a small public office; this included order writing, bill collecting, banking and public relations.

1956–1964 Operator/Instructor–Operator Services
* Conducted training classes.
* Operated switchboard handling emergency, long distance, overseas, and special assistance calls.

EDUCATION

BELL SYSTEM TECHNICAL AND MANAGEMENT TRAINING,
UNIVERSITY OF COLORADO, Denver, Colorado.
Curriculum: Real Estate

Systems Administrator

LUCILLE DOMINGO

2252 Mariposa Street

City, CA 00000

000/000-0000–home   000/000-0000–office

8/88 to present
SYSTEMS ADMINISTRATOR
Newport Harbor Art Museum, Newport Beach, CA
Manage the implementation of the museum's computer system: accounting, capital campaign, art inventory and desktop publishing. This encompasses project management, system design and programming, development of administration of system policies and procedures, training and troubleshooting.

Systems knowledge includes IBM compatibles, Novell network, dBase, Clipper, 1-2-3, WordPerfect, various application packages and networking.

11/86 to 8/88
SYSTEMS SUPPORT SPECIALIST
Imperial Corporation of America, San Diego, CA
Supported the 120 PC's (IBM compatibles) and the McCormack and Dodge mainframe system for the Finance Division. Support for both areas consisted of application development, training class development and instruction, and user assistance/troubleshooting.

2/86 to 11/86
MICRO COMPUTER ASSISTANCE for Imperial Corp.
Eastridge Temporary Service, San Diego, CA
Assisted the Financial Management Systems group with the implementation of the company's new accounting system. PC software utilized was Wordstar, Lotus, Symphony, and dBase.

9/85 to 1/86
MARKET RESEARCH COORDINATOR
Cushman & Wakefield of California, San Jose, CA
Researched and maintained a data base on the condition of the Silicon Valley real estate market. Generated statistical reports from this data base which were used by the company's brokers, and published locally to substantiate Cushman & Wakefield's reputation as a source of reliable market information. dBase and Lotus 1-2-3 were used in the development of these reports.

7/81 to 7/85
ADMINISTRATIVE ASSISTANT
PERSONNEL CLERK/RECEPTIONIST
Coordinated the 1984 and 1985 Sales Meetings, planned and implemented all activities involved in the production of the sales newsletter and worked as the editor of the corporate newsletter.

Education:
B. S. in Business Administration/Marketing.
San Jose State University, 1983.
GPA: 3.7/4.0

Job Application Letters

A job application letter is basically a sales letter; therefore present yourself with confidence. This type of letter is sent instead of a résumé—do not send both. It is another approach to obtaining an interview.

Before writing a job application letter, however, it is wise to complete a résumé. Doing so requires that you review in detail your job experience and organize it in a rational way. Having done that, you have the facts for your application letter.

The model letters that follow are suggestions, and none will fit you exactly because your letter must reflect your personality as well as your qualifications. Emphasize your strongest ability, then describe two or three others, but don't get carried away trying to mention all the applicable experience you have. Rely on your highlights. The purpose of this letter is to obtain an interview. It is there that you can add details.

Application letters should be sent to the president or highest company officer of the department to which you are applying.

How to Do It

1. Specify the job you are seeking.
2. State your accomplishments and abilities.
3. Ask for action from the employer.

Answering Ad for Accounting Manager

Dear Mr. Franklin:

This is in reply to your advertisement in the *Chicago Tribune* for an Accounting Manager.

I have twenty-five years experience, the last twenty with one corporation, in all phases of plant accounting. My responsibilities included: closing the accounting books monthly, followed by preparing the profit and loss statement and the balance sheet; preparing journal entries and supervising their preparation by others; preparing monthly cost statements for materials, labor, administration, selling, and selected cost centers; making detailed reports of costs and their variances from budget for top management.

Additional responsibilities were calculating a mid-month estimate of profit for the current month; reconciling bank statements; furnishing annual reports of SEC data; year-end tax data, Federal Census of Manufacturers, and sales and use tax reports;

writing accounting and workflow procedures; training and supervising accounts payable and billing clerks and junior accountants; overseeing inventory records and control systems; approving vendor invoices for payment, with check-signing authority to $10,000.

My accounting experience was preceded by two years of stock control and ordering, and three years as a combination purchasing agent and cost accountant.

I am available for an interview at your convenience to discuss these accomplishments and how my experience will help you. I will call you next week to arrange a meeting.

Sincerely,

Answering Ad for Market Research Trainee

Dear Mr. Gosnell:

The position advertised in the *Morning Gazette* for a market research trainee is the one for which I have been trained. In June, I graduated from the University of Washington with a major in marketing. The courses covered retail, wholesale and manufacturing marketing as well as the many other aspects of business operations.

I was one of four students selected by our adviser, Dr. Holmstead, to study marketing problems in companies that had asked the university School of Business for help. We worked with the employees and owner of each company to learn their problems and to suggest in written reports a solution or solutions.

That practical experience, in addition to my general business education, will help me serve Grace Motor Company.

I am eager to start work, and am available for an interview to discuss my qualifications and your requirements at your convenience.

Sincerely,

Cold-Call Application Letter for Private Secretary

Dear Mr. Finkenstein:

When you are ready for a new private secretary, I am interested in that position.

In your busy office, speed, accuracy, and broad-based competence are paramount. During my secretarial career, I have developed a typing speed of 100 words per minute. My five years in good standing as a legal secretary for Smith, Alexander & Wingate vouches for my accuracy.

During my six years as a private secretary with Waterford Manufacturers, I handled many responsibilities in addition to typing and taking dictation. My statistical and accounting training from the ABC Technical School helped with the preparation of seven monthly reports and a comprehensive annual report. My English skills helped in the proofreading of approximately thirty letters sent out weekly. My two years' experience teaching office procedures at ABC also proved invaluable when training new and temporary personnel.

Mr. Finkenstein, I look forward to applying my skills, energy, and enthusiasm to the challenge of a busy office such as yours. Can we arrange an interview at your convenience?

Sincerely,

Cold-Call Application Letter for Computer Systems Manager

Dear Mr. Kowalski:

I am seeking an opportunity to work with World Destiny as a Computer Systems Manager. My professional experience and my awareness of your unparalleled reputation and accomplishments have led me to want to work for World Destiny.

Since 19__ I have focused on computer system design, implementation, maintenance and training. As Systems Administrator for Newport Harbor Art Museum for the past two years, I have directed accounting, capital campaign, inventory, and publication production. We designed the system from scratch, developing all applications, policies, procedures, and training programs. I was well prepared for such a challenge by my previous positions as a Systems Support Specialist and MicroComputer Assistant for the Imperial Corporation of America.

Over the years, I have worked with Novell networks, IBM PC compatibles as well as McCormack and Dodge mainframes, using programs including dBase, Clipper, Lotus 1-2-3, Word-Perfect, Wordstar, and Symphony. This familiarity with a variety of hardware and software has helped me to get up to speed on nearly any computer with a minimum training period.

Additional experience in other fields also reinforces my value to World Destiny. As a Market Research Coordinator for Cushman & Wakefield of California, I not only researched and maintained a comprehensive database of Silicon Valley properties, but also generated statistical and written reports that substantiated Cushman & Wakefield's reputation. Previously, I coordinated companywide annual sales meetings and publication production for Qualogy, Inc.

Mr. Kowalski, while this experience more than qualifies me to join any number of successful companies, it is my personal goals that spark my interest in being part of the World Destiny team. I believe my computer, promotional and organizational skills, fueled by my convictions, make World Destiny and me right for each other. Can we arrange an interview at your earliest convenience? I will call within the next week to arrange a meeting.

Sincerely,

Application Letter For Job Suggested by a Present Employee

Dear Mr. Cibron:

Mr. Ralph Andrews, production manager of your Los Angeles plant, suggested that I contact you about an upcoming opening in your Redwood City plant for an assistant plant manager.

I have seventeen years experience with corrugated box making operations, including manufacturing, assembling, installing and repairing the machinery, as well as supervising machine operators, scheduling orders, and computing costs of major machine installations.

Five years experience selling boxes has acquainted me with the customer's viewpoint.

One day's notice is all I need to arrange an interview at your convenience.

Sincerely,

Dear Ms. Chu:

Ms. Beverly Compton, who is executive secretary to your marketing vice president, Mr. Watkins, suggested that I apply for the position as your executive secretary.

I have a business degree with a major in accounting. While attending school and during the four following years I held positions that significantly improved my skills in both accounting and secretarial work. I enjoy both fields a great deal and hope to continue the combination rather than specialize in one or the other. The merger of abilities will be helpful to an executive secretary to a financial officer.

I look forward to the privilege of meeting you and discussing my qualifications in much more detail. I am available for an interview at your convenience.

Sincerely,

Thanking an Employer

The five categories of letters that follow: Accepting Offer of an Interview, Thank You for the Interview, Thank You for Your Recommendation, Accepting Job Offer, and Rejecting Job Offer, are basically thank you letters. Even when rejecting a job offer, you are thanking the employer for having accepted you.

The basic outline for all these letters is the same.

How to Do It

1. State what the thank you is for.
2. Mention the appropriateness of what you have received or been offered.
3. Be sincere, brief, and pleasant.
4. When appropriate offer something in return.

Accepting Offer of an Interview

Dear Ms. Martinez:

Thank you for making an appointment for an interview with me to discuss the executive secretary position.

I will be there promptly at 9:00 a.m. on Monday, December 10, 19__.

I am quite interested in secretarial work, and will be happy to explain my past experience and how it will help me become an effective member of the Zollar Corporation team.

Sincerely,

Dear Mr. Rose:

Thank you for scheduling an interview on January 16, 19__ at 10:30 a.m. I look forward to reviewing your Industrial Engineering opening with you at that time in your Detroit office.

I feel sure you will find my twelve years experience definitely applicable to your needs.

Sincerely,

Thank You for the Interview

A follow-up letter after a job interview can often be the extra push that gets you the job. Indeed, some human resources managers consider the thank you note an essential step in the job-hunting process. A letter received two or three days after the interview will keep your name in front of the employer. The letter also provides an opportunity to add what you wish you had thought of during the interview.

A short thank-you for the interview is sufficient for the introductory pleasantries. Then mention the main topic of the interview—the main topic from the *interviewer's* point of view—and what you can contribute to that situation. Follow this with helpful information that you may not have included in the first discussion. You can then add reminders of your strong qualifications and abilities. End with a statement of when you will contact the company to schedule a second interview.

Keep in mind throughout the letter that you are selling your ability to help the company you wish to work for.

Dear Mr. Arlington:

Thank you for the interview on the 22nd. I am confident I can fill the position of purchasing assistant. I agree that with your expanded activities, you need someone who can devote time to comparing prices and researching alternate sources of supply, and I have a program in mind that has been used successfully by other firms. Because it could easily be adapted to your operation, I would like to present this procedure for your consideration.

In my previous job we purchased from several of the same suppliers that you use. I believe I can adapt quickly to your purchasing procedures.

I will phone your office on the 30th to see if we can set a time to continue our discussion.

Sincerely,

Dear Mr. Edwards:

Thank you for explaining the opening in your hardware department. The position sounds interesting, and I believe I can help you. My experience with Baker and Hamilton is directly related to the work you require. Also, my school background and my work with Jones Simpson Company provide a strong base in retail marketing.

I am enclosing the completed application. My school transcript will be sent directly from San Jose State University.

I enjoyed our talk yesterday, and will call you next Friday morning.

Sincerely,

Dear Mr. Becker:

Thank you for the interesting interview on Monday, April 14. We did find an amazing number of similarities between the accounting operations of your company and the one I am now involved in, although the two industries are shipbuilding and paper finishing.

You mentioned several difficulties in getting data necessary for accurate cost controls. Most of the same difficulties were experienced where I work. Several problems were solved and others are being solved. I would like to present these solutions in more detail when we meet again. I am sure that many can be adapted without any changes in your accounting procedures, merely changes in details.

I will phone you Wednesday, the 30th to see what we can arrange.

Sincerely,

Dear Mr. Allis:

Thank you for the interview yesterday. I certainly appreciate your evaluation of my education and experience.

I will enroll in the two courses you suggested at the Ace Technical Academy and also obtain a couple years of practical experience in electrical assembly. You may expect at that time for me to ask for another interview.

Again, thank you for your helpful suggestions.

Sincerely,

Dear Mr. Goodwater:

Thank you for the opportunity to meet with you on Tuesday to discuss your corporate accounts payable position.

I am interested in that phase of accounting, and my previous computer experience will be of great help in reorganizing your present procedures.

Looking forward to another interview with you.

Sincerely,

Thank You for Your Recommendation

Dear Mr. Marconi:

Thank you for letting me use your name as a reference on my job application.

Your confidence in my character and my learning abilities must have convinced the Anderson Hardware Company that I could help them a great deal. I got the job!

I am proud to have your friendship and am thankful for your help.

Cordially,

Dear Mrs. Howell:

I deeply appreciate the letter of recommendation you wrote to Westminister Clothiers. I am sure it was a determining factor in their hiring me as their office manager, a wide-scope management position.

I am sure they will be pleased with my work, as you were. I learned a great deal from you that will be applicable here, and I approach this opportunity fully confident of success.

Sincerely,

Accepting Job Offer

Although accepting a job is usually done verbally and the acceptance formalized when personnel records are completed, it is a polite gesture to mail a letter of acceptance. Adhere to any deadlines suggested by the employment offer.

Dear Miss Chang:

Thank you for offering me the position of branch manager of the Regan Department Store in Marquette. Your confidence in my ability is gratifying.

The decision to grant me full control of all the facets of the store operations will provide the means of initiating needed changes in both merchandising and advertising. These two areas will become my first priorities in improving the image of the store.

I am eager to begin work as soon as possible.

Sincerely,

Dear Ms. Walters:

How can I thank you for the joy that your letter gave me? I checked the mail daily for the last month, eager to know if you had found a way of utilizing my talents and experience. Your response justified every moment of anticipation.

Although employment with *Bank* magazine will only be part-time, I intend to involve myself fully in the operation of the magazine. As I mentioned in the interview, the position is of great value to me as a means of reentering the job market after taking time out to raise my children. Therefore, you will find me willing to accept all manner of assignments.

I will report to your office at 9:00 a.m. Monday, July 16, 19__.

I look forward to beginning work.

Sincerely,

Dear Mr. Dray:

I am happy to accept a position in your Market Research Department. Your organization is the type I can readily fit into.

I've completed the application forms you gave me; they are enclosed.

As you requested, I will report to the personnel department at 9:30 on the morning of June 1. I am pleased to be working with you and the Anderson-Wells Corporation group.

Sincerely,

Dear Mr. Williams:

I was pleased to receive your letter offering me the position of purchasing agent with S&A Parts. The offer is particularly enhanced by the fact that a large number of applicants vied for the position.

Your confidence in me will prove well founded. Experience and judgment gained in past years will guide me in conducting an efficient operation.

I look forward to working with you.

Sincerely,

Rejecting Job Offer

As a job applicant, you may find yourself in the position of having to reject a good job offer, either because you don't want the job or because another offer is more attractive. You may at that time be inconsiderate of the employer's viewpoint, thinking that your unfavorable response is just one of the trials of being an employer until you realize that your refusal may be only temporary. A few years hence you may want to apply again or find that you have to work closely with the firm you are now rejecting. A polite letter stating a plausible reason for your declination is the accepted way to end the negotiations.

Dear Mr. Chun:

It was a pleasure discussing your marketing opportunities. I thank you for your insights into the range of possibilities at Jones & Johnson.

However, as I indicated, my primary interest is in production, and although I recognize the connection between the two fields, I prefer to start with a production job.

Thank you for your consideration.

Sincerely,

Dear Mr. Bruce:

Thank you for your offer to start as a Junior Engineer for Rollins Consultants on March 1, 19__.

On February 17, I was offered another position, which I accepted.

I appreciate the efforts you made on by behalf.

Sincerely,

Resignation

See Chapter 9, Termination and Resignation.

SECTION II—LETTERS WRITTEN BY EMPLOYERS

How to Do It

1. If the subject, from the reader's viewpoint, is positive or neutral, state the purpose of the letter in the first sentence.
2. If the subject, from the reader's viewpoint, is negative, make a related, positive statement in the first sentence. State the negative fact near the middle of the letter.

Tentatively Accepting Applicant

With this type of letter, the employer is hedging his bets and buying time. The applicant is not an ideal choice, but may be acceptable if the first or second selected employee doesn't work out. Also, the interest of the applicant is retained while the employer searches for a better candidate.

Dear Mr. Hart:

Thank you for your résumé.

So many applicants have responded to our advertisement, that we will need from two to three weeks to evaluate them before scheduling interviews.

We sincerely hope this delay will not be inconvenient for you.

Sincerely,

Dear Mr. Gilbert:

Thank you for your job application letter (for your résumé) (for returning our job application form).

Because we review each one in detail, we will need up to three weeks to set up a timetable for interviews. We will let you know as soon as possible if you will be invited to discuss your qualifications.

We apologize for the delay necessitated by the large number of applicants.

Sincerely,

Requesting Data from References

To avoid possible legal complications, some companies decline to provide any other information than dates of employment about former employees. Sometimes, however, you may receive helpful information, especially if it is complimentary to your applicant. Often a letter requesting, "Any details that may be helpful in our decision to hire John Jones will be sincerely appreciated," may get better results than a prepared questionnaire. Also, a person other than an employer may be more willing to share his personal observations and to provide details than a business concern might be.

Dear Mr. Wheadon:

Your name has been given us by ___(employee's name)___ as an employment reference. We would appreciate an early response because _(his or her)_ continued employment depends in part upon the receipt of appropriate recommendations from former employers.

Our company has employed ___(employee's name)___ in the position of _(position)_ which requires skill in dealing with the day-to-day behavior of mildly disturbed adolescents.

We would appreciate receiving a straight-forward appraisal of _(his or her)_ ability to provide professional quality social work services to such children in a residential group home setting.

Would your company be willing to hire _(him or her)_ again?

We greatly appreciate your assistance.

Sincerely,

Dear Mr. Collar:

Janet Austin has applied here for a secretarial position. She stated that she worked for your company from 19__ to 19__.

Could you give me the exact dates of her employment and any other details you can that would be helpful to us and to her?

Your help will be sincerely appreciated, and we will reciprocate any time you ask.

Sincerely,

Requesting Data from Applicants

Dear Mr. Terry:

Thank you for your reply to our advertisement, and for your résumé.

We wish to learn more about your abilities and how you might fit into our organization.

Please complete the enclosed application form. If the answers to some questions repeat what you have already sent us, please repeat the data.

The enclosed pamphlet will help you become better acquainted with our company.

We look forward to your prompt reply.

Sincerely,

Providing References to Another Employer

You may be asked to provide a reference about a former employee. Often this presents no problem, but occasionally compliments cannot honestly be given. When this occurs, be especially careful about what you write. Because recent federal laws permit people to examine their personal files, precautions are necessary to prevent a legal suit against your company. An attorney or your company's legal department should be consulted before you put anything derogatory about a person in writing.

Some personnel departments give references by phone only. Even then, any uncomplimentary statements should be general and vague. Such mild words as, "John Allison has worked here for seven years and except for some personal problems his work has been satisfactory," could be the basis for a legal suit by John Allison, and, although true, the "personal problems" statement would have to be proved in court. Litigation could be avoided by writing, "John Allison was employed here from January 15, 19__ to March 31, 19__," ignoring any reference to character or performance. If you feel you can write only a negative recommendation, don't write any!

Examples of a wide variety of letters are included in the section that follows.

Dear Mr. Heiman:

I am sorry we cannot provide any information on Miss Alice Wooden except that she was employed here from October 14, 19__ until December 31, 19__. We treat personal data about our employees as confidential material.

Sincerely,

Dear Ms. Culver:

Your letter to Mr. Samuel Collier was referred to me for reply.

I'm sorry to inform you that we cannot supply you with the information you requested. James and Holcomb does not permit the release of personal data.

Sincerely,

Dear Mr. Faulkner:

Ms. Eleanor Scott is highly recommended as a secretary. She worked for me for six years as secretary and statistical clerk. Not many will surpass her as a take-charge confidential secretary, and her statistical work is accurate. Her attendance is above average, she is on time, and she willingly works late when I ask her. Her handling of telephone calls and personal callers is most efficient and pleasant.

Sincerely,

Dear Mr. Hansen:

I am happy to recommend Norma Bellson, who has worked under my supervision for the past four years as a billing clerk. She does her work on schedule and is more accurate than most billers. In addition, her work is neat and thorough. She is always on the job a little ahead of time and her absenteeism is nearly zero.

Norma grasps new ideas and instructions quickly. She has a bookkeeping background and would be excellent as a billing clerk or junior accountant.

Sincerely,

Dear Ms. Wiles:

Theresa Anderson receives my hearty recommendation as an accounts payable clerk. She did excellent work under my supervision during the last six years. She got the bills paid on time, was cooperative and willing to do other assignments—mostly in the area of accounting reports. She has no accounting background but was extremely helpful with routine reports. Her typing is top quality. She was on time and had a better than average attendance record.

I wish I had her back.

Sincerely,

Dear Mrs. Amos:

Arlene Arnold is a precise statistical clerk; her work is fast and accurate. She is consistently pleasant, tackling all assignments with a smile. She usually comes to work early, and she was absent only five days in the four years she worked here.

She learns quickly but is not really analytical or research minded. On the other hand, after being shown step-by-step how to do a report or assignment, few can better her performance.

I recommend her highly for a position working with numbers.

Sincerely,

Dear Mr. Cunningham:

As vice president of this bank for eight years, I have overseen John Sands in his capacity as loan officer. He is a serious and dedicated worker, and his reliability and integrity are above question. He is well respected in local banking and real estate circles.

I highly recommend John Sands to you. He is a man who will help your organization grow.

Sincerely,

Invitation to an Interview

Dear Mr. McConnell:

Thank you for returning your completed application form.

We have scheduled an appointment for you at 10:00 a.m., Monday, March 20, 19__ at our Wilmington office. Transportation, meals, and lodging will be reimbursed to a maximum of $550.

We look forward to a pleasant and informative discussion with you.

Sincerely,

Dear Ms. Won:

Our fashion designer, Miss Warner, would like to discuss your application further at 1:00 p.m., Wednesday, April 22, 19__.

If you cannot keep the appointment, please call her at 000-0000.

Sincerely,

Rejecting Tentatively Accepted Applicants

Dear Mr. Fritz:

To keep you up-to-date on the status of your résumé, it has been further reviewed by managers directly interested in your specific abilities.

Although our needs are constantly changing, we have not been able to identify an appropriate opportunity for you at this time.

We thank you for your interest in the ABC Corporation, and wish you well in locating a position.

Sincerely,

Dear Mr. Bokeman:

Your application has been carefully considered again by our corporate management team.

Your qualifications are impressive; however, we have made an offer to a candidate who has a background in this industry and whose recent experience is directly related to the available position.

Thank you for your time and interest in pursuing employment with our company.

Sincerely,

Rejecting Applicant

Dear Mr. Gallatin:

Just a short note of thanks for visiting me in regard to our present opening.

You have a fine business experience with Jansen Manufacturing of which you should be proud. However, comparing the business we have here at Walkup Corporation and your overall capabilities with a much larger firm, I think this would be the wrong place for you.

Thank you for taking the time to come in, and the best of luck in finding just the opening you want.

Sincerely,

Dear Mr. Pappas:

We have received your recent inquiry concerning employment with Winston Developers and appreciate your interest in our company.

We have reviewed your experience and education against our current requirements. Although your qualifications are impressive, we feel that our current opening does not offer a close match to your background.

As you might imagine, our operations and employment requirements are continually expanding and changing. We have placed your résumé in our future reference file where it will be reviewed again as openings in your area of interest become available.

We sincerely appreciate your interest in becoming associated with our organization. We regret that this response cannot be more favorable, and we wish you well in locating the opportunity you desire.

Thank you for considering Winston Developers as a potential employer.

Sincerely,

Dear Mr. Langley:

Thank you very much for giving us the opportunity to consider you for employment.

After carefully considering your background and qualifications, we find that we do not have an appropriate position for you at the present time. Should one develop, we shall be in touch with you.

We appreciate your interest in Riverside Construction and wish you well.

Sincerely,

Dear Mr. Wilson:

Your interest in Stanford Corporation is appreciated. I read your résumé with considerable interest and it has been evaluated carefully by our personnel and marketing departments.

Your qualifications are excellent, but I regret that we do not now have an position open that fits your obvious abilities.

We thank you for considering Stanford Corporation, and I know you will find a suitable position soon.

Sincerely,

Dear Mr. Lattler:

Thank you for sending your résumé and giving us the opportunity to consider you for the accounting manager's position.

Our personnel and financial officers have thoroughly reviewed your qualifications. They are excellent but do not quite fit the position we have in mind at the present time. Your technical experience is notable, especially in the area of tax accounting, but right now we need someone who is stronger in supervisory experience.

We will keep your file active, and when promotions create an opening to fit your qualifications, we will write or call you.

Yours sincerely,

Accepting Applicant

A written record of being accepted for a job is appreciated by the applicant. The letter eliminates doubt and confusion and clarifies details such as where and when to report. Information about lodging availability and what to expect the first day will be of help in some situations.

This type of letter affords a great opportunity for a sentence or two (no more) of good impression building. Make the new employee glad to have accepted a position with your firm.

Include a congratulatory statement.

One word of warning, however. Do not lead the employee to believe his or her acceptance is a "contract" for employment by using such words as "guaranteed employment," "permanent employment," or "tenure." Do not use such phrases as, "you can stay and grow," "as long as you do your job," or "a long and successful career." A mere hint that a contract exists could put future attempts to terminate the employee into a tangle of legal difficulties.

How to Do It

1. Make a congratulatory statement.
2. State or imply that selection was made from many applicants.
3. Present a low-key sales pitch for the employer.
4. List any special conditions: when, where, and to whom to report; temporary lodging; first assignment; or other.

Dear Miss Garcia:

Your recent application for office clerk has been approved by the Personnel Department. Your abilities appear suitable to the needs of J. P. Sundstrom and we offer you a position beginning immediately at the salary discussed.

At J. P. Sundstrom, every employee is an important member of the firm. All employees have the opportunity to rise according to their abilities. Thus, even entry-level employees are selected with great care.

Congratulations on being selected. If you accept our offer, please report to the Personnel Office on Wednesday, September 17, 19__ at 8 a.m.

Sincerely,

Dear Ms. Rhymer:

I am happy to inform you that Burns School can offer you the position of instructor for the 19__–19__ school year. Selection from among so many qualified applicants was difficult. However, the results of your interview, coupled with the fine recommendation we received, led us to decide in your favor.

You should arrive the Saturday before classes resume. Temporary lodging will be available at Beogan Hall. Just call ahead or ask at the gate. We can also help you to locate an apartment in the area. Our classes begin September 7, and the first few days will be rather hectic. Be prepared. I will assume that you accept our offer unless I hear from you in the next week. Once again, congratulations on your selection.

Sincerely,

Dear Mr. Berg:

Congratulations on being selected as our new Parson store manager. I hope that you will accept our offer and that the salary offer is commensurate with your expectations.

The decision was a tough one since many qualified people were being considered. However, your creativity and enthusiasm won out over the others. I personally feel that the right choice was made.

We're a difficult store to work for since the public eye is always on the image projected by both our fashions and our employees, but you should have no problem in these areas.

Try to arrive in town by September 2, so you can get settled before the big season really begins and your duties multiply by the hundreds. Call when you're ready to begin work. My best to you in this new undertaking.

Sincerely,

Welcome to New Employee

A welcome letter sent to an employee shortly after he or she starts work projects a positive image. It also displays courtesy, consideration, and, of most importance, friendliness.

Say something nice about your organization and that you are proud to belong. This will help the new employee feel the same way.

Give your assurance that the reader has become a member of a strong team. Tell how you will assist in his or her orientation or what the employee can do to get off to a good start.

Dear Mr. Larson:

We at Aatel are glad to welcome you to our financial staff. We admire the work you did at Pierce Tractor and believe you can do as much for us. You will find a professional and cooperative staff here, and I am sure you will enjoy working with them.

I will arrange to have lunch with you soon to discuss some aspects of your work. In the meantime you will find Mr. Bond most willing to answer your questions.

Welcome aboard,

Dear Miss Ellis:

It is a pleasure to welcome you to Farnsworth, Inc. We are sure that you will find working here a pleasant and rewarding experience because we work especially hard to ensure that our employees and their jobs are compatible.

Our progress and growth are the result of each person's taking responsibility for a share of the work that needs to be done. As responsibility increases, so do the rewards. We take pride in our accomplishments, and I am sure you will too.

Sincerely,

Dear Ms. Romoglia:

I am very pleased that you have decided to join Bastone Leather Company as our Accounting Manager. I am confident that your years of experience will meet the needs of our company and of this position.

We hope that you enjoy a long and fruitful employ at Bastone Leather.

If you have any questions, please feel free to let me know.

Sincerely,

Performance Appraisal

It might be more accurate to describe a job performance evaluation as a memo rather than a letter. The evaluation is written by a supervisor who reviews it verbally with his superior and then with the employee.

How to Do It

1. Summarize the appraisal in the first paragraph.
2. Include a statement of advancement potential.

3. Make judgments based on relevant data, not broad, general statements.
4. Use positive statements. Negative performance should be stated in a way that suggests improvement is possible.
5. Make suggestions for ways to improve.
6. Include the employee's reaction to your evaluation.

Performance Evaluation

If Martin Willard continues his present rate of on-the-job learning, he will be ready for promotion from production foreman to production superintendent in one year.

Positive Aspects He has a clear grasp of production scheduling, its planning and follow through from operation to operation as well as the importance of timing in meeting scheduled dead lines.

He understands the function of each machine and how to make adjustments to control the scheduled flow of the product and how to maintain quality.

Negative Aspects He needs more training in cost control. Schedules and quality are well controlled but the cost of supplies and labor to do so is sometimes excessive. Separate seminars are to be arranged with the purchasing and accounting departments to broaden his awareness of these two factors. His use of this education will be monitored by the production manager.

Some subordinates complain of his harshness while admitting his effectiveness as a supervisor. The corporate director of labor relations will assist Willard in how to use a more tactful approach when instructing machine operators.

Michael Rosen	Martin Willard
Production Manager	Production Foreman

Job Performance Review

Another approach to job evaluation is to use a list of qualities. Each one is given a grade, 1 through 5 (highest being 1), followed by a brief comment if appropriate.

Date:
Name:
Present job:
Years at present job:
Evaluator:

Job Duties

Accuracy
Knowledge
Understanding
Meets deadlines
Attitude
Initiative
Analytical ability
Judgment
Planning
Flexible to change
Ability to present facts or ideas
Cost awareness
Accept responsibility
Safety awareness
Telephone etiquette
Housekeeping of work area

Leadership

Enthusiasm
Drive to "get it done"
Self confidence
Willingness to make decisions
Follow-up
Ambition
Delegates authority
Ability to organize work load
Training subordinates
Motivating people
Supervisory ability
Ability to assist supervisor

Personal Characteristics

Work habits
Judgments made calmly
Contacts with others
Punctuality
Appearance
Dependability
Personal habits

Overall Grade

__ 1. Outstanding   __ 4. Marginal
__ 2. Good   __ 5. Unsatisfactory
__ 3. Acceptable

General Comments

————————   ————————
Evaluator   Subordinate

Recommendation for Promotion

Dear Mr. Human:

Robert Winslow has developed at an accelerated pace during the past two years. In his capacity as Sales Service Manager, he has displayed much decision-making ability. Leadership is one of his strongest qualities.

Although the youngest person in the Sales Service Department, both in age and seniority, Robert was able to assume command upon promotion to his present position. He is rated as a No. 1 performer.

Robert has indicated a desire for line management and is willing to relocate. He is capable at this time of functioning as a Field Sales Manager.

Sincerely,

Dear Mr. Chan:

Rosa Ramada is ready for a promotion to Laboratory Manager.

She has worked under my supervision for five years as a laboratory technician, many times assuming my responsibilities when I was away. She is quite capable in that position. Her technical knowledge in both chemical and physical testing fields is without peer.

Ramada has received excellent training in cost control and administrative management. She is ready to move upward.

Sincerely,

Notice of Promotion

NOTICE

We are happy to announce that Arlene Britton has been promoted to Finance Manager. She has been our Accounting Manager for the past four years in charge of all accounting and statistical reports.

In her new position she will assume the additional responsibilities of corporate banking, capital structure, and stockholder relations.

Congratulations, Arlene. You have our full support.

(signed)

Congratulations on Your Promotion

Dear Alice:

Congratulations on your promotion. It has always been a pleasure working with someone as competent as you.

We look forward to more of the same fine work in the future.

Sincerely,

Dear Bud:

It was great to hear of your recent promotion. There is no doubt you have earned it, and I am confident it will not be the last.

I have always felt you handled the problems we sent you exceptionally well.

We look forward to working with you in the future.

Sincerely,

Reprimand

Begin a reprimand with a compliment. A statement such as, "Your work record in the past has been excellent," or, "Your attitude is commendable," will put the person being addressed in a more receptive frame of mind than a caustic remark.

Make the letter short: that will eliminate unrelated ramblings. Make negative statements in a positive way. For example, rather than saying, "You are making too many mistakes," say, "We believe a little more effort will improve your work."

Suggest specific corrective action, goals the person can accomplish, such as 95 percent attendance, 200 units per hour, or Report 57A completed by the 11th of each month.

When one employee's performance improves, his or her accompanying new attitude often carries over to other workers.

Dear Jim:

Cintex plant reports sent to Headquarters during the past six months have been on time, and have raised no significant problems, with one notable exception: The sales invoice processing has steadily deteriorated. This has delayed our receipts of data for the Sales Statistical Reports. It is also delaying our cash receipts because customers are getting their invoices late.

While some of the problems can be attributed to the Headquarters Data Center, the major problems are being created by the Cintex plant. The problems at Headquarters will be resolved, and I am confident that the future support from the Data Center will meet our standards.

The problems being created by the plant are in three categories: (1) late receipts past cutoff date, (2) month-end bunching of sales invoices, and (3) illegible documents and invalid data.

The attached schedule details the receipts in the Data Center for the month of February. As you will note, 22 percent of February's invoice volume was apparently billed on the last two days of the month. With 20 billing days, the expected percentage of billings on the last two days should not have exceeded 10–12 percent. Additionally, over 3 percent of the month's invoices were received after the cutoff date.

I am going to monitor future closings more diligently. Each month we will publish a report on the prior month's closing to highlight problems and take corrective action as necessary.

Please give this your personal attention. We must resolve this problem.

Sincerely,

Dear Howard:

Your work during the past four years has been excellent, but lately that is being offset by your absentee record. I am aware that your health has not been the best, but regular attendance is one requirement of your job. Something must be done to improve your attendance, because we cannot schedule our workloads efficiently when we cannot depend on you to be here.

If you need to see a doctor, we can easily schedule time from work for you to do that. Please give this serious thought; we need you on our team.

Sincerely,

Dear Jim:

I have a complaint from H&H Pallet Co. that you used abusive language toward their purchasing agent when asked to clear up a mistake on one of their orders.

Who was at fault is of little importance, but what is important is that you violated a company policy and came close to destroying a potentially profitable relationship. There is nothing you need to say to a customer that cannot be said politely.

I have straightened out the difficulty, and Mr. Johnson is reasonably pacified. Now that you both have had time to cool off, I want you personally to apologize to Mr. Johnson, and remember the importance courtesy plays in persuasive selling.

Sincerely,

Dear Dave:

I know you have been trying, but upon reviewing the first three months of 19_3, we find ourselves running 20MM units behind our Budget, and your short-range forecast shows no improvement in the next few months. Last January, I suggested you consider 19_1 costs for 19_3 rather than your budgeted figures, since your volume for 19_1 and 19_3 are similar. For the first three months of 19_3 you are behind 19_1 by 6MM units; therefore your costs should be as low or lower than 19_1.

If you will evaluate your Profit Analysis Report, you will see how the loss of volume has lowered your profit. Besides the loss of profit resulting from loss of volume, your salesmen are not obtaining last year's average price level, let alone the price they projected for this year.

Comparing the first three months of 19_3 with the first three months of 19_1, you have spent $7,000 more for printing, $19,000 more for cutting tools, and $18,000 more for packing—all of these are higher expenses with lower volume.

The only area in which you have reduced costs is wrappings, to the tune of only $930. This is the only sales controlled item in which any improvements have been realized.

I would like to know by May 7 what steps you have taken to:

1. Bring your sales volume up to your 19_3 Budget level.
2. Bring up your depressed average price level.
3. Decrease your printing costs and bring them in line with 19_1 costs.
4. Decrease your cutting tool costs and bring them in line with 19_1 costs.
5. Decrease your packaging costs and bring them in line with 19_1 costs.

Also please advise me by May 7 when these objectives will be accomplished.

Sincerely,

Termination Warning

See Chapter 9, Termination and Resignation.

Termination

See Chapter 9, Termination and Resignation.

Accepting Resignation

The acceptance of a resignation should be with sincere regrets. Only ill will can be gained by implying that the resignation was anticipated or that it is eagerly accepted. Say something nice about the person resigning. If nothing else, say that he or she did a fine job. End with an expression of good wishes for the future.

How to Do It

1. Express sincere regrets.
2. Say something complimentary.
3. Express good wishes for the future.

Dear Bill:

We are sorry to see you leave and accept your resignation with regret.

You accomplished a great deal for us during your six years as our mechanical engineer. You deserve much of the credit for our smooth running and profitable operation.

We do, however, understand your desire to be near your family. We know you will do as much for your new employer as you did for us. The best of luck to you.

Sincerely,

Dear Susan:

Mixed feelings well up in me when I accept a resignation. We never like seeing our associates leave, but at the same time we want you to know that our best wishes go with you.

We are proud that you received a promotion to Nursing Administrator at Wesley Medical Centre and know you are looking forward to your new surroundings and an interesting challenge.

Thank you for your valuable contributions and years of faithful service to our hospital. Our sincere good wishes to you, and if you are ever in this area again, please stop in for a visit.

Sincerely,

Notice of Employee Leaving

The occasion will arise when a company terminates an employee but wishes the real reason hidden. This may be prompted by controversy that would affect employee morale if brought into the open. These notices are brief, nonncommital, and pleasant. All signs of irritation, disgust, or "serves-them-right" feelings are omitted.

NOTICE

Mr. Albert Johnson, manager of our Arlington plant, has left the company to pursue other business interests. He will be replaced by Mr. Gerald Norgard, presently manager of the Sutherland plant. This will be effective July 1st.

NOTICE

Ms. Georgia Hayes had chosen to take early retirement. She preferred not to transfer with us when we move to Willows in August. She joined James & James in 19__ as secretary to Mr. Arnold James.

We will miss Georgia, and I am sure all of you join me in wishing her a pleasant retirement.

(signed)

Retirement Congratulations

Dear Tony,

I want to congratulate you and extend my best wishes for your retirement next month. You are to be commended for forty-seven years of productive and innovative work. Many of the procedures you established will continue for years to come.

You should have all the time you want now to play golf with your buddy, Charlie; no more waiting for the weekend.

We will miss your smiling presence, but do enjoy your leisure.

Sincerely,

Dear Ms. Landers:

It will seem strange here without your cheery "good morning" each day. Our customers will miss you too (but I hope not enough to forget us).

Let me say once again how much you have done to give our store its reputation for friendly service. After thirty years of being so helpful, I doubt that anyone can replace you.

Please accept my personal gratitude for your devoted service and my best wishes for an enjoyable retirement. Come to visit us as often as you can; we think of you as one of our family.

Sincerely,

Dear Tony,

I want to extend my best wishes for your retirement next month. You are to be commended for thirty-five years of productive and innovative work. Many of the procedures you established will continue for years to come.

We will miss your smiling presence, but do enjoy your leisure.

Sincerely,

Dear Frances,

When you started your career here, retirement seemed an endless distance away, but here it is. It seems to me that anyone who devotes that many years to public service deserves the most hearty congratulations!

You probably won't stay retired long, I can see you becoming deeply involved as a volunteer and keeping busier that when you were working.

Best wishes for a long-deserved change.

Sincerely,

Dear Rozanne:

Your approaching retirement, I am sure will not mean idling and relaxing. You have been too active in too many projects for that, and I believe that the only way to retire is to stay as active as ever, but restrict the activity to pleasurable things.

I am sure you will enjoy yourself, and let me add my congratulations to the many others you receive. You deserve them all.

Sincerely,

Dear Employees:

Alfred Parton, general manager of the Western Core Division, will retire June 30 after a long and distinguished career with Antelope Machine Corporation.

I know you will join me in extending to Alfred our appreciation for the leadership he has provided in developing the West Core Division into the strong organization it is today. Our best wishes go with him in his retirement.

Sincerely,

SECTION III—LETTERS INVOLVING THIRD PARTIES

Thanks for Helping Me Get a Job

Dear Ms. Mitchell,

I really want to thank you for all you did for me in your legal secretary class. I followed your suggestion and registered with Temporary Service. With the help of your recommendations, I was employed by the District Attorney's office for five weeks, by the trust office of Bank of California for two weeks, and by Marsh & Marsh for four weeks. The experience could not have been better. Next week I start a full-time job as a legal secretary for the law firm of Moyan, Lane & Watson.

Sincerely,

Dear Mr. Mapes:

Thank you for your most helpful suggestions about my entering the field of financial planning. Recent publicity about that profession has been mixed, with many firms emphasizing sale of securities rather than planning for the future.

By following your guidelines, I have established a business that helps others in the way I had hoped.

Again, thanks for your professional approach and your personal courtesy.

Best regards,

Recommending a Job Applicant

Dear Mr. Archer:

This is in response to your letter of March 4, 19__ requesting a personal letter of referral on Robert R. Riley.

I have personally known Robert for a number of years. He is a good friend of my son. I also know his family well because his father is my wife's doctor.

Robert is a tenacious young man and seems to be a determined, straightforward individual who knows where he is headed.

If you need further information, please write or phone.

Sincerely,

Dear George,

Harry Watson recently graduated from Stanford Law School. I have known him for over seven years and can honestly say he is one of the most intelligent, ambitious and likeable men available. Had he studied engineering, I would take him without a moment's hesitation.

I hope you can find room for Watson in your office. Someone will start him on his certain, brilliant career in law.

At the least, he will appreciate a visit with you because he greatly admires your work.

If you learn of any bright and ambitious engineers, send them to me. I'll be happy to return the favor.

Cordially,

Dear Mr. Baker:

Mrs. Lee Andry has been with us as secretary for three engineering managers for five years. For personal reasons she has found it necessary to move to Atlanta. Because she is a highly qualified secretary and administrative assistant, I thought you might be able to use her in your company. If not, perhaps you could offer her some suggestions for continuing her career in the Atlanta area.

If you or any of your staff should be coming to the Northwest, please call me; we can set up a business dinner.

Cordially,

Rejecting Applicant Recommended by a Third Party

Because this is a "bad news" letter, couch the decision in the middle. Courtesy and goodwill suggest that this is a letter that *should* be written, even if it seems to be an annoying obligation.

Dear Mr. Fenwick:

I thank you for recommending that Ms. Allison Walters see me about our computer opening. Your interest in our company is appreciated.

At the present time, in spite of her excellent academic training, we require someone with more on-the-job experience.

Thanks again for your interest in our operation.

Cordially,

Dear Mr. Thurber:

We appreciate your sending Mr. Edward Todd to see me about employment here. I can understand why you recommended him. He would be a great addition to our team, but right now we just don't have a place for him.

But I thank you for considering our company as a place to work for someone you obviously regard highly.

Sincerely,

Congratulations on Promotion

Dear Mr. Mosk:

Our entire family cheered when we learned of your advancement to Regional Manager. Congratulations! It is a good feeling when a former neighbor—and such a friendly one—is given a big promotion.

Sincerely,

Dear Ms. Bonfiglio:

I'm delighted to hear that you have been appointed to the Board of Directors. Perhaps I should also congratulate Lenkurt Co. for recognizing such a good woman.

Regards,

Dear Arlene:

Congratulations on your recent promotion. It has always been a pleasure working with someone as competent as you.

We look forward to more of the same fine work in the future.

Sincerely,

Dear Bud:

It was great to hear of your recent promotion. There is no doubt you have earned this promotion, and I am confident it will not be the last.

I have always felt you handled the problems we sent you exceptionally well.

We look forward to working with you in the future.

Sincerely,

Dear Mr. Rosen:

Congratulations on your promotion to Manager of the Converting operations. I know you worked hard for that promotion and no one is more deserving of the position you have attained. We are all proud of you.

Sincerely,

Dear Ben,

Congratulations to the new Manager! You are certainly deserving of the promotion.

I look forward to congratulating you in person in two weeks.

With regards,

Dear Tom,

We were thrilled when we heard of your promotion. Congratulations! We hope the added responsibility will not keep you too tied down. When you are more settled, please call us, so we can congratulate you in person.

Sincerely,

Dear Henry,

I was more than pleased this morning to hear that you are now a vice president. It couldn't happen to a nicer or more deserving person.

We both wish you continued success.

Sincerely,

Dear Tim:

The good news of your appointment as president of Saxxon Company came to me today from our friend Bob Anslowf. Hearty congratulations, and may I wish you every success. I agree that you are the best one to keep the company on its profitable course. The work, I'm sure, will be hard enough to be interesting and let's hope light enough not to be a burden.

Cordially,

Congratulations on Retirement

Dear Tom,

Congratulations on your retirement! I recall when you started work for Bullwright Construction, over 40 years ago. I even remember your first day: you complained about your sore arms from pushing a heavy wheelbarrow all day. Must seem like ancient history to the immediate past president.

Regards,

Dear Anne,

I learned yesterday from Joan Bartlett of Semiconductor Supplies of your recent retirement from Woodstock & Sons. Congratulations!

You worked long and hard for them for too many years and certainly deserve a few months at the beach. I say a few months because I know you won't stay idle long, but perhaps you can work in a more relaxed atmosphere. You're entitled to that.

The best to you,

Chapter 9

TERMINATION
AND RESIGNATION

TERMINATION

A letter announcing termination of employment should be a model of fairness. No matter how angry the writer is with the employee, it should be remembered that a letter is a written record that can come back to plague the writer if it is not reasonable and polite. The company needs complete documentation of the reasons for the dismissal because some dissatisfied employees take their cases to the National Labor Relations Board, the Equal Employment Opportunity Commission, or to their attorneys. The letter should also be brief in order to eliminate a tendency to present the sad news slowly, and thus painfully, to the recipient.

Here are a few "just causes" for terminating an employee:

— The employee has been forewarned of disciplinary measures for actions or lack of actions.
— The company's requirements are reasonable.
— All employees are treated equally.
— The employee's performance justifies termination.

The letter, however, must be positive. Leave no doubt in the reader's mind that he or she is being fired. The first question that comes to the reader's mind is "Why me?" This must be explained in order to make the letter complete. The explanation must sound reasonable and plausible, as well as being true, so the employer's goodwill (as much as possible under the circumstances) is retained. Terminating an employee is an integral part of any business, but it is also a painful experience for both parties. Treat the situation as even-handedly as possible. This can be done by including all the following points in the termination letter.

How to Do It

1. State regrets at having to terminate the employee.

277

2. State the fact of termination.

3. Explain why the decision to terminate was made.

4. Make a comment that will retain the employer's goodwill.

5. End on a note of encouragement.

Plant Closed

Dear Mr. Perez:

The recent reorganization and increasing inflation have forced AZE Corporation to close down several of its operations. Your department will cease operation effective January 10, 19__.

I regret having to terminate your association with AZE, as I believe that your work and enthusiasm have made you an asset to the company.

Rest assured that I will recommend you highly to potential employers as a most competent individual.

Sincerely,

Company Cutbacks

Dear Jean:

I regret having to tell you this, but due to a corporate program of cutbacks, your services will have to be terminated. The effective date will be May 31.

This cutback is being made companywide and will affect about 150 salaried employees. Seven or eight will be laid off in this branch. When deciding whom to let go, seniority was the primary factor. However, headquarters management has determined that certain occupations will be affected more than others.

We are sorry to see you leave and will certainly provide a good reference when you need it.

Sincerely,

Dear Mr. Mullen:

As you have become aware during the past six months, economic conditions have hurt us badly, forcing us to eliminate certain positions. This is unfortunate but we see no alternative. Regretfully, your position is one of those to be eliminated. A lot of hard thinking and long discussions with your supervisor, Mr. Thomas, preceded this decision.

We hope that as economic conditions improve we will be able to consider you for another position when one becomes available. We wish you every success in locating a new position and extend our thanks and appreciation for the good work you have done for us.

Sincerely,

Company Merger

Dear Mr. Grossman:

The recent merger of AZE and BFG Shoe Companies has created a large pool of employee talents, many of which duplicate one another.

It is unfortunate, but many faithful employees of AZE will have to be released by the end of fiscal year 19__ in order that a more efficient, cost-effective operation be established.

It is my sad duty to inform you that your position is one which will be terminated.

This unfortunate occurrence is not meant to reflect upon either your competence or productivity, both of which I would personally vouch for.

If there is any way in which I can be of assistance, please let me hear from you.

Sincerely,

Financial Problems

Dear James Calabar:

It is with deep regret that I must inform you of the recent decision to terminate your association with J. Alcove, Inc., as of December 30, 19__. Recent financial problems have forced us to scrutinize our manpower resources carefully, and several employees have, unfortunately, suffered in the process.

Your work here has been admirable and I will certainly provide you with the highest of recommendations if called upon to do so.

With your skills and abilities to work with people, I have no doubt that you will soon secure a position with another organization.

Sincerely,

Indiscretions

Dear Mr. Ludding:

The decision has been made to request your resignation effective June 5, 19__.

Recent publicity regarding alleged indiscretions with several of our members has made effective functioning in your position close to impossible.

Although individual board members maintain a belief in your innocence, public opinion has made our decision inevitable.

You are highly competent in your field and we trust that several new positions will open for you.

Sincerely,

Project Completed

Dear Mr. Evans:

You have done a fine job for us this summer. The Emerson project was a masterpiece of thoroughness and provided our top management with just the information needed.

We would be fortunate to have you back with us next season—and, we hope, for longer. We know you will do well wherever you go.

Sincerely,

Personal Friend

Dear Tommy:

We have been good friends for several years now, which makes this the most painful thing I have been asked to do in my business career. After long discussions with Ron Alyn, he has concluded that the best thing for all concerned is that you leave the company.

I know you will be leaving many friends, but conditions are such that this seems the best thing to do. Your severance pay will allow you time to locate new opportunities, and I'll be glad to help you in any way I can, now and in the future.

Sincerely,

Performance

Dear Allan:

I am sorry to be the one to tell you this, but your service will no longer be required. However, your pay will continue for two full months. The time is based on your years of service.

We have repeatedly asked you to put more effort and willingness into your work. We believe you have the potential to do a competent job, but your last three reports were late, incomplete, and inaccurate, and therefore useless to our managers who rely on these reports for operating decisions.

Perhaps you should seek a job that is less demanding and has less critical deadlines. I am confident you will soon find work more suited to your abilities.

Sincerely,

Classroom Procedures

Dear Mr. Weeks:

The school board has recently received several strongly voiced complaints regarding your procedure in the classroom. After a thorough investigation into the charges, the board has voted not to renew your contract for the coming academic year.

Admittedly, Milltown is not an avant-garde town, and many unusual approaches to education are not fully appreciated by the parents of the school children.

I trust that you will locate a position in a school system that is more receptive to your techniques, and we wish you well in your endeavor.

Sincerely,

TERMINATION WARNING

Some adults retain the childhood characteristic of needing a superior to restate their limits. A child may extend his limit of walking one block from home to two blocks unless constantly reminded. A teenager will stay out until midnight unless reminded often that the limit is 11:00 P.M. An adult employee will arrive at work later and later unless occasionally reminded that work starts at 8:00 A.M. Coffee breaks increase from 15 minutes to 20 or 25 minutes. Reports will be completed late unless the deadlines are restated each month. Employees overcome by these habits often respond to a less subtle reminder. The direct approach is required.

When these employees reach the line requiring a warning of possible termination, skip over the calm, subtle tones and state directly the reason for the warning letter, the potential consequences of the employee's actions (or lack of actions), and how the employee can avoid termination.

How to Do It

1. State regrets at having to consider termination.
2. Give reasons for considering termination. Mention *specific* reasons or actions or lack of actions or instances or examples.
3. Make clear that the reader is in a probationary situation.
4. End on a note of encouragement.

Personal Problems

Dear Mr. Bowen:

Termination of an employee is never a happy chore, and we make all efforts to avoid the situation. However, unless your work performance shows substantial improvement, AZE will be forced to terminate our association.

Personal problems affect all of us periodically. When these occur, help should be sought so that such problems do not affect work performance to the point that an individual is unable to function effectively.

Unless you seek professional help and make the effort to perform well once again, we will have no choice left but to sever the relationship.

The excellence of your past record cannot be overlooked, and I trust that your future efforts can be equally successful.

Sincerely,

Poor Performance

Dear Ms. Gallo:

We pride ourselves on being a "family store" and regret whenever we have to let an individual go because of poor performance or other difficulties.

Unfortunately, unless several flaws in your performance are eliminated immediately, we will have to terminate your employment with us. Customers have registered dissatisfaction with your rudeness, careless appearance, and reluctance to assist them in obtaining merchandise.

I'm sure that all of this can be worked out without any further complaints occurring, and with no further reminder required.

Sincerely,

Dear Mr. Sorbert:

It is with reluctance I inform you that, unless conditions improve measurably, AZE will have to terminate your association with the company.

Personnel performance and productivity rates have shown steady declines in the past twelve-month period. Frankly, unless improvement is observed, the department will have to be revamped and several other employees released in order to make up our losses.

To be realistic, we estimate that such improvement will take a minimum of six months to become visible. Given your excellent performance record in the past, there is no reason to assume anything but success.

Sincerely,

Dear Mr. Phillips:

This is a written record of our discussion following the accounting audit by the Sano Company on May 22, 19__. You have a copy of the 52 errors in accounting procedures and policies noted by the Sano Company auditors.

We discussed with you our concern and disappointment with these errors as well as your performance as an office supervisor. Company management will share this concern, especially because your position as assistant office manager places you in line for promotion to office manager. Your limited experience has been considered, but of more importance is your evident weakness in accounting skills and your lack of ability to organize procedures. In addition, while discussing procedures with members of your staff, we found morale to be unduly low.

At present, you may consider yourself on probation. Your performance will be carefully monitored, and if, in our opinion, a definite improvement is not forthcoming, there is a possibility that steps will be taken to replace you. You have begun to correct some of the problems, but a review of your progress will be made in four months. We expect to determine your permanent status at that time.

Sincerely,

Dear Mrs. Deyo:

Although with regret, I feel it is necessary to inform you that the following items concerning your supervision of the Baywell House of our youth agency need your immediate attention:

1. The amount of gasoline consumed from Friday to Friday should not exceed $25. Special field trips are excluded. No trips are to be made in the agency vehicle that are not agency related.

2. Mileage forms should be turned in at the end of every month completely filled in. Trust receipts and allowance receipts must be turned in weekly.

3. The phone bill is not to exceed $70 for agency calls. This is separate from your personal calls, for which you pay. This means that all calls need to be monitored *before* the number is dialed and a record should be kept for each boy stating whether or not his one long-distance, five minute call was made for that month. A log should be maintained for all calls.

4. The grocery list is to be filled in according to needs listed on the menu form ONLY. The grocery list should indicate the quantity needed. Food is ordered Friday through Thursday.

Improvement must be shown in these areas by March 9 or employment will be jeopardized. By this date, there should be enough improvement made that these issues will no longer be a problem.

I have read this and understand its contents.

_____
Francine Deyo   Date: _____

Classroom Performance

Dear Mr. Chaffee:

The school board has received several strongly voiced complaints regarding your practices in the classroom. Unless modifications of such procedures are undertaken, renewal of your contract cannot be a certainty.

In particular, your suspension of all homework assignments and the assignment of comic books as reading material in senior literature seminar have been cited. Parents also allege that numerous individual class sessions have become no more than verbal free-for-alls, with little direction by you.

Unannounced teacher evaluation will be utilized within the next two weeks in an effort to clear up this matter. I trust that you will make every effort to conform to the standard of education of this school.

Sincerely,

Tardiness

Dear Mr. Torr:

Promptness is important to the management and the customers at Rich Savings and Loan Association. Therefore, while we make allowances for occasional lateness, consistent lateness cannot be tolerated and offenders must be dismissed.

You have reported late to work for 17 out of the last 23 days. Unless this situation is remedied immediately, you will be asked to leave our organization.

Should there be extenuating circumstances, please come in and speak with me. If there is a problem, perhaps we can work it out together. Rich S & L never likes losing a good employee. I'm sure that the problem can be eliminated.

Sincerely,

Absentee Record

Dear Harvey:

Your work has been excellent, but your absentee record is about to overshadow your work record. I don't doubt that your health has been poor, but one requirement of a job is regular attendance. We have difficulty scheduling our operations when we cannot depend on your attendance.

This subject has been discussed several times before, and now your attendance must meet our requirements or termination will result.

Sincerely,

RESIGNATION

A letter of resignation must be fair to both parties involved. Show tact and consideration for the person or parties from whom you are resigning.

Regardless of the reason for resigning—you hate the boss, the work is too hard, the hours are too long, the work is boring, or you *did* get a better offer—tact is always required. A blatant statement of the facts may arouse the ire of the reader and preclude a good recommendation should you ask for one at a later date. The resigner should assume full responsibility and not blame the boss for causing the resignation.

A socially acceptable reason should be given for resigning. It may be because of poor health, someone in your family is being transferred, you wish to change directions, you want to spend more time with your family, or you have served for a number of years. The occasion may arise, however, when a one-sentence statement of resignation with no explanation or comment is all that is required. The recipient of the letter would already know the reason.

Avoid self praise. It is well to mention the pleasant aspects of having worked for the organization, but do so by mentioning how your associates made work pleasant for you, not how you helped them.

Mention the specific date of resignation.

How to Do It

1. State the effective date of resignation.
2. State an acceptable reason for resignation.

3. Briefly mention the good points of having worked there.

New Position

Dear Mr. Larson:

With great reluctance I am submitting my resignation, effective July 31, 19__.

My association with Wiley Company has been a pleasant one, and I will miss the friendship here. However, as I mentioned in our brief discussion last week, the offer I have received cannot be ignored, considering the financial benefits to my family and the future potential of the position.

I appreciate your understanding of my decision to leave Wiley Company.

Sincerely,

Dear Mr. Aurner:

I have been offered a position that includes a wider range of accounting tasks and one that will lead to a supervisory position,

I am eager to accept this new challenge and will be leaving October 1, 19__. Meanwhile, my best efforts will go into training a replacement.

Sincerely,

Seeking New Challenge

Dear Bill,

Harper Clean Air has grown rapidly during the past fifteen years. The problems of growth presented an intriguing challenge. The challenge was met, and I enjoyed my part in meeting it. The future promises more growth, but I have been at my desk handling the same problems over and over for the past five years. I need a fresh challenge.

Thus, with mixed feelings of leaving an old friend and of needing my own "Clean Air," I am offering my resignation, to be effective November 30. I will join the new firm of Hoskins and Halloid. They manufacture air valves and plan to expand into related lines.

We have several people here who could take over my position with a minimum of training. Please accept my thanks for the opportunity you gave me to work with you in meeting the challenges of the past fifteen years.

With regards,

College Training

Dear Mr. Carlyle:

To make full use of my college training in business finance, I have accepted a position with the Norcross Development Company, builders of shopping centers. My resignation will be effective March 31, 19__. I will be glad to help in any way possible to train a replacement.

Over the past few years, I have given serious thought to making a change. I sincerely appreciate the opportunity you gave me here at Johnson's Hardware to learn about business and the importance of work, and especially the help this job provided in financing my college education.

I have enjoyed working here and will continue my personal friendship with you and your staff.

Sincerely,

Ill Health

Dear Ms. Willis:

Resigning was the furthest thing from my mind when I worked so vigorously to become director of the City Youth Program. However, I must leave the position at the end of December.

Ill health and growing burdens in other areas have drained me of the energy and enthusiasm needed to conduct such a program.

The young people and those with whom I've worked have added immense meaning to my life. I only wish I could continue to work with them.

Sincerely,

Heart Problem

County Planning Commission:

With much reluctance and regret I ask to be released from the position of County Planning Director.

Because of a heart condition I have developed, my doctor has instructed me to slow my pace of work.

As you may imagine, this is somewhat of a blow to me, but my doctor knows this condition better than I. During the past six years I've enjoyed working with the fine people of our county. It is difficult for me to resign, but I must do so effective August 15.

Let me extend my good wishes to all of you for success on the riverfront project.

Sincerely,

Allergies

Dear Mr. Newell:

Circumstances require that I resign my position as quality control supervisor, effective March 18, 19__.

My unique susceptibility to the materials worked with makes continued employment in this capacity at Jones Company an impossibility. In addition, I have been ordered by my physician to detoxify my system by isolating myself from the substance for several months.

I am appreciative of the patience and kindness shown to me by both co-workers and management as I have sought to deal with this difficulty. Unfortunately, fairness to myself demands that I resign rather than continue.

Sincerely,

Personal Problems

Dear Mrs. Aldridge:

For nine months, I have enjoyed the pleasure and benefits of being vice president of the Milltown Businesswomen's Club. Thus, it is with great regret that I must resign.

Recent personal difficulties are creating more demands on my non-professional hours. As a result, I cannot give full attention to my responsibility as vice president, and I feel that I am shortchanging the Club.

Working with the other officers has provided pleasure as well as insight into the skills and competence of today's business-woman. Please accept my regrets.

Sincerely,

Disagree with Goals

Dear Mr. Deihl:

Recent occurrences demand that I resign my position as Vice President for Public Affairs, effective February 9, 19__.

Disagreement with the goals and philosophy of the company has hindered my performance and negated my ability to assist in furthering those goals.

I will miss the challenge and adventure my role offered, as well as the many people with whom I worked.

Sincerely,

Want Less Travel

Dear Mr. Davis:

It is with deep regret that after eight years with Atwater Shoe Company, I must resign my position effective August 6, 19__.

Financial considerations, and the increased needs of a growing family, require that I accept a position that demands less travel and time spent away from home.

The opportunity for growth and continuing challenges offered by Atwater in these past eight years have been of great personal and professional value to me. I will miss the personal closeness and the consideration shown by all members of the company.

Sincerely,

Credit Union

Board of Directors:

I hereby submit my resignation as chairman of the Credit Union Supervisory Committee effective March 1, 19__.

Sincerely,

RESIGNATION ACCEPTANCE

The acceptance of a resignation should be with sincere regrets. Only ill will can be gained by implying that the resignation was anticipated or that it is eagerly accepted. Say something nice about the person resigning. If nothing else, say that he or she did a fine job. End with an expression of good wishes for the future.

How to Do It

1. Express sincere regrets.
2. Say something complimentary.
3. Express good wishes for the future.

Dear Bill:

We are sorry to see you leave and accept your resignation with regret.

You accomplished a great deal for us during your six years as our mechanical engineer. You deserve much of the credit for our smooth running and profitable operation.

We do, however, understand your desire to be near your family. We know you will do as much for your new employer as you did for us. The best of luck to you.

Sincerely,

Dear Jim,

All the Church School members and teachers will miss you very much. Your eleven years as Church School Superintendent was an uplifting experience for all of us—in our faith and in our attendance.

No one can replace you, but we will find someone to carry on the work.

We wish you well in your retirement and your move "back to the old homestead," as you put it.

With God's blessing,

Dear Bob,

The Board of Directors regretfully accepts your resignation as the Chairman of the Supervisory Committee of the Credit Union.

You worked many long, hard hours auditing the books and the operations of the other committees. We got many new insights through your willing efforts. Your judicious handling of the special meetings during our troubled times of changing managers will never be forgotten by the Board.

We want you to know of our deep appreciation of your work during the past five years, and although our acceptance of you resignation is reluctant, our best wishes go with you.

Sincerely,

Acknowledgment of Separation Pay and Release

I, (Employee), have received from (Employer Company) the net amount (after standard deductions) of (write in the amount) dollars ($____)—consisting of (write in the amount) dollars ($____) in severance pay and (write in the amount) dollars ($____) in vacation pay. In exchange for this payment, I will release (Employer company) as well as their directors, managers, staff members, program coordinators, supervisors, and other agents from any claim or causes of action that are connected in any way with my employment or the termination of my employment by (Employer company).

I have read this release and understand it. I also accept the payment described above as a final and complete settlement of all claims and causes of action that I have or may have against (Employer company).

Signed this _____ day of _____19__.

(Signature of employee)

_____

Witness

_____

Witness

(Reprinted from *"Wrongful Discharge" and the Derogation of the At-Will Employment Doctrine* by Andrew D. Hill, Wharton Industrial Research Unit, University of Pennsylvania, with permission.)

Chapter 10

SYMPATHY
AND CONDOLENCE

The first essential of a letter of sympathy is a feeling of respect for the reader. He or she has lost a loved one or suffered an accident or succumbed to an illness. A respectful mood is called for. The sympathetic situations covered in this chapter are those in which a cheery greeting or humorous get-well card is not appropriate. The letter should be written from the heart, and should be warm, human, and kind. The writer needs a feeling of empathy with and consideration for the reader. All of these feelings, however, need not be put into one letter. In fact, the second essential is brevity. Long eulogies and maudlinism are out. Do not burden the grief-stricken with more grief or long explanations of unrelated matters.

The third part of a letter of sympathy is an offer to help. This does not fit into all situations, but if the intent is sincere and follow-up certain, an offer to help at the end of the letter is a real comfort, especially at the time of the death of a loved one.

The use of the word *death*, along with *died* and *killed* in a letter of condolence is objectionable to some people, because these words seem unnecessarily strong. The word *deceased* is also used as a substitute for *dead*, but is hardly an improvement. References to sorrow, grief, tragedy, or loss can be used, and the meaning remains clear to the reader. Some of the examples that follow use the word *death* and some do not. The decision to use it or not will be based upon the writer's understanding of how the reader will react.

When the cause of death seems so traumatic the writer is uncomfortable stating it, a simple sentence such as, "May we express our sympathy," or "We are truly sorry," will reveal the writer's feelings. The cause need not be mentioned.

Some letters of sympathy include phrases similar to these: "there is nothing anyone can say at a time like this," or "words cannot express our feelings," or "we don't know what to say at this time." Such phrases should be eliminated. They seem to be put in to lengthen a short statement of sorrow, and they express helplessness at a time when the reader needs help.

How to Do It

1. Mention the person about whom the sympathy is being expressed: for example, Henry, Dr. Miller, your boss, or your sister.
2. State your relationship with this person: for example, our friend at work, my acquaintance of many years, or all of us here.
3. Make a complimentary statement: for example, he was loved by all, he was a warm friend, she was always cheerful, she was helpful, or we spent many pleasant hours together.
4. If appropriate, offer to help the reader.

Sentences Expressing Sympathy

A list of sentences appropriate for letters of sympathy follows. In instances where they seem to fit, they can be added to the sample letters. These statements can also be substituted for statements in the sample letters in this chapter or can be the starting point for a self-composed letter.

We hope our caring will make your sorrow easier to bear.

We hope that time will ease the sorrow of your recent loss.

We know that memories will keep your lost one close to you.

May our sympathy help to comfort you.

May you find comfort in knowing that we care.

Our thoughts are with you in this time of sorrow.

We wish to express our deepest sympathy.

May the love you feel for the one you lost lessen your sorrow.

May the love that surrounds you be a source of comfort at this time.

May your memories be a source of comfort.

It may help to know that our thoughts are with you.

May the sympathy of those who care make the sorrow of your heart less difficult to bear.

Some things are hard to understand.

No one is ever ready for death.

We know death is certain, yet it remains hard to accept.

Those who have not experienced the death of a close one cannot comprehend the loneliness.

There is an emptiness that only those who have lost a close relative can understand.

Our sympathy and love go out to you, Mrs. (Mr.) Smith.

We shall miss her (his) smiling presence.

The loss of a son, (daughter, wife, husband) is giving up a part of one's self.

When one spouse leaves a loving partnership, it's always too soon.

Until you have suffered the loss of a loved one, you cannot fully understand the pain of separation.

Sentences Thanking the Reader for an Expression of Sympathy

Without you I wouldn't have known where to turn for the endless number of decisions one must make in a time of grief.

You were such a comfort to us following Edward's death.

Jon always thought of you as a real friend, and that you proved to be during my period of grief.

How much I appreciated your kindness and help when Alexander died.

I just couldn't have managed without your help.

The letter you sent at the time of Andy's death continues to be an inspiration to me.

Thank you for your kind words and your understanding heart.

Your kindness overcame the self-pity I was beginning to feel.

Your words of encouragement stayed with me during my bereavement.

Thank you for your understanding sympathy.

Your love and help during my recent difficulty have meant more than words can express.

We wish to thank you for your kind thoughts.

My husband and I wish to thank you for your kind thoughts.

We wish to thank you for your letter. The kind messages sent by friends have been a great comfort to us.

We appreciate your thoughts of us and your sympathetic note.

We appreciate your kindness in writing to us at this time.

We gratefully acknowledge your kind expression of sympathy.

We appreciated your sympathy in our bereavement.

We thank you for your kindness and sympathy.

Your note of sympathy helped me to accept Tom's death more courageously.

Your sharing of your recent sorrow helped me to bear my present bereavement. Thank you.

It is a comfort in a time of sadness to receive such a beautiful expression of sympathy.

Thank you for your kind expression of sympathy.

Your sympathetic note reminded us of the many kindnesses you have extended to our family through the years.

We are grateful to you for helping us bear our grief by your kind letter of sympathy.

I appreciate the kind thoughts that prompted you to send such lovely flowers.

The family of Joan Anderson accepts with sincere appreciation your kind expression of sympathy.

Letters to Hospitalized People

When writing to a person in a hospital, be pleasant and optimistic while expressing an interest in the patient's welfare. Do not refer to the specific illness or injury—that is the doctor's job.

Hospitalized for Illness

Dear Will,

When I called at your office today, I was surprised to hear that you were in the hospital. With your usual spunk I can't see an illness holding you down very long. Take it easy and enjoy the rest while you can. I'll be looking for you to be back at work soon.

With regards,

Dear Al,

Word of your illness just reached me, and I want to wish you a quick return to health.

Your many friends will be sorry to learn that you will be in the hospital for a few weeks. I am sure it helps to know that you have a large group of well-wishers.

When you return home I'll be over to see you. In the meantime, please ask Mrs. Jacobs what I can do for her here. I'll be glad to help in any way possible.

I hope the next few weeks will pass quickly and you'll be home again soon.

Sincerely,

Dear Eilene,

Gloom hangs over the office since we received news of your sudden illness. We send our wishes for a fast recovery. (We need you here at the office.) We hope the flowers will brighten your room in the hospital and cheer your spirits.

Sincerely,

Hospitalized for Accident or Injury

Dear Margaret,

Your mother called this morning to tell me of your accident Saturday and that you will be in the hospital for three or four weeks. We will miss you but don't concern yourself with your work here. We will take care of it for you.

Rest as much as possible under the circumstances. We all hope for a full recovery.

Sincerely,

Dear Mr. Allison:

I am sorry to learn of your injury. Please accept my best wishes for a quick recovery.

Since you will be confined for a few days, I believe you will enjoy this new book on your hobby of boating.

Cordially,

Other's Illness

Dear Ron,

Your friends at Elton Corporation are sorry to learn of your wife's serious illness. Please accept the flowers we have sent with our sincere wishes that she will have a fast and complete recovery.

Sincerely,

Death of Business Associate

Dear Mrs. Appleton,

All of us here at Sear's Lumber are saddened by the death of your president, Andrew Jennings. You have our most sincere sympathy.

Mr. Jennings was a real community leader and served as an example to all of us. His work with the Boy Scouts will long be remembered.

Sincerely,

Dear Linda,

It is with great sadness that we learned of the death of Thomas. I had worked with him in Denver and then in Atlanta until his transfer last August. We will all feel the loss.

Sincerely,

Death of Business Friend

Dear Mrs. Jader,

It is difficult to tell you how deeply I feel about Mr. Jader's untimely death.

What started many years ago as a business relationship between Harold and me quickly became a warm friendship. It was a privilege to have known him so well, and I will never forget his thoughtfulness and kindness.

With great personal sorrow, I ask to share your loss and to extend my heartfelt sympathy.

Sincerely,

Dear Mrs. Reinhardt,

It was with heartfelt sadness that I learned of William's passing. Bill and I worked so well together on the Bonner Bridge project in the late sixties. We spent many pleasant hours together, off the job as well as on. He was a great companion and a warm friend.

Sincerely,

Death of Spouse

Death of Husband

Dear Jean,

Losing one's husband can cause a loneliness unlike any other, but having your children near will help ease the difficulty of the days ahead.

With your fortitude and courage I am sure you will adjust to your new situation. I know you are grateful for the many happy years you shared with Tom.

Love,

Dear Eldrid,

Your John made friends of everyone he met, even during his last days in the hospital. But this was only a part of his personality. We all will remember him for his generosity. He often involved himself in worthwhile civic projects. The community is richer for his having lived.

I wish we lived closer together so I could be with you at this time. I send my love.

Sincerely,

Dear Mrs. Nunan,

Please accept our heartfelt sympathy in your time of great sorrow. Only those who have lost a husband can know the depths of your feelings. We send you our love to give you strength to bear your sorrow.

Sincerely,

Dear Mrs. Emerson:

Mr. Franklin and I wish to express our deepest sympathy to you and your family.

I came to know Dr. Emerson well these last few years. I had no friend whose wisdom and kindness meant more to me. We shall miss him.

Sincerely,

Dear Mrs. LaCosta,

We wish to express our sympathy on the untimely death of your husband. He was a great asset to our company for many years, and all of us old-timers will miss his steadfastness.

If I can be of any help at all please call me.

Sincerely,

Dear Mrs. Bascomb,

I was stunned yesterday to learn of Fred's untimely passing. I have known Fred since coming to work here nearly twenty years ago, and have enjoyed these many years of friendship with him.

Fred was loved by all his co-workers, and his friendliness cheered us all. He will be greatly missed.

Mrs. Bascomb, our thoughts are with you, and we extend our deepest sympathy.

Sincerely,

Dear Mrs. Sanders,

We were both grieved to hear of your loss. Mr. Sanders was the one person we could always go to in time of trouble, however slight. He was so warm and wise and understanding.

If there is anything at all we can do to help you, please let us know.

Sincerely,

Dear Adele,

When there is love, any life is too short. Fred had a way of making the joys of life contagious. We remember especially his help with our basement—a problem was turned into a pleasant and companionable experience.

We know you are grateful for your life with Fred, and we feel fortunate to have known him.

With sympathy,

Death of Wife

Dear Bob,

Perhaps it will help to lessen the sorrow of Mabel's death to realize that so many of her friends share your grief. We all appreciated the happiness she so willingly shared and inspired in her friends.

I know your courage will help you through this rough time. Our love is with you.

Sincerely,

Dear Mr. Gordon,

I wish to express my deepest sympathy. Mrs. Gordon was one of the loveliest women I have ever known. No one who knew her could ever forget her charm and warmth.

Sincerely,

Dear Mr. Jenkins,

Bereavement is so personal that few of us, unless we have experienced it ourselves, can comprehend its grief. Your wife, Jackie, was loved by all of us who worked with her. Her pleasant vitality was a continuous inspiration. We hope that our caring will lessen the sorrow that you bear.

Sincerely,

Dear Jerry,

We were sorry to hear about Maryanne's death. We will always remember her for her fascinating interest in the environment and the people around her. She will be missed by many.

Cordially,

Death of Relative

Death of Mother

Dear Mr. Donaldson,

We extend our most sincere sympathy to you upon the loss of your mother. If there is anything at all that we can do to help, please call us.

Sincerely,

Dear Ms. Rutherford,

There is a lonesomeness after the death of one's mother, but I want you to know that your friends are thinking of you and sympathizing with you in this time of your great loss.

I will never forget the friendliness and kindness your mother extended to me. She was loved by all who knew her.

With sympathy,

Dear Robin,

My love for your mother will last as long as my memory of her. During the many years we were neighbors, she shared her smiles, her flowers, her recipes, and most of all her pleasing personality.

No one who knew her will ever forget her. I want to share my sympathy with you.

With love,

Death of Father

Dear Miss Elwood,

May I send you my deepest sympathy at this time and say that my thoughts have been with you since I heard of the death of your father. I admired him greatly. You must be even prouder of his devotion to you. I know you will be brave in your sorrow as he would have wanted you to be.

Sincerely,

Dear Mrs. Lansing

We were truly sorry to read of your father's death yesterday. We will be over tomorrow to help with whatever we can.

With sincere sympathy,

Death of Daughter

Dear Alice,

No person or experience will ever replace the happy days and love little Lana gave you.

We hope it will be of some comfort to know that you gave her all the love and care possible and that your many friends share your sorrow.

Love to you and Jim,

Dear Mr. Arronson:

It was with sincere regret that I heard this morning of the loss of your daughter. I know what a shock you have suffered. I wish to express my deepest sympathy and the hope that the kind thoughts of your many friends will make your grief a little easier to bear.

Sincerely,

Dear Kevin,

I was surprised and saddened to hear from Mrs. Addison that your daughter succumbed to the injuries from her recent accident.

I want you to know how terrible we feel that you have lost a lovely and talented daughter at such an early age.

Please call me if there is anything I can do to help you.

Sincerely,

Death of Son

Dear Brad,

Please accept my sincere sympathy on the death of your son, Jerry.

Sincerely,

Dear Mr. Welch,

The loss of your son comes as a shock to us at the Boating Club. We all had the greatest respect for him and will miss his cheerfulness and lighthearted humor. We realize our loss is small compared to yours.

We offer our heartfelt sympathy in a time of sorrow.

Sincerely,

Death of Sister

Dear Jane,

I have just learned with sorrow of the death of your sister. Because you and your sister were so close, I realize how deeply this loss will touch you. I know you will be able to adjust, and please accept my sincere sympathy.

Cordially,

Death of Brother

Dear Mr. Mantell,

The death of your brother brought profound sorrow to me as well as to his many friends. During the many years I knew him I often thought of him as my own brother.

May I extend my deep sympathy to you and your family.

Sincerely,

Death of Others

Dear Mr. and Mrs. Inland,

We were shocked to learn of your recent loss. Louis had such promise and was so well liked that it seems hard to believe he is no longer with us. His passing will be mourned by those of us who loved him so much.

Most sincerely,

Dear Madolyn,

We wish to express our deepest sympathy upon the untimely death of Jim.

He was one of our great managers as well as a personal friend to so many of us who worked with him. The many years he devoted to community services will be long remembered by the people of Little Rock. May your memories be a source of comfort.

Sincerely,

Dear Benny,

I am deeply grieved when I think of your loss. Janice was a wonderful friend who always did more than was expected of her. She made this world a little better for me and for all the others who knew her.

Sincerely,

Dear Mrs. Solons,

It was a distressing shock to learn of Howard's death yesterday. We worked together here for many years. If there is anything I can do to help you, please don't hesitate to give me a call.

Sincerely,

Dear Janette,

I just learned in a letter from Dave about Jim's accident and the misfortune you are suffering. It's hard to face the loss of a long-time friend even from far away. If I were closer, perhaps I could be of more help to you at this time to ease your strain. But I do send my deepest sympathy to you and your family.

With sympathy,

Belated Condolences

Dear Mabel,

I was deeply shocked and grieved to hear that Edward passed away last month. I will always remember his pleasant ways and how he made us feel so much at home whenever we visited with you folks.

I think it is great, and a great help to you these days, that you are spending so much time at the Convalescent Hospital as a volunteer helper.

Sincerely,

Dear Ellie,

I learned only yesterday of your father's death. I always admired the cheerful way he helped your neighbors and his willingness to get involved in the town's activities.

I will always think of him with fondness.

Sincerely,

Death by Suicide

Dear Alice,

Word has just reached us of Jerry's tragic death. As impossible as it must be to understand, Jerry must have felt in his own mind that this was the best alternative.

You have the courage, I know, that you will need to face the days ahead.

We send our love
and sympathy,

Dear Ron,

I am deeply moved by the news of Marie's most shocking death. None of us understand it. I am sure she gave a great deal of thought to her decision to depart at a time of her own choosing.

It will require an untold amount of courage for you to carry on, but I have faith that you can surmount the tragedy.

Bless you

Death—from a Business Firm

Gentlemen:

I am sure the death of Allen Rogers is almost as great a shock to the entire accounting profession as it is to the members of your organization.

Few men have been held in as high esteem as he was for many years. No man deserved it more.

As a member of our profession, I share with others this tragic loss.

Sincerely,

Dear Mr. Johnson:

  We at Basker Company were saddened to hear of Mr. Condon's death. We extend our deepest sympathy. Mr. Condon's leadership in our business community will be sorely missed by the community as well as by his numerous friends.

Sincerely,

Dear Mrs. Addison,

  Just a quiet word to extend our deepest sympathy to you and your family, and to let you know we are thinking about you.

Sincerely,

Dear Mr. Browne:

  Your great loss has saddened my staff and me. We wish to express our deepest sympathy to you.

Yours sincerely,

My Dear Mr. Lawrence:

  We at Jordan's were very sorry to hear of the death of your daughter. Only one who has lost a lovely, young daughter can know the tragedy of this loss.

  All of us here wish to extend our heartfelt sympathy. Please let me know if there is anything that we at Jordan's can do to be of help to you.

Sincerely,

My Dear Mrs. Robertson,

  Everyone at our company was surprised and saddened by the sudden death of your husband.

  Although sympathy is only a small consolation, even from the hearts of us who share your sorrow, I want you to know how deeply Tom's loss is felt here. He was respected and admired by everyone who worked with him.

  We cannot eliminate your sadness, but each individual of our company joins in this expression of our deep sympathy.

Very sincerely,

Dear Mrs. Smith:

No one can take the place of a devoted husband, and only one who has had a like sorrow can understand the grief that you are experiencing.

My words can bring only slight comfort when your grief is so great, but I did want you to know that we at Watson Corporation extend our deepest sympathy.

We share your personal grief as we have lost a needed and valued member of our team.

Sincerely,

Dear Mr. Sanders:

We have just heard of the great personal loss suffered by you in the tragic tornado that brought death and destruction to your city.

Buildings and even cities can be restored, but the death of your son is an irreparable loss. We are willing to do what we can by shipping you anything you may need to rebuild your business. We'll gladly extend any length of credit necessary. Will you let us do that much for you?

To hear of a friend and customer losing his store and his son brings home to us the heartaches and sadness from which many people in your city are suffering. May you have the strength and courage to carry on.

Sincerely,

Birth Defect

Dear Anne,

A birth defect seems so terrible now, but since I also have a child with a birth defect, let me assure you that it won't be as bad later on as it seems now.

Some physical defects cannot be changed, but control of expressions, revealing a return of your love, can be learned. With your wisdom and patient understanding, your precious baby can develop so her personality shines right through the handicap.

I'll be glad to share my experiences and learning with you. I'll call you soon.

Cordially,

Divorce

Dear Annabelle,

We were surprised and deeply disturbed to hear that you and Jim are getting a divorce.

We don't know your intimate differences or the deep reasons for your decision, but as long as we have known both of you, we didn't realize there were any serious frictions or problems.

We have written a short note to Jim, also, to let you both know that we are ready to help in any way we can.

With love,

Marriage Separation

Dear Janet,

As a lifelong friend of your mother—and of you, too—I am greatly concerned about your separation from George.

I know you are taking this step after serious consideration, but if it should be because of something that could be ironed out, please give the separation another thought or two. I am concerned that such a promising marriage should not endure. All marriages take a lot of work and compromise, but whatever your decision, I will always remain your close friend.

Love,

Misfortune

Dear Brother,

Misfortune hits each of us at some time or other. Hang in there and don't let this drag you down. You have recovered before from setbacks by driving ahead with the next project. Although right now this may seem worse than before, I know your persistence and stamina will propel you to the top again soon.

We here are all rooting for you and know we can expect the best from you.

Regards,

Personal Reverses

Dear Ben,

A stone wall may be all you see now, but out of your adversity I know your tenacious courage will find a gateway opening once again to the success you have achieved before.

Your friend,

Unnamed Tragedy

Dear Mr. and Mrs. Alder,

I saw the report in the paper about Jim, and want to tell you how sorry I am. Jim was three years younger than I, so we didn't play together often as kids. But when I met him at your daughter's wedding last month, I realized what a fine son you have and how proud you must be of him. You'll just have to take my word for how badly I feel.

Sincerely,

Thank You for Your Sympathy

Dear Mr. Cooly,

We appreciate and thank you for your expression of sympathy upon the death of Mr. Olson.

Sincerely,

Dear Beth,

It was heartwarming to receive your comforting letter of sympathy.

Sincerely,

Dear Mr. Nelson,

Thank you for your warm expression of sympathy upon the death of Hugh. The pain is lessened by your kind offer to help, which I may accept soon.

Sincerely,

Dear Mrs. Coulson,

Thank you for your thoughtfulness upon the death of my sister, Ellen.

Sincerely,

Dear Mrs. Eberly,

We were pleased to receive your letter of sympathy. It was a comfort to us. Eleanor always mentioned you with the greatest respect and admiration.

Sincerely,

Dear Mr. Franklin,

We appreciate your kind expression of sympathy.

Sincerely,

Dear Jane and Roy,

Thank you so much for the gift of your friendship. It is a great comfort to our family to know that Dad had such good friends at work. The spray of pink carnations you sent was just beautiful.

With appreciation,

Dear Joan,

Thank you so much for your thoughtfulness in sending me the beautiful dwarf pine. I appreciate your caring.

Sincerely,

The Sanford Office Group

I wish to thank all of you for remembering me in my time of need. The plant you sent is beautiful.

Sincerely,

Gentlemen:

On behalf of all of us at Morton, Martin, and Grove, I wish to thank you for your kind expression of sympathy upon the death of our Mr. Allen Rogers.

It is true that we have sustained a shock and a great loss by his sudden passing. We believe the greatest tribute to him will be maintaining the high professional standards he represented and so strongly encouraged.

Very sincerely,

Chapter 11

APOLOGY

Writing a letter of apology is an ego-deflating task: you just hate to admit a mistake. Because the other party already knows of the error, the best approach is to take a deep breath and plunge in. To be effective, an apology must be genuine; the regret must be sincere but not overly emotional. To say, "I am sorry," "I am truly sorry," or "I am sincerely sorry for my mistake," is a genuine expression of feeling. But to expound, "I don't know what to say, but I ask your forgiveness for my terrible error of sending the wrong replacement parts. I know this has slowed your production startup and has probably cost you a lot of money. We are extremely sorry," is just too much for any reader.

In most instances, make the statement of apology at the beginning of the letter. It is inconsiderate to the reader to hide the purpose in the middle or at the end. Use the middle of the letter for an explanation of the mistake—if an explanation is deemed necessary. Make the explanation as brief as possible while keeping it clear. Omit long, detailed, or technical explanations. The middle of the letter is also the place to relate what is being done to prevent a recurrence of the mistake, or to thank the reader for being tolerant while a confusing situation is straightened out. If an explanation isn't feasible, don't ramble on saying nothing. The whole letter can say, in effect, "We're sorry; we'll work to avoid repeating the error."

Close a letter of apology on a forward-looking and positive note. If something has been delayed, state the new delivery, completion, or approval date. Make a promise of future promptness and fewer errors. Relay to the reader your confidence that relations will improve.

How to Do It

The following sequence is suggested for a genuine, goodwill-retaining letter of apology:

1. Apologize at the beginning of the letter.

2. Explain the error and the determination to prevent further errors.
3. Close on a forward-looking, positive note.

Sentences of Apology

Here are some statements that will prove helpful when composing a letter of apology:

We appreciate your patience in allowing us time to research the information and respond to your complaints.

We are sorry that this is one of the few instances in which we cannot make a refund.

We are sorry for any inconvenience we caused you.

We are proud of our excellent service, and you should expect it at all times. We apologize for our failure and will try not to let this happen again.

We try our best, but occasionally errors do slip by. We will try even harder to prevent future errors.

This is one of a very few areas of loss that Forward Insurance Company does not cover, and we are sorry we are unable to help you in this time of need. We suggest you contact Hanford Insurance of Brooklyn for this type of coverage.

Thank you for your patience while we straightened out the confusion about your order. We are sorry for the inconvenience.

Thanks for staying with us while we contacted all parties involved in this confused situation. Your understanding has helped us clear the many tangled ends.

Again, we are sorry for the inconvenience we caused you.

We appreciate the amount of work you put into your bid, and we are sorry we could not offer you the contract.

For an efficient operation, we have found that our policies must be followed in detail. We are sorry we cannot make an exception for you.

Please accept our apology.

Reasons for an Apology

The following are acceptable reasons for making an apology:

I am sorry I missed our scheduled dinner meeting yesterday in Kansas City. Because of stormy weather there, the plane did not stop over but went directly to Chicago.

I am sorry to hear about the poor printing on your last order. The printer acknowledges the faded-out appearance and will credit you for the full amount.

There was a delay in shipping because the demand exceeded our expectations, and we had to order a second printing.

The delay in shipping was due to a local trucker's strike and alternate carriers were busy beyond their capacity.

The delay was due to our error, for which we have no excuses. If you cannot use the belts sent, please return them for a full refund.

Please accept our apology. We have no explanation for our obvious error.

Mr. Johnson has been ill for the past week.

An unexpected field trip kept me away from the office.

The Chicago trip required two days more than I anticipated.

Unfortunately, due to my oversight this notice did not go out sooner, and I must apologize.

Mr. Sanders is away for two weeks but Ms. Lawson will do the report and have it for you as soon as possible, probably by next Wednesday.

We regret the delay in getting copies to you, but our copying machine broke and we had to send your work to another printer.

We are sorry we omitted the samples when we sent your package yesterday. We made the mistake, but the samples are on the way now.

Unexpected developments prevented my being there.

Bad Behavior

Dear Mr. Hall:

I am sincerely sorry for what happened Wednesday, and especially for my actions. I hope you will accept my apology, and rest assured that nothing similar will occur again.

Regretfully,

Dear Mr. Hallen:

My behavior at the party following our recent dinner meeting was deplorable, I assure you it will not happen again. I was wrong, I have no excuses, and I am sorry.

Regretfully

Billing Error

Dear Mr. Rodgers:

You are right and we are wrong. We apologize for the error and thank you for calling this to our attention. A corrected bill is enclosed.

Sincerely,

Sorry for the error . . .

We're enclosing for you, Mr. Silva, one invoice not included with your February statement. We are sorry this invoice was omitted. The total of the invoices will now equal the statement amount of $150.65.

We appreciate your being a customer since 1957.

Customer Service Division

Company Procedure

Dear Ms. Arthur:

I am sorry we cannot write you a check from our local plant for your past due freight bill No. 278-089789 as you requested.

We received the copy of the bill on Wednesday, November 21. We have matched it with our purchase order and will mail it today to our headquarters in Detroit for payment.

Although the bill is overdue, because we have not received the original bill, our corporate procedure requires that our headquarters office pay the bill. This procedure speeds payment in practically all instances and includes an audit of all paid freight bills.

You should have your money in less than a week.

Sincerely,

Confusing Word Usage

Dear Mr. Dunbar:

I want to apologize for not helping to sponsor the TV program on containers and the environment that we discussed last Wednesday. We were favorably inclined until we realized that the word *containers* as you used it meant beer cans, pop bottles,

and plastic bottles used to contain thousands of varied products.

In the paper and forest products industry, the word *containers*
means corrugated boxes (often called cardboard boxes).

I hope you understand our confusion and appreciate that
we do not wish to help sponsor a program not related to this
association's industry.

Sincerely,

Declining Dinner Invitation

Dear Mr. Hamilton:

Julie and I appreciated your invitation to dinner on July 10,
and it is with regret that we find we have another engagement
on that date.

Thank you for thinking of us.

Sincerely,

Dear Mr. Peters:

We are sorry we can't accept your invitation for dinner and
the Snappers show on May 3. I have a budget meeting scheduled for that night and there is no way I can skip that meeting.

With regret,

Dear Mr. Jones:

Since accepting your kind invitation to dinner and the theater
on March 2, I have learned of the serious illness of my mother
and I will be leaving for Chicago tomorrow.

I am sorry to have to forego a delightful evening with you.

Sincerely,

Delayed Answer

Dear Ms. Gaines:

I deferred writing to you until I had all the facts, and I am
glad that I did. New developments show that you were correct
in stating that you have not missed the deadline for submitting

the manuscript for the article. I was surprised to learn that your arrangements with Mr. Anderson were not communicated to me. I was, therefore, under the impression that you and Mr. Anderson had also agreed on the original date of May 1, rather than the revised date of August 1.

I apologize for the inconvenience I caused you. I am looking forward to seeing your manuscript by August 1.

Cordially,

Dear Ms. Ralston:

Please excuse my delay in answering your letter of February 13, but this has been one of those busy, hectic periods beset with all kinds of deadlines.

I am glad you found some of my survey data useful, and look forward to seeing your report on condominium growth in San Diego.

Sincerely,

Dear Mr. Wilson:

I hope you will forgive the long delay in answering your letter of June 9. We are temporarily understaffed, but we *are* getting inquires answered—although admittedly somewhat slowly.

The information you requested will be mailed early next week. We are happy to send you records of our experience with the Anhold starch maker, which we find exceptionally efficient.

Thank you for your patience.

Sincerely,

Dear Mrs. Wiseman:

We regret that the item described above has been temporarily misplaced in our files. When located, it will be mailed to you promptly.

Your patience is greatly appreciated.

Sincerely,

Dear Ms. Herlock:

I apologize for not writing sooner about the letter you objected to receiving, which pertains to an unpaid bill for $239.79.

I was away from the office for almost two weeks with a severe cold and have just returned. I checked your account with our bookkeeper, and I am happy to say that you are correct: you don't owe us any money.

The error was caused because we have another customer whose name is Jan Herlock. We are correcting our records.

We apologize for any unpleasantness and concern this may have caused you. We value your goodwill.

Sincerely,

Delayed Credit

Dear Mrs. Sanders:

I am sorry you had to wait so long for your credit of $51.20. We had some difficulty tracing the sale and return of part of the merchandise. The refund check to you is now in the mail. Again, please excuse the delay.

Sincerely,

Postponed Dinner

Dear Mr. and Mrs. Rulless:

Mr. Webb and I regret that, due to the illness of our daughter, the dinner arranged for Friday, September 28 must be postponed.

Regretfully,

Delayed Order

Dear Bill:

I don't have any excuse for the delay, and I am truly sorry.

The booklets you ordered are being mailed today, and I'm sure you will find them worth waiting for. I enjoyed working on them for you, but they did take a little more time than I had anticipated.

I would appreciate hearing how well they are received by your clients.

Sincerely,

Delayed Paper Work

Dear Ms. Sampson:

Thank you for reminding us of the credit due you. We ran into unexpected delays, but the accounting department has notified me that your check for $51.20 will be in the mail today.

Thank you for your understanding.

Sincerely,

Dear Mr. Childress:

My apologies to you for not getting the Ward Company freight claim information to you earlier. I was sent to Chicago to work on a machine installation for six weeks and got back just yesterday.

I called Ward Company this morning and Mr. Andrews said he had a detailed listing of the expenses for your claim. He will mail a copy to you. If you don't get it by Tuesday of next week, call me and I will follow up with Mr. Andrews.

Again, sorry for the delay.

Sincerely,

Delayed Return of Borrowed Item

Dear Ms. Sanders:

Let me apologize for not returning your folder and two pamphlets on the collection of delinquent accounts.

I have found the information of great benefit but was slower in getting through it than I had promised.

It is really helpful when two credit unions can exchange information.

I hope you haven't been inconvenienced by my delayed return of the data. I thank you so much for you generosity.

Sincerely,

Dear Mrs. Stone:

I'm really sorry I didn't return your book sooner. I put it in the bookcase when I returned home from the hospital and completely forgot about it. The book was just lively enough to keep me in good spirits while spending so much time flat on my back.

I appreciate your lending me this interesting book, and I apologize for keeping it so long.

Sincerely,

Dear Mr. Parker:

Last year's issues of *Business* magazine that you lent me are being returned. I owe you an apology, as well as a thank-you, for not returning them sooner as intended.

I found the articles I was looking for and got much useful information from them.

It was kind of you to lend me these magazines, and I hope the delay has not been an inconvenience to you.

Sincerely,

Delayed Thank You

Dear Mr. Carswell:

Please excuse my delay in thanking you for the interesting visit with you and your staff on June 16 and 17.

I found our contract discussions helpful: we now have a better understanding of your needs. I know we are a little behind schedule, but we are working on the proposed contract for your approval and expect to have it ready by the end of the week.

Again, thank you for the information tour.

Sincerely,

Dear Mr. Simon:

Please let me apologize for not writing sooner to thank you for your assistance with the Bradford Associates account while I was in Phoenix. Your previous experience with them proved a great help in putting across my proposal.

Don't hesitate to call me when I can be of some help to you. As they say, I owe you one.

Sincerely,

Indiscretion

Dear Mr. Stamm:

Please forgive us for the indiscreet inquiries we made. After I explain the reasons for the questions we asked, I hope you will accept our apologies.

For open credit of $100,000 that you requested, we investigate our customer's credit potential thoroughly, often following seemingly insignificant leads. Our forty-seven years of experience have proven this to be beneficial to both us and our customers. A customer suffers as much as we do from overextended credit.

We apologize for any inconvenience and hurt we have caused you. You will be glad to learn that your open credit line for $100,000 has been approved.

Sincerely,

Dear Mr. Tunney:

I am sorry that we seemed indiscreet in making inquiries about you. Let me explain the reasons and then I hope you will forgive us.

For a life insurance policy as large as $250,000 we investigate our clients rather closely. Issuing such a policy is a risk to us. To lessen our risk and to ensure our financial stability, we sometimes check references two or three people removed from the references given by you. We have found this to be a sound business policy, and we are sorry for the concern we unintentionally caused you.

You will be pleased to learn that your policy has been approved.

Sincerely,

Ignoring a Customer

Dear Mr. Avery:

I was surprised when I heard that you feel you haven't been getting the same attention you received when we were a smaller company. I was wondering why we hadn't seen you lately.

I am truly sorry if anyone in our organization has been giving you less service than you deserve, since you have been one of our most loyal customers for many years. If this is the case, I offer my personal apology, and trust you will give us another chance.

I look forward to seeing you personally the next time you stop in. I would enjoy discussing our business relationship, and I will see to it that you are taken care of to your satisfaction—and incidentally to mine as well. Our relationship has been very pleasant and profitable for both of us, and I would feel hurt—less for business than personal reasons—if through some fault of ours that relationship were changed in any way. See you soon.

Sincerely,

Incomplete Instructions

Dear Mrs. Wordsworth:

We agree that the blouse you returned shrunk in your washing machine. This particular blouse is not washable although some blouses of similar appearance are. Our sales staff has been instructed to make each customer aware of how each blouse must be cleaned. Sometimes a clerk will forget.

Whether or not this was the case, we are sorry, Mrs. Wordsworth, for the disappointment and inconvenience to you.

Please let me know if you wish a replacement of the blouse or a credit to your account. Above all we want our customers happy.

Sincerely,

Incomplete Project

Dear Mr. McGuire:

We have just discovered that it will be impossible to complete the project for you as we promised.

My colleagues and I spent many hours collecting the data you requested. Most of it was in a car that was stolen, and to date the local police haven't recovered it.

Please accept our sincerest apologies for any inconvenience to you. Enclosed is a refund of your $100 retainer fee.

If our property is recovered soon, we will send the data to you without charge.

Sincerely,

Late Report

Dear Opal:

You're absolutely right; my project report is due this Wednesday, the 7th. I'm embarrassed to say I haven't finished it. In

error, I had noted on my calendar that it was due next Wednesday, the 14th. I just confused the dates.

I'll start working on the rest of the report today, and it will
be on your desk Monday. In the meantime, is there something
I could do to alleviate any problems my lateness may have
caused you?

I appreciate your patience.

Sincerely,

Missed Appointment

Dear Mr. Fowler:

Please accept my apology for not meeting you for lunch
Tuesday. At 11:30 our press had a breakdown and I had to be
there to help locate the reason for the breakdown.

Could you have lunch with me on Friday? I don't anticipate
any maintenance problems then, and we should be able to
enjoy a leisurely lunch.

Sincerely,

Missed Meeting

Dear Mr. Denton:

Mr. Anderson was called to Houston unexpectedly and asked
me to express his regret at not being able to attend your dem-
onstration of the Hasting-Allison process. He was looking forward to an interesting afternoon.

Sincerely,

Dear Mr. Donaldson:

There is no excuse for my not meeting you for lunch yesterday
or at least getting word to you. I had the appointment written
on my calendar, and I was looking forward to the occasion,
but somehow I thought our date was for next Thursday. It was
just one of those days.

Please forgive me. I am anxious to talk with you, and will
phone you Tuesday to see if we can arrange a meeting before
you leave town. I won't let you down this time.

Cordially,

Dear Miss Sampler:

This is an apology I feel embarrassed at having to make. I have no excuse for not checking my appointments calendar before dashing off to Denver—even if it was an emergency call.

After looking forward for six weeks to meeting you and discussing your latest research results of the Matson project over lunch, I feel bad about forgetting to even notify you of my absence.

I will call you next week when I return and perhaps we can get together in San Francisco at your convenience.

Please accept my apology.

Sincerely,

Missing a Caller

Dear Ms. Englund:

I am sorry I was out of the office when you called Tuesday. I had told you I would be available any time during the week, but a labor problem at the Northside plant required my presence Tuesday afternoon.

Please phone and let me know when you will be in town again. I'll try to forestall any emergencies that day.

Sincerely,

Project Failure

Dear Mr. Anwar:

I have never before experienced the failure of a project like the Atchison project. I assure you it will not occur again. All our people feel bad about it and have reviewed in detail with me the reasons for failure, and, more important, ways of preventing mistakes in the future.

My apology at this time cannot undo past damage, but my regret is sincere, and my efforts in the future will be guided by this experience.

Sincerely,

Quote Error

Hello Mr. and Mrs. Watson:

I am sorry to report this, but I made a mistake on your homeowner's policy. The policy will cost you $428 per year rather than the $379 I told you.

I confused the policies issued by two of the several insurance carriers we write for.

I am sorry for the mistake. You have the option of canceling the policy if you wish, or having us rewrite the policy for coverage that will cost you only $379 per year. Please let me know which you decide.

Kindest regards,

Shipping Error

Dear Mr. Banter:

Will you accept our apology? We made an error in putting your shipment of May 22 together. Thank you for calling this to our attention. We work very hard to please our customers, but obviously we must work even harder.

The chair you ordered is being shipped today. You may return the other chair, collect, at your convenience.

Sincerely,

Dear Mrs. Montez:

You are certainly justified in being angry about our blunder in returning the unordered merchandise you had returned to us. Please let me apologize. The error was ours, but it would help us when you return merchandise if you would enclose a note to me or our sales representative stating why it is being returned. This will ensure proper credit to you.

You will receive immediate credit for this returned merchandise and all shipping charges.

Again, I am sorry for the inconvenience to you. We do value your business and your friendship.

Cordially,

Slow Payment

Dear Mr. Allison:

We are sorry to have caused you a financial inconvenience by not paying a group of your invoices sooner. We have had internal problems, but these are resolved now. We will start paying your invoices tomorrow.

You could ensure quicker payment in the future by extending us terms of 1 percent, 10 days. Invoices marked this way are paid as soon as received. Invoices with no payment terms are paid in 30 days.

Again, we are sorry for the past inconvenience, and future payments will be on time.

Very truly yours,

Small Reward

Dear Frank:

It was an exciting year, struggling to overcome our many difficulties. You are given much of the credit for the turnaround toward profitability.

I realize a thank-you is small reward for your diligent work, but next year we expect to make our thank-you more tangible. Meanwhile it's great having you on our team. We are running strong and in the right direction.

Sincerely,

Statement Error

Dear Mr. Wendell:

A corrected statement of your account is enclosed. We are sorry about the error and hope that it didn't cause any great inconvenience. We check every step in our processing of accounts, but even then clerical errors occur at times. Please accept our apologies. And we do appreciate you giving us the opportunity to be of service to you.

Sincerely,

Our Apologies . . .

The finance charge information for 19__ is not printed on this statement, but will appear on your statement next month.

Please use your February, 19__ statement for income tax preparation.

Thank you for being our customer.

Sincerely,

Dear Customer:

Hello! Here we are again. We recently mailed you the Statement of Account for your mortgage loan for 19__.

Our face is red because that Statement of Account appeared
to have had some errors.

The Revised Statement of Mortgage Account, enclosed, is
current and the errors are eliminated.   Please review the
amounts under Taxes and Interest.

Again, we wish to apologize for any inconvenience our error
may have caused you.

Sincerely yours,

Wrong Information

Dear Customer:

OOPS! WE GOOFED!
Our order blank states: "All offers expire April 30, 19__."
It should read: ALL OFFERS EXPIRE JULY 31, 19__.

Sincerely,

Chapter 12

CONGRATULATIONS

We enjoy sharing our enthusiasm and delight with friends who have won awards or have been recognized for outstanding work. This special accomplishment is an occasion for a letter of congratulations, a time to send good wishes. Your friend will appreciate a little boost to his or her ego. If you are writing to a business acquaintance or associate, a letter of congratulations can do much to stimulate cooperation between the two of you or to strengthen an existing good relationship. Goodwill should be nurtured at every opportunity

Many occasions are appropriate for a letter of congratulation: winning a hole-in-one golf tournament, winning a skating championship, receiving a superior rating in a music contest, earning an appointment to an office, doing the best selling job last month, receiving a job promotion, or winning a bride.

Write a letter of congratulation as soon as possible after the event. Six months later, your friend may feel let down that it took you so long to recognize his or her promotion.

Along with your bubbling enthusiasm, sincerity must come through to the reader. Use expressions that would be natural in a conversation with the reader; don't overblow the occasion or smother it with flowery phrases. The tone of the letter, however, will depend on your relationship with the reader. To a staid business acquaintance, straightforward and conservative statements may be appropriate, while to a sorority sister or fraternity brother, jocular informality may be just the thing.

Now for the easy part: make the congratulatory letter brief; from three to six sentences is sufficient.

How to Do It

1. State the occasion for the congratulation in the first sentence.
2. Make a comment that links the person and the occasion.
3. Write or imply your expectation of continued success.

Sales Volume

Dear Bob,

Your successful sales efforts have secured an annual sales volume of $1 million from Amsterdam, Inc.

My congratulations to you for this fine job. As you know, business conditions being what they are, the Amsterdam account is doubly important. Keep up the good work!

With best regards,

Dear Tom,

Congratulations on establishing a new sales volume record in the month of March. I recognize that this is the result of work done during the past year by your sales staff, but it looks great on our financial records, and I know you played a big part by inspiring your sales staff.

Sincerely,

New Customer

Congratulations, Jim—

on securing this new account!

I know you worked hard on this one and it is great that you were able to close the deal before being transferred out of the territory.

Again, let me say, "a job well done."

Regards,

Job Well Done

Dear John:

About the Baker's Dozen account:

GREAT!

Sincerely,

Dear Mr. Mullen:

I would like to congratulate you and your people for the fine job that has been done in reducing our raw materials inventory in the recent months.

This result, so effectively presented by the graphs that were prepared, turned out to be a high point during the recent manager's meeting.

I would appreciate receiving these graphs each month.

Sincerely,

Dear Joe:

Please note the attached copy of Mr. Robinson's letter of congratulation.

To it I wish to add my own congratulations for the outstanding achievement in inventory reduction.

Keep up the good work.

Sincerely,

Top Salesperson

Dear Janet,

Congratulations on being the #1 salesperson in the Northwest sales group last month. Your volume and the gross margin dollars were the highest for any November in the Company's history.

Good luck in December,

Exceeding Goal

Dear Joe,

My congratulations to you and the sales force for having surpassed our 19__ goal on scrap recovered from our customers. During the month of October we collected 485 tons which amounts to 5,800 tons on an annualized basis. This is well in excess of our 4,000 ton goal.

Regards,

Graduation

Dear Jack,

Congratulations! and an extra hurrah for making the top ten! Our family is proud of you.

We regret, Jack, that earlier commitments prevent our attending your graduation ceremonies.

Best wishes for continued success as you start your new career.

Sincerely,

Dear Mrs. Long,

We just heard that Patricia graduated from the University of California at Berkley with honors. You must be extremely proud of her accomplishments, and I am happy right along with you.

Please give Patricia our best wishes for continued success as she enters law school. (. . . pursues her career.)

Sincerely,

Dear Lynn,

I was delighted to receive the announcement of your graduation from Stanford. Congratulations on your well-earned degree.

My blessings go with you as you face a new career and new challenges.

Cordially,

College Degree

Music

Dear Howard,

Your long years of study, practice, playing, and teaching have finally won you a coveted Master of Arts degree in music from Mills College. My hearty congratulations on an honor that does not come easily. The degree will certainly enhance your opportunities for teaching; you are already widely recognized as one of the best.

Keep up the good work; we are all proud of you.

Sincerely,

Specialized Teacher

Dear Jean,

Congratulations on your graduation! I understand you already have a position teaching blind children. It is most encouraging to you, I am sure, having the opportunity to apply your specialized training so soon. With your interest in children, you and they will surely have a pleasant learning experience.

I am confident you are equal to the unusual challenge.

With best wishes,

Handicapped

Dear Kathy,

You'd be the last one to want special recognition for graduating from college, but with your handicap you deserve the highest praise for your accomplishment.

Your hard work and courage will carry you far in this world. You are a heartening example to many others.

Sincerely,

New Position

Dear Mike:

Congratulations on your new position as an aeronautical design engineer. You must be glad to get back to a familiar line of work. Around here, we will miss your cheerful personality and most sorely miss your willingness to help in any problem areas.

Please stop by any time you are in town: we don't want to forget you.

Again, congratulations,

Service Award

Dear Marge,

I quite agreed with the members of the Golden Years Club when they honored you with this year's Special Service Award.

You have made many contributions to the club and to this community with your long hours of dedicated work—a beautiful example of unselfish love.

We are all proud of you.

Sincerely,

Five Years

Dear Andy Colfax:

Five years of service with Jacobs Company deserves recognition. The continued success of our company depends on loyal employees who pull together. Your work and loyalty are appreciated.

Your five-year pin will be presented at the general office meeting on February 26 when several others will join you in receiving service awards.

In another five years, I hope to see you receive your ten-year pin.

Sincerely,

Twenty Years

Dear Donald,

Congratulations on your twentieth anniversary with Fibre Containers.

Your steady progress is a result of your many accomplishments, but the one that stands out is your success in getting cooperation from co-workers as well as subordinates.

We would find it difficult, Don, to get along without you. Best wishes for many more rewarding years with us.

Sincerely,

Golf Tournament

Dear Tony,

Congratulations on winning the company golf tournament. A champion manager can also be a champion golfer. Keep up the good work.

Sincerely,

Industry Award

Dear Mr. Miles:

Let me congratulate you on winning the Hartford Award! Your leadership in our industry has long been known to many of us, and I am happy to see you receive the nationwide recognition you have earned by your years of diligent work.

Best regards,

President of Rotary

Dear Mr. Briney:

It was a pleasure to read in last night's *City Ledger* of your election as president of Rotary.

Let me offer my sincere congratulations upon your receiving this honor. I wish you success in your new office.

Sincerely,

Anniversary

Dear Mary and Joe,

Congratulations on your anniversary!

May the past happy memories be a prelude to future memories.

Happy Anniversary,

Honorary Sorority

Dear Joan,

So you made the Honorary Sorority! Congratulations to a hard working (as well as bright) girl. I know your pleasing personality played a large part too.

Best wishes for the continuing scholastic achievements I know you will earn.

Cordially,

President of Association

Dear Mr. Ramsey:

My hearty congratulations to you on your election to the presidency of the Western Management Association. Your election is earned tribute from your colleagues, and is recognition of the outstanding work you have done for the Association and for your profession.

The Association chose the right man in my opinion. Best wishes for success in your new position.

Sincerely,

Opening Store

Dear Andy,

Congratulations on the opening of your own hardware store! I know it has been a dream of yours for many years. With your know-how and willingness to work, there is no reason why you shouldn't have a booming business in a short time.

We are happy to see you make the big step.

Good luck,

City Councilman

Dear Ray,

Congratulations on your election to Concord City Council. I am pleased that we now have a financial expert in our city government. We can look forward to a closer scrutiny of fiscal matters, something we have needed for a long time.

Sincerely,

Loan Paid

Dear Mr. Crown:

Congratulations!

We are pleased to notify you that you have fully paid the enclosed loan.

Now—why not continue making regular payments into one of our savings accounts? You have already discovered a convenient, safe place to save money—and be paid for saving it—and a friendly place to borrow money at a low interest rate.

                                              Sincerely,

Marriage

Dear Andrew,

Congratulations on your marriage.

Let me wish you and your bride your full share of happiness as the years go on.

                                              Sincerely,

Dear Alice,

It is somehow hard to believe you are no longer the pretty little girl down the street, but have already grown up to become a happy bride.

Please congratulate your husband for me, and tell him I think he is most lucky.

You both have my best wishes for a long and happy life together.

                                              Affectionately,

Chapter 13

THANK YOU
AND APPRECIATION

A thank-you letter should be sincere, expressing appreciation without excessive flattery. The tone should be pleasant. Clearly state what the thank-you is for and, if appropriate, offer something in return.

Business people appreciate receiving a thank-you letter because it adds a touch of warmth to the cold world of business. The letter reveals consideration and appreciation. Large manufacturers often receive letters from students asking about products, processes, or procedures. These are usually answered with pamphlets, brochures, and letters from production managers or administrative executives. One corporate executive complained that after sending our large quantities of printed material and innumerable letters, no thank-you letters were received. He lamented that even a post card saying, "Thank you for the materials," would have shown consideration for his company's efforts. The goodwill of your company, and also of yourself, can be enhanced by a letter of thanks.

A thank-you letter should be short. The sincerity of the thank you is emphasized by brevity. Basically, all that need be said is, "Thank you for this," or "Thank you for that." A long thank-you letter may be a sales letter in disguise, or it may be loaded with unnecessary flattery, lowering the reader's opinion of the party sending the letter.

Pleasantness is another requirement of a good thank-you letter. One way to accomplish this is with an informal opening, for instance:

> Enjoyed meeting with you and appreciate the time given to Don and me.
>
> Just a "thank you" for being a customer this past year.

Any harsh thoughts or words should be eliminated because their inclusion will completely destroy the purpose of the letter, which is to show gratitude for help that has been given.

While thanking a person for something he or she has done, it is often possible to return more than just words of thanks. This will emphasize the writer's gratitude. When a person has spent time showing you his or her company's operation or the sights of the city, offer to do the same when that person visits your company or city. When giving thanks for information received, it would be appropriate to relay how the information is being used; for example:

> The sketch fits so well in our den.
> I would never have heard of the exhibit otherwise.
> Your suggestion led to this fabulous job.
> Your recent payment clears your longstanding debt.
> Your work made it possible for us to catch up.
> The information is exactly what I need for my report.
> Your suggestions enabled us to increase our machine speed 20 percent.

When an organization has helped your group in some way, volunteer your group's help as a return favor.

Thanking someone for a favor indicates polite manners—and is good business practice. But thanking in advance is considered, by some authorities in the use of the English language, an objectionable habit. For example, it is common to write:

> Send the completed project to Mr. A. B. Andrews at Headquarters by September 15.
>
> Thank you.

This seems to imply to the reader that the project was of so little importance that a thank-you for an excellent and timely submission will not be worth the effort of writing again. To overcome this possible adverse reaction by the reader, start the letter with, "Will you please" or "I would appreciate your sending . . . " or "Please." An alternative is to open the letter with a paragraph stating appreciation, for example:

> Your sending this project to Headquarters by the 15th of September will be greatly appreciated.
> Your sending this freight bill to Friedman, Inc. is greatly appreciated.
> Sending me the samples will be truly appreciated.
> Your cooperation and hard work on this project is really appreciated by us.

When a letter expressing thankfulness is appropriate, a prompt answer will make the reader aware of your thoughtfulness. Three months later, the reader shouldn't be reminded that he or she had been piqued by not having received a deserved note of thanks.

While writing the letter, assume an attitude of polite sincerity.

How to Do It

1. State what the thank-you is for.
2. Mention the appropriateness of what was received.
3. Be sincere, brief, and pleasant.
4. When appropriate, offer something in return.

Gift

Dear Friends in Albany,

My heartfelt thanks (no pun intended) for the beautiful terrarium you sent while I was in the hospital for heart bypass surgery. It will remind me for years how nice friends can be.

Sincerely,

An alternate last sentence might be:

It will remind me for years of my many friends in Albany.

Dear Mrs. Patterson,

The sketch of a cowboy is a beautiful gift and fits so well in the den. A special gift from a special friend is always appreciated. Thank you for your generous thoughts.

Sincerely,

Dear Mrs. Orland,

Thank you for the wedding gift. I have the black ceramic vase on my mantel. It is always nice to receive an item unique to a certain part of the country. It has a history of its own, and we love it.

Cordially,

Dear John,

You have that rare ability to select just the right gift. The puzzle you sent kept me up half the night—I'll get it yet.

Sincerely,

Pamphlet

Gentlemen:

Thank you for the illustrated pamphlet on personnel forms. We are considering changes in our personnel reporting and will find the samples useful.

Sincerely,

Information

Dear Mr. Arronson:

Thank you for your prompt reply to my inquiry about scheduled tours of Redwood Furniture's Pittsburgh Plant.

Because of our commitment to the Martinez Boy's Club as volunteers, we are unable to schedule a tour as a group.

Sincerely,

Dear Marge,

Thank you for your letter and the announcement of an antique dealers' convention in New England. I would not have learned of the meeting otherwise. It was nice of you to take the time to send it when you knew I would be interested.

I'll see you there.

Cordially,

Materials Received

Dear Mr. Benson:

Thank you for the materials you sent with your letter of September 25. The samples will be helpful.

Sincerely,

Dear Mr. Latter:

Thank you for the brochure *Trees are Forever*. It contains exactly what I need for a speech I am preparing.

Sincerely,

Thank you . . .

For your interest in our Plain English Multicover Policy. I am pleased to enclose an information kit for your review.

Cordially,

Advice

Dear Mr. Manning:

You helped me a great deal with my future plans only six years ago as we sat in your office working to eliminate my frustrating uncertainty.

I took your advice—probably the best thing I ever did. Since then I have advanced several times with this company. The cooperation of the people here is better than I should really expect. I am sure my future is here.

I want to express my sincere gratitude for your consultation and help and to wish you and your family a happy holiday season.

Cordially,

Recommendation

Dear Ellis:

Just a short thank-you for the recommendation you gave me yesterday. Your well-chosen words were a big boost in getting me the transfer I wanted.

I sincerely appreciate your help.

Regards,

Dinner Invitation

Dear Tim,

It was certainly a privilege to be with you and your friends at the excellent Service Club dinner last night. Tom Powers had a message to give and he gave it superbly.

Thanks ever so much for inviting me!

Sincerely,

Recognition

Dear Jan,

Thank you for mentioning my Music Teacher's Conference award. It is a great feeling to receive recognition for work covering a period of years, and I appreciate your mentioning it in your daily column.

Sincerely,

Dear Jan,

Thank you for mentioning my Music Teacher's award in your column. The award means a great deal to teachers and I appreciate your giving it public recognition.

Sincerely,

Going Away Party

Dear Lois,

Frank and I are most appreciative of the dinner party given for us last Saturday. We really enjoyed your efforts, the good drinks, the good food, the friendly chats—and the bridge cards.

Leaving a group of such good neighbors and friends after 15 years fills us with a puzzling mixture of nostalgia and appreciation.

We will try to get back from time to time, but meanwhile, our phone number is 000-000-0000.

Sincerely,

Companionship

Dear Katy,

This gift is only a token of how much your friendly companionship this summer has meant to me.

There will always be love in my thoughts of you.

With affection,

Friendship

Dear Don,

This gift is just a small thank-you for the friendship you showed me this summer.

I will always think of you as a kind friend who took a real interest in both my work and play.

Sincerely,

Dear Sandy,

You have that rare knack of making strangers feel right at home. Sharing your friends with me yesterday certainly made a newcomer feel like a comfortable old-timer. I know I will like this friendly city, and I hope Ron and I will be here for a long time.

Thank you so much for all you have done for me.

Sincerely,

Appreciation

Dear Tommy,

It was thoughtful of you to write me and let me know how much you enjoy working at Exxon. It really doesn't surprise me, because I well remember your enthusiasm as well as your record here at the University—and also your popularity among the students. I was glad to be of help in setting your career course.

Kindest regards and best wishes for your continued success.

Cordially,

Dear Mr. Watson:

Your letter of appreciation for my work on the recent project was warmly received. It was a time of struggle for both of us. If you need any data from me during my short absence, please call and leave a message. I will be able to pick it up in the evenings.

See you in November.

Sincerely,

Dear Dave,

Thank you for your letter of appreciation for my work during the past year. It was generous of you to give me so much credit for the company's operating improvements.

Our struggles and difficulties certainly did add interest to the year's activities. I do enjoy working with and for you, and am sure next year will be economically better for the company.

Sincerely,

Illness

Dear Fred:

Thank you for the letter you wrote to me while I was in the hospital. It really helped to brighten my days.

I am now back to work on a half-day schedule, but will be working full-time next week. The operation went well and the recovery period gave me a chance to relax. I was a little disappointed though that the office got along so well without me.

When you are in Los Angeles again, please stop by and we can share a couple of hours over lunch.

Sincerely,

Dear Nadine,

No one but you would have thought of having a comic card delivered each Sunday during my convalescence. What a terrific morale booster. You are so thoughtful.

With love,

Job Well Done

We would like to thank you, Mark,

and all the other people there at Tomkin's for a job well done this past year, especially during the Christmas rush when we were adjusting our orders so frequently.

Your interest in Samuelson Company and the courtesy and cooperation you have extended is sincerely appreciated.

Best regards,

Dear Andy,

Just a note to let you know that your hard work during the past year has been sincerely appreciated.

I hope that you and Theresa enjoy a happy holiday season and vacation in the West. You both deserve a good rest and I trust the weatherman will cooperate to make your stay in Phoenix truly relaxing.

Cordially,

Dear Jim,

We know you will be pleased to hear that your June sales broke all previous records. It's great to have you on our team.

Sincerely,

Dear Mr. Ludwig:

Your decision to retire as director of Ableson Corporation has been received with deep regret by the directors and officers of the Corporation.

Leaving after nearly half a century is not easy, but during your tenure you played an important part in doubling our market coverage. Your annual market survey trips endeared you to many throughout the corporation.

I look upon your retirement as a real personal loss. Your example and counsel has been most beneficial to my work as officer and director. For that I thank you.

I sincerely hope that your retirement from many years of cares and tensions will be a pleasant experience for you.

Cordially,

Dear Mr. Walton:

I have just read of your retirement from the Alameda Real Estate Board. I would like to express my appreciation for the work you have done, especially in acquainting the public with the variety of ways a real estate agent can be of help to a buyer, seller, or investor in real estate.

Your contributions have been great, and though you will be missed, you deserve an enjoyable retirement.

Sincerely,

Dear Mr. and Mrs. Hancock:

Your daughter, Jo Ann, has worked for us for six months now. I thought that you would like to know that she is doing a remarkable job, and we are extremely pleased with her work attitude.

Jo Ann is a credit to you, her parents. We are proud of her and we know you are too.

Sincerely,

Dear Frank:

It was an exciting year, struggling to overcome our many difficulties. You are given much of the credit for the turnaround toward profitability.

I realize that a thank you is small reward for your diligent work, but next year we expect to make our thank you more tangible. Meanwhile it's great having you on our team. We are running strong and in the right direction.

Sincerely,

Being Our Customer

Dear Mr. Smith:

Just a "thank you" for being a customer this past year.

We want you to know we appreciate the business you have given us, and we hope to continue serving you during the coming year.

With regards from
Hamilton's Heavy Hardware,

Thank you

I want to let you know how much we value your business. The prompt manner in which you maintain your account makes it a pleasure to do business with you.

I hope Ralph's can continue to serve your motoring needs for many years to come.

Sincerely,

Dear Mrs. Wamsley:

Thank you for the confidence you have placed in us.

We will always do everything possible to continue to earn your trust and goodwill.

Cordially,

Charge Account Requested

Dear Mrs. Warner:

Thank you for the opportunity to add you to the growing number of satisfied charge account customers of Long's Department Store.

The privileges of a charge account are many. You have 25 days to enjoy your purchases before paying for them. You are notified of special sales before a general announcement is made; and often, by presenting the mailed announcement, you may purchase sale items a day or two before the sale officially begins. Special delivery and layaway services are open to charge account customers. When you wish to place an order by phone, or want a special favor, please mention your charge card and just ask. We are always pleased to do a little extra for the convenience of Long's customers.

Sincerely,

Dear Mrs. Wilson:

Thank you for requesting a charge account at Ansell's. Your credit has been approved and you may use the enclosed charge card at any time. It will add convenience and enjoyment to your shopping.

You will be pleased with the fine quality merchandise and pleasant service always available at Ansell's.

Sincerely,

Sales Presentation

Dear Mr. Wyley:

The "shoe box size" package you lost and inquired about in your letter of June 7 was found behind a chair in the lobby.

We are happy to return it to you via United Parcel, and wish to thank you again for your informative presentation of your computer line.

Sincerely,

Accounting Help

Dear John:

Thank you for coming to San Jose Wednesday to help us straighten out our accounts with you. We have been short-handed for several months and just couldn't seem to get our payables accounts right. Your help in reconciling the differences got us on top of the work and I believe we can keep our records in agreement with yours from now on.

Again, thank you for your help.

Sincerely,

Payment

Dear Mr. Evers:

Thank you for your payment of $327.80. This clears your delinquent account.

We appreciate your cooperation and look forward to serving you again.

Sincerely,

Dear Mr. Jones:

Thank you for your partial payment of $200. This leaves only $92.40, which will be due in 30 days. By making this payment on time, your account will be open again.

We look forward to having you as an open-account customer again.

Sincerely,

Referral

Dear Mrs. Mayer:

Thank you for referring Peter Seller to me for an eye examination. I certainly appreciate your thoughtfulness and want to assure you that your confidence in me will be justified.

If at any time in the future I may again be of service to you, please feel free to call me.

Once again, thank you for referring Mr. Seller.

Sincerely,

Attending

Dear Mr. Ronald:

Thank you for attending our meeting last Thursday and for sharing your suggestions based on your long years of experience. Being new, our group found your suggestions and recommendations extremely helpful.

We hope we can return the favor by doing something for your group. Please call when we can assist in any way.

Sincerely,

Dear Mr. Alberts:

The Business Elders group wishes to thank you for your inspiring remarks at our dinner last Wednesday. You gave us some good ideas that we will discuss at our next regular meeting, and I believe we can successfully act on some of them.

We will let you know the outcome of your ideas. The dinner committee is already planning to ask you to speak again.

Cordially,

Visiting

Dear Mr. Hanson:

I wish to thank you for giving me the opportunity to visit your plant and to have discussions with you and with your friendly staff.

The visit to your plant was one of the highlights of my visit to your country and I hope to see some of the Fireboard people in Australia at some future date.

Yours sincerely,

Dear Mr. and Mrs. Lyons:

Thank you for visiting Highland Estates.
If I may be of any help, please call me.
My home phone is 000-0000 and my office phone is 000-0000.

Sincerely,

Dear Bill:

Enjoyed meeting with you and appreciate the time given to Don Allen and me on such short notice.

As we discussed, we are going to pursue the problems you are encountering with various materials you purchased from us. We anticipate that when you visit our mill in the near future, our technical people will have some answers.

Thanks again for the time and courtesies shown Don and me.

Sincerely,

Dear Bob:

It was a pleasure meeting with you last Friday and having the opportunity to visit the Centrex production facility. Your operation looked quite good. The volume produced in that one location is surprising.

When you are in Washington this fall, I hope a tour can be set up for you to see a fully integrated paper mill operation.

Thanks again for your time and hospitality.

With regards,

Dear Mr. Greenland:

I really enjoyed my visit with you during my recent trip west. You were more than considerate to rearrange your schedule on such short notice and to spend the afternoon with me.

When you come to Chicago next time be sure to call me and we can have another pleasant visit.

With regards,

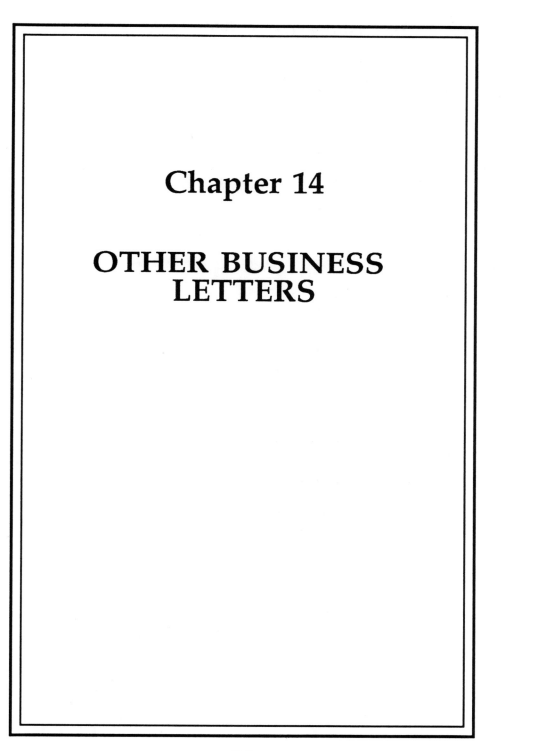

Chapter 14

OTHER BUSINESS LETTERS

Only the imagination of the reader can limit the number of categories for business and personal letters. It is hoped that the variety this books presents and suggests is enough to fulfill your needs. Many letters fit neatly into more than one category; a little thumbing through related areas may turn up just what you need. Perhaps parts of different letters can be combined to provide one better suited to your need.

Regardless of how the letter is classified, remember that it is the reader who must play the starring role. Forget I and me and we: think *you*. Give full consideration to the feelings of the reader. Be pleasant and sincere. Revealing an attitude of sincerity is the art of writing a letter that accomplishes its purpose. Along with attitude, correct technical aspects of word usage will help the reader respond positively to your letter.

GOODWILL

A letter of goodwill is basically a low-pressure sales letter—low-pressure because no particular product or service is being pushed, only a friendly relationship. The letter can also be thought of as a public relations gesture—something that is often neglected with good, steady customers—or as a reaching out for a kindly feeling of approval and support. If we express kindly thoughts towards our customers and friends, we hope to receive consideration (and increased business) in return. The expressions or impressions of goodwill may be combined with a thank you, appreciation, request, apology, regrets, or just pleasant thoughts.

The letter can vary in length from a short statement of appreciation to the several paragraphs appropriate for a year-end holiday season letter. A combination of the occasion and the mood of the letter writer will determine the length—but don't overburden the reader.

Goodwill is not a one-time thing, but a continuing relationship. With this in mind, do not make the letter a conclusive statement, but indicate a desire to continue the friendship. For example, the model letter headed "Sales Agreement Ended" expresses regrets that a customer has ended a sales agreement, but the writer is not ready to admit that this is a lasting decision. He ends the letter with the upbeat, "I know our paths will continue to cross in the future."

How to Do It

1. Begin with a complimentary or pleasant statement.
2. Make a comment that relates to or expands upon the first statement.
3. Express anticipation of continued good relations or of a future meeting.

Seasons Greetings

Dear Mr. Anderson:

Do you recall some of your childhood fantasies? A high tree stump would be your throne; you were king or queen of all you surveyed, and everyone obeyed your wishes no matter how whimsical. The rays of a sunset would glisten from the walls of your make believe castle. The snow-covered ground was your peaceful paradise, completely void of screaming kids and demanding parents.

These imagined experiences are a part of growing up and the rewards of their success seem real.

The display of lights, the warmth of fireplaces, the trimming of the tree, the preparation for Santa's descent down the chimney, or the glow of Hanukkah candles all become a part of our children's fantasies. But the gathering of families to celebrate love and being together is no fantasy.

My wish for you this year is that as your children's imagination—and yours—dances freely this holiday season, you will appreciate the reality of your family's love.

Cordially,

Good Work

Dear Frank:

It was an exciting year, struggling to overcome our many difficulties. You are given much of the credit for the turnaround toward profitability.

I realize that a thank-you is a small reward for your diligent work, but next year we expect to make our thank-you more tangible. Meanwhile, it's great having you on our team. We are running strong and in the right direction.

Sincerely,

Free Bulletin

Dear Miss Conrad:

Here's a copy of our latest news bulletin. I think this one will keep you completely informed about our industry. Other publications lack many of the special features that we include.

If you'd like to receive it monthly, just drop me a note and I'll put your name on our mailing list—no charge to you.

Sincerely,

Golf Invitation

Dear Bart,

We enjoyed having you with us Saturday.

Since I know you will forgive the photography, I am enclosing some pictures of you and Ray at the Yacht Club.

If you happen to be in the Bay Area and have time for a game of golf, please let me know and maybe we can get together at the Westlake Course.

Sincerely,

To a Salesperson's Spouse

Dear Ann,

Rick is a great guy. I'm sure you have known that for a long time, and now we know it too. His sales volume is rocketing. We planned on some increase when he took over the Salinas area, but his sales have far exceeded our expectation.

I just want you to know that we appreciated the encouragement you have given Rick. Your interest in his work has meant a great deal to us. Thanks again.

Sincerely,

Dear Mrs. Wentling:

Welcome to the Sun Ray Distributors family.

As the wife of one of our new salespersons, you become a part of our growing family. We are pleased to welcome you.

We are a new company, but the selling and installation of solar heating systems is expanding rapidly, making the potential for growth almost unlimited. We know Ted Wentling will play a large part in our growth. He was carefully selected as one who will dig in now to get us going and continue his enthusiasm as he participates in our growth.

We have a quality product to sell; our engineering consultants made sure of that, and our growing list of satisfied customers points to the truth of their findings.

As will all salespersons in a new position, Ted Wentling will find a few tough spots and discouragements at first, but we have found that wives are a real source of understanding, encouragement, and cheer during the initial period of adjustment to a new job.

Ted will also find you a help in entertaining an occasional customer and in recognizing that selling is not a straight 8-to-5 job. Some late hours will be required as well as a small amount of traveling.

We are sure that these few inconveniences will be worked into your time schedule and you will derive pride and satisfaction from contributing to Ted's success with Sun Ray.

Sincerely,

Dear Mr. Quintana,

We are pleased to have your wife join our sales staff. We select only people who have demonstrated a willingness to learn and work hard. I am sure you are proud that Diana qualified for the position, and we are enthusiastic about her potential.

You are aware, no doubt, that selling is not a nine-to-five profession. Our sales personnel are asked to work occasional nights, to attend evening seminars, and sales staff meetings. Some traveling will also be involved. We do our best to keep late and away-from-home hours at a minimum, but Diana will not be home every evening to share dinner with you.

We ask that you lend your support to her efforts to become one of our top sales people, as I know she will. Your cooperation is sincerely appreciated—by us and especially by your wife.

Our best regards,

Sales Agreement Ended

Dear Ben:

We are sorry to learn of your desire to terminate our sales agreement, which has been in effect for nine years. We can understand your position and appreciate the reasons.

Although nothing was said in your letter, I assume you wish this agreement to terminate as of October 22, 19__ without the ninety day cancellation notice mentioned in the contract.

It has been a pleasure to work with you, Ben, and although our formal arrangement is terminated, I know our paths will continue to cross in the future.

Sincerely,

To Parents of Young Employee

Dear Mr. and Mrs. MacMahon:

Your daughter, Lynn, has worked for us six months now. I thought you would like to know that she is doing a remarkable job, and we are extremely pleased with her work attitude.

Lynn is a credit to you, her parents. We are proud of her and we know you are too.

Sincerely,

Enjoyed Meeting You

A candidate for an elective office made a personal visit. The candidate follows up with a goodwill note.

Dear John:

I enjoyed meeting you this past weekend.

Sincerely,

Real Estate Service

Dear Mr. Robinson:

Just a note to say thank you for thinking of me for real estate service.

I look forward to working with you in the future if your move to Denver works out.

I'll be seeing you Saturday.

Sincerely,

Fishing Trip Invitation

Dear Rick:

Glad to hear you are all fine and that the trip was uneventful. There is nothing worse than car trouble when you are out in the middle of nowhere.

Yes, I know Elvis Waters. He is in charge of our printing sales and annually fishes in Canada for salmon. Maybe the next time I get up there we can both do some fishing.

Please give my best to Cheryl and let us hear from you if you plan another trip to Detroit.

Regards,

Gift Received

Dear Danny:

Just received your "volume of songs" and want to thank you for the many hours of pleasure and elbow bending they will provide for me. Cheers.

Hope you are beginning to make plans for a trip to the East Coast after the first of the year. We should again visit our Southern and possibly our Northern mills.

Hope all the family is well, and give my regards to Alice.

Kindest personal regards,

Requested Information

Dear Dan:

It was a pleasure meeting you on my recent visit to San Diego. My wife and I always enjoy ourselves on a return visit. The changes in the city leave us in awe as we remember the "old home town" of the 1940s.

I will look forward to receiving your mailings on scuba diving trips to Mexico. It is a certainty that some members of our household will be participating in this activity.

My family anticipates spending two weeks in San Diego during Easter. If you are about, I will be happy to share a pitcher of Margaritas.

Best Regards,

Sending Information

Dear Walt:

Please forgive me for not answering your letter sooner, but both my travel and my secretary's being on vacation have postponed most of my correspondence.

I am glad to hear that things are going well with you and that you are busy with new packaging developments. You may find the attached reprint of interest, although it is more appropriate for more expensive equipment than you use in your particular manufacturing operation. Should I come across anything else, I will send it along to you.

Please give my best to Jill and everyone in Denver.

Sincerely,

Making Contribution

Dear Mr. Haggard:

I have provided medical treatment for many of the handicapped boys since my arrival in City two years ago. I have found them to be very courteous and responsible. It has been a pleasure serving them.

Enclosed is a contribution. I wish you and all of them a Merry Christmas!

Sincerely,

INTRODUCTIONS

The purpose of an introductory letter is solely to introduce one person to another. It is not a reference letter, which can be used to sell the qualifications of one person to another, so get right to the point with a letter that is brief.

The tone of the letter will depend on the relationship between the writer and the reader, and the anticipated relationship between the person being introduced and the reader. This will usually be a friendly and informal relationship, requiring a letter with a touch of warmth.

Provide at least the first and last names of the person being introduced, and, when possible, background, or at least some interest common to both parties. An explanation that is reasonable to the reader should be given for the introduction. This is often really asking for a favor; therefore give full consideration to the feelings and probable reaction of the reader.

In commenting about the person being introduced, make the reader *want* to meet him or her. Without overdoing a good thing, make the person sound interesting.

How to Do It

1. Provide the full name of the person being introduced.
2. Give a reasonable explanation for what is really a request for a favor.
3. Make the reader *want* to meet the other person.

New Sales Representative

Dear Jack:

Our new sales representative, Andy Watson, will be calling on you soon.

Andy has a wealth of background in bag-making machinery, including manufacturing, assembling, and repairing, as well as supervising machine operators and scheduling orders—and even sales. Not many people have such thoroughgoing experience with a machine they are selling and servicing.

You will find Andy as pleasant and helpful as he is knowledgeable. We are proud to have him represent us, and I know you will soon think as highly of him as we do.

Sincerely,

Friend for Sales Position

Dear Mr. Gibson:

Mr. Jack Stanton is a long-time acquaintance of mine. He has been a successful salesman for many years in the industrial equipment field. I believe he would fit well into your organization and cover the needs you described to me last month.

Please give him your consideration. You will find him worth it.

With regards,

A Friend

Dear Mr. Blackman,

Marvin Melville is a good friend of ours. He will be in Minneapolis about the middle of next month for a few days, and I would like him to meet you. You both have a strong interest in juvenile runaways. Marv is doing research in San Francisco now, and I told him about the study you did on juveniles in Chicago last year. I'm sure you both would have a lot to talk over. You'll find Marv extremely pleasant.

May I give him your phone number? Please write and let me know.

Best regards,

Dear Charlie,

My good friend Jim Hoskins will be in Atlanta the week of February 10. Jim is director of marketing for a large folding carton manufacturer. I told him you are doing research for a textbook on the use of graphics designs in advertising. Jim was more than a little interested in your project and how it might apply to the sales of folding cartons, which his company makes and prints.

If you have time, give him a call at 000-0000, room 000. I told Jim you might be tied up that week, so he will understand if he doesn't hear from you.

I know you would enjoy each other's company.

Regards,

Academic Assistance

Gentlemen:

This will introduce Mr. Joe Phillips, who is studying for his master's degree at the University of Washington. We believe you can help him in the area of foreign trade. Your help would be greatly appreciated by him and by us.

Sincerely,

New Employee

Dear Mr. Spanol:

It's our great pleasure to introduce to you Gary Nelson, our new Senior Vice President, who came to us in January, and is in charge of Sales, Acquisitions, and Finance. Mr. Nelson comes to us with a wealth of experience in the acquisition and operation of syndication properties. We are delighted with Gary's immediate and expert command of our remarkably complex organization.

Sincerely,

INVITATIONS

A letter of invitation is one of goodwill. It is a friendly letter (even if solely for a business purpose) because you wish to retain the reader's good thoughts about you. It is also a personal letter because you are writing to one person who will feel pleased to be singled out. To attain this good feeling, the letter must be warm and express an honest wish for acceptance, as in these sentences:

We will be waiting to hear from you.
Please let us hear from you soon.
We are anxious to get together with you again.
Please confirm by May 4 that you can attend.
It will be so good to see you again.

The degree of formality to use in the writing depends on the relationship between the writer and the reader. It can vary from "old buddy" jocularity to third person formality, from "Hi Skip, I hear you'll be back in town next week. How about pouring a few with Don and me at Morland's," to "The Onward Civic Club cordially invites you to attend . . . "

As well as being specific about when and where you will meet the recipient of the invitation, it may be appropriate to mention why you have invited the reader. This is primarily true in business invitations: you wish to discuss a specific aspect of your business relationship, or you have a particular reason for inviting this person to speak or to join an organization.

How to Do It

1. Mention the purpose of the invitation.
2. State when and where and, if appropriate, why.
3. Request confirmation or express anticipated acceptance.

Luncheon for Old Friend

Dear John:

Tom Hardy, "dear old Tom," will be in town next week. I am getting several of his friends together for a luncheon at the Aztec Hotel Fireside Room on Friday, November 23 at noon.

I sure hope you can join the old gang; there will be an empty spot without you. I look forward to seeing you there.

Cordially,

To Do Advertising

Dear Mr. Callby:

We have a new line of coated stainless steel cookware ready to market. Would you be interested in discussing the product and the possibility of advertising it for us?

Please phone me before Friday to arrange a date for further discussion. I will be waiting for your call.

Sincerely,

Use Company Hotel Room

Dear Mr. May:

When you come to Minneapolis for your sales meeting next month, perhaps you would enjoy staying at our company hotel room. I can reserve it for you for March 17, 18 and 19.

I think you would enjoy the location (as well as the room) because it is only three blocks from your meeting place.

It will be a pleasure to reserve the room for you. I must have your decision by the 15th of this month.

Please let me hear from you.

Most sincerely,

Ball Game

Dear Barbara and Bob,

Jan and I would like to have you attend the Cal-Stanford Big Game with us. (I just happen to have two spare tickets.) It would be a great reunion for us after your many years in the South.

You could meet us at our house the morning of __, 19__ for a snack before leaving for the game.

We are looking forward to hearing from you.

Your old buddy,

Dinner Guest

Dear Jim,

The East Bay Accounting Society is having an exciting guest at its dinner meeting next Thursday. The guest is Ben Stoddard, who has won fame as a tax-avoidance authority—not tax *evasion*, he will point out.

I thought you would be interested in attending as my guest. The meeting is at 7:00 p.m., Thursday, the 24th, and will be over by 10:30 p.m.

Please let me hear from you. I can pick you up on my way there, and I know you will enjoy the evening.

Best Regards,

Accepting Invitations

A letter accepting an invitation should emphasize warm gratitude and anticipated enjoyment. It was really nice of the person to invite *you*, and in return you should say you are grateful by writing:

I shall be happy to accept . . .
It was thoughtful of you to invite me to . . .
Thank you so much for thinking of me.
Thank you for your invitation to . . .

An invitation is written only to those who are expected to enjoy the occasion, and it is appropriate for the acceptor to concur with the writer's statement or impression that a good time will be had by all. For example:

> We look forward to seeing you again.
> We always enjoy the Michigan State games.
> It will be a pleasure to meet your club members.
> You can count on my being there.

The degree of formality or informality in the acceptance letter would normally follow closely the tone of the invitation.

How to Do It

1. Express thanks for the invitation.
2. State acceptance.
3. Confirm time and place.
4. Express pleasant anticipation.

To Speak

Dear Mr. Lawson:

Thank you for the invitation to speak at your fund-raising committee meeting. You suggested reviewing last year's successful campaign. I think that is a great idea. I plan to emphasize the positive aspects and suggest how you can build upon the successful techniques to strengthen this coming year's campaign.

I will be at your meeting place a little before 7:00 p.m. on Friday, May 17.

I am happy to do what I can to help your campaign.

Sincerely,

Football Celebration

Dear Dave,

Thank you for the invitation to celebrate the A's victory at your home.

Doris and I will be there about 4:00 p.m., Saturday, the 24th. We always enjoy visiting with you, and it seems like a long time since our last get-together.

See you Saturday,

Retirement Dinner

Dear Sharon,

Thank you for inviting Cheryl and me to attend a retirement dinner at the Aztec Restaurant on May 4 at 7:30 p.m.
We will be there.
I think it is nice of you to add something special to our standard retirement activities.

Cordially,

Dinner Invitation

Dear Mr. Sheridan:

In reply to your mailgram invitation of May 24, 19__, I would be pleased to meet with you and Mr. Hanson on Wednesday, June 6th at 7:00 p.m. at the Marboro Hotel Dining Room.

Sincerely,

Join a Group

Dear Alice,

Thank you for inviting me to join the Women's Hospital Auxiliary. I do have many years of enjoyable experience in this line of work and am sure I can be of much help to your organization as well as to the patients we serve.
I will be able to attend your meeting on August 4 at 4:00 p.m.

Sincerely,

Declining Invitations

See Chapter Two, Declining Requests.

ACCEPTING A POSITION

When accepting an office or position with a social organization, the acceptance letter will be probably the only written record of either the offer or acceptance.

The first sentence should include an acknowledgement of the acceptance and an expression of appreciation; having accepted the position, you should have no trouble feeling appreciative. Here are some examples:

> I am happy to accept your offer to join Lending Hands charity.
> I am pleased to accept the position of program manager.
> Your acceptance of my bid for the position of committee chairman is greatly appreciated.

An expression of thanks for being considered can enhance the employer's confidence in you and in his or her judgment in selecting you.

> Your confidence in selecting me will be well founded.
> I appreciate your selecting me from the large number who applied.
> I am happy that you found a way to utilize my varied experience.

In some acceptances of a position, you may be able to include what you hope to accomplish. This lets the group know you are looking ahead, but be general and cautious; many unknowns await the new volunteer. You may, however, be able to include statements similar to these:

> Your decision to grant me full control will enable me to give first priority to improving the annual fund raiser.
> I have some procedures in mind for improving control of the accounting data.
> There are effective promotion programs that can be implemented with a minimum of change in your current procedures.
> I am aware that long hours will be required to accomplish your immediate goals.
> Although this is a part-time activity, I will involve myself fully.

How to Do It

1. State with enthusiasm what is being accepted.
2. Express thanks for being considered.
3. Indicate what you hope to accomplish.

Committee Chairperson

Dear Mrs. Brown:

Your eagerly awaited letter stating that I have been selected for the position of chairperson of the Fund Raising Committee arrived today. Your confidence in me is appreciated and I heartily accept your offer.

As soon as it is appropriate, I would appreciate discussing the function and duties of the position with the outgoing chairman, Jim Smyth.

Please let me know when I can start.

Sincerely,

Lions Club

Dear Mr. Samuelson:

Thanks for passing on the word that I've been selected as the next president of the Lions. With so many good men in the running, I hardly expected to make it to the top five, let alone the presidency itself.

A training period will be necessary, however, to familiarize myself not only with the official duties but also with the ceremonial aspects of the position.

My efforts are aimed toward making this the most successful one in a long while by promoting unity as well as service among members.

Sincerely,

COVER LETTER

The purpose of a cover letter is to help the recipient save time and effort. Rather than having to read the first part of a written document or a group of papers, then having to decide what they are and what they are for, the reader can read a cover letter and know immediately what is enclosed.

A cover letter should be brief. For example:

Four copies of the May 1 revision of the 19__ Budget are enclosed.

That statement tells what is enclosed and how many. In this case the reader was expecting the budget revisions, but some cover letters must include a little more information. If several different items are enclosed, a listing is helpful. It may be appropriate to mention who requested the enclosures or who instructed the sender to mail them. If the receiver is not expecting the item, an explanation of its purpose may be required.

A job résumé cover letter should also be brief, but long enough to mention what job you are applying for and one or two of your strongest selling points.

People given the task of reading résumés usually do this infrequently; it is an added-on task. They are still busy with their regular work. The cover letter, therefore, should be brief, to the point, include an applicable selling point, and, of absolute importance, make the reader anxious to turn to the résumé itself.

How to Do It

1. State what is enclosed or attached; if in answer to a request, name the person who made the request.
2. If applicable, mention the quantity enclosed or make a brief listing.
3. The purpose of the enclosure may be mentioned.

Expenditures Request

Dear Mr. Wade:

Attached for your consideration is our Capital Expenditure Request No. 400-32, covering installation of cooling units ahead of the roof ventilators. At present, the ventilating air picks up a large amount of heat from the tar-covered roof.

Regards,

Lists

Dear Mr. Holmes:

Enclosed are three (3) copies of lists showing miscellaneous items in Warehouse Inventories.

These lists have been revised to October 31, 19__.

Sincerely,

Dear Mr. Erwin:

Enclosed is our Division's list of items normally expensed that could be carried as inventory, as requested in J. P. Connor's letter of February 28, 19__.

Regards,

Agreement for Signature

Dear Mr. and Mrs. Custom:

Enclosed is the Modification Agreement as proposed in our letter of April 30, 19__.

If you agree to the change, please sign the agreement, have your signatures notarized, and return the document to this office.

Sincerely,

Warehouse Report

Dear Ms. Anwan:

Enclosed is Ashton Warehouse Co. Commodity Report covering the inventory for Ren Bearing Co.

Will you please reconcile this report to your records.

Sincerely yours,

Certificate of Incorporation

Gentlemen:

Enclosed for filing is the certificate of incorporation of H.H.H. Associates, Inc., together with our check for $60 to cover the filing fee, ($50) and two certified copies of the charter ($10).

Sincerely,

Statement Requested

Dear Ken:

Attached is the signed Compliance Statement requested in your letter of December 14.

Sincerely,

Commodity Codes

Dear Mr. Sanders:

The attached copy of the Master Commodity Code carries an effective date of January 1, 19__. Will you please cross-index your working files with these codes so that your purchase invoices will be properly classified.

Sincerely,

Savings Statement

Dear Miss Donner:

Enclosed are sealed envelopes containing individual Savings Account statements as of December 31, 19__ for:

C. O. Sanders   A. T. Younts
B. B. Wankel

Please mail the statements to these individuals.

Sincerely,

Insurance Renewal

Dear Mr. Matson:

Your insurance renewal is enclosed, continuing this important protection for you over the coming months. This renewal protects you against lapse of coverage and is in force from the expiration date of your present policy. After looking over the coverage, should you have any question or if any corrections are necessary, please call or write our office promptly.

Our sincerest appreciation for your continuance of this business. Do not hesitate to contact our office if there is any way we can be of further service.

Once again, thank you,

Price Increase

Dear Ms. Waterford:

The Abel Company has announced a price increase of approximately 6 percent effective July 1, 19__. Attached is their National Account Price List No. 17.

Two account changes have been made in this latest price list:

1. Chemical Coatings have been added.
2. All products are now listed alphabetically by name, making them easier to find in the list.

Sincerely,

Valuable Document

Dear Mr. and Mrs. Frame:

We are pleased to enclose your Policy of Title Insurance. This important document should be placed for safe keeping with your other valuable papers.

Sincerely,

FOLLOW-UP

A follow-up letter can be a reminder, a progress report, a request for an explanation, or even a sales letter. Examples of each of these are in this section.

Start right off with a statement of the event or situation you are writing about. State the topic in the first sentence. This is followed by facts, figures, or a description of what has occurred between now and your prior contact with the reader. End with a statement of what action you will take or what specifically you are now requesting.

If the time interval between contacts is short, the facts and descriptions in the second step may be omitted, assuming there is no doubt in the reader's mind about what has occurred, as in this introductory sentence:

Is my face red! I just read your letter of January 17. How we could make a mistake like that I don't know, but we did, and here's what we are going to do about it.

How to Do It

1. State the situation or event that is being followed up.
2. Describe what has been learned or what has happened since prior contact with the reader.

3. Stipulate what action you will take or what you are requesting.

Correct an Error

Dear Ed:

As a follow up, I am attaching copies of two letters dated April 19 and May 27, 19__ to which we had no reply.

The letters relate to incorrect shipments to our Charleston and Richmond offices.

We would appreciate your looking into this and letting us know what you find.

If you require copies of the backup material sent with the letters, or any other information, please let me know.

Sincerely,

Additional Information Requested

Dear Mr. Naughton:

Stanley Company's quote on the cost of relocating two presses appears to be more general than specific. Working with our local engineers, you will have to take the information supplied by Stanley, get what information you can from sources within our company, and come up with some hard dollar figures on the cost of this project.

I think it's important that we give this our immediate attention.

Sincerely,

Additional Information Provided

Dear Mr. Dearborn:

Following up on the problem of building a stacker behind the Wallington machine, which I discussed in my letter of January 15, we have reviewed the situation and have a plan. The problem now is getting maintenance time to get the job done.

We will move this job up on our priority list and see if we can't come up with the solution within the next month.

Sincerely,

Inactive Charge Account

Dear Mrs. Walters:

Have we disappointed you?

We hope not, but we are disappointed . . . that you have not been using your open credit account recently. When an account is active, we know you are pleased with our merchandise, our service, and the convenience of charging your purchases.

If there is something in particular we can do to make your shopping more convenient, please let us know on the postage-paid card enclosed.

Our goal is to have happy customers.

Sincerely,

Power Lawn Mower Purchase

Dear Mr. Morton:

Your Huston Power Lawn Mower dealer, J & J Warner Bros. of St. Louis, has written us of your recent purchase of a Huston mower. We at Huston headquarters, as well as J & J Warner, appreciate your decision to buy a Huston. We are sure you will become a satisfied owner.

We are proud of our dealers: they are responsible business people, they operate sound businesses, and they participate in community activities. They help make your city a better place in which to live and grow.

Your Huston dealer is trained and qualified to assist you with any maintenance problems or operating questions. J & J Warner stands ready to help you.

We are enclosing three Western prints for your enjoyment. Every three months for a year we will send you a small gift to show our appreciation and continued interest in you, our customer.

Sincerely,

QUERY LETTERS SEEKING PUBLICATION

A query letter is designed to convince an editor that your article or book is worthy of serious consideration. It is primarily a sales letter that, for non-fiction writers, helps sell your composition before it is written. The piece can then be written to meet the requirements of that publication.

The query letter is the editor's first impression of *you* as well as of your writing ability. Do it carefully. Concentrate on the following when writing a query letter.

— Study the publication for which you are writing.
— Do enough research to convince the editor you know what you are writing about.
— Address the letter to a person, not a title.
— Arouse the editor's interest in the first sentence
— Keep the length of the query to one page.
— Mention the title in the query letter.
— Include samples of your work. If you have none, make no mention of them.
— Proofread: errors in your query letter will imply errors in your manuscript.
— Include a self-addressed, stamped envelope.
— Ask yourself, "Would I be favorably impressed if I received this letter?"

How to Do It

1. State what the article or story is about.
2. Describe who the intended audience will be.
3. Present your qualifications for writing this particular piece.

Book

Dear Mr. Wilson:

Improve Your Business Letters is designed as a text book for the college level business student or the serious business person interested in improving communications. It is not intended to be a complete book on Business English but rather a supplemental text specifically to teach effective written communication.

There is a difference between *Improve Your Business Letters* and other business letter books. This book not only provides examples of effective and ineffective letters but in addition:

— analyzes the examples.
— lists reasons for the letters being winners or losers.

— lists techniques for improving the letters.

— illustrates the improvement by rewriting the letters.

The following parts of my book are enclosed:

Preface
Contents
Chapter I, The Chaos of Words
Chapter II, Brevity
Chapter III, Straight Arrow Information
I will be pleased to submit a detailed outline.

Sincerely,

Magazine Article

Dear Ms. Duston:

How do you handle the rapid turnover of low-wage employ-ees? Often after the three-day training period and a couple of days on the job, your new employees quit and your staff has to work overtime to fill in for them and train replacements. How can you arrest this debilitating cycle?

Sandra Olinger, head of a direct response phone agency named Call Central, answered that dilemma with a double punch. By combining efforts with the Oklahoma state correc-tions administration, she arranged for female inmates on good behavior to work as Call Central operators in an innovative program that was recently awarded the "Best New Program for Business" honors by the Rockefeller Business Institute.

It's a winning situation, benefitting inmates, companies, and taxpayers. The inmates learn marketable skills, the companies stabilize entry-level jobs, and the taxpayers save because par-ticipating inmates pay the institution one-third of their wages for room and board. This solution could mean the difference between fortune and failure for businesses caught in today's vicious wage-employment conflict.

Would *Business Solutions* readers like to know more about how Olinger and her team are bringing former Supreme Court Justice Burger's dream of "factories without fences" alive in "Cons are Entry-Level Pros?" The story would run 1,500 to 2,000 words. A sidebar about the Call Central management team, which turned a one-horse service into a full-steam contender in their field, could run 750 to 800 words. Interviews would include participants; Fred Boscoe, CEO of the state agency monitoring the program; and Justice Burger. Photos are available.

My more than 150 published credits include contributions to *Saturday Review*, *The Wall Street Journal*, and *Tulsa Living*. I also have a business degree, and am ready to begin working on the article.

Looking forward to hearing from you,

(With thanks to Mary Westheimer, author and former Executive Director of the Arizona Authors' Association, with permission.)

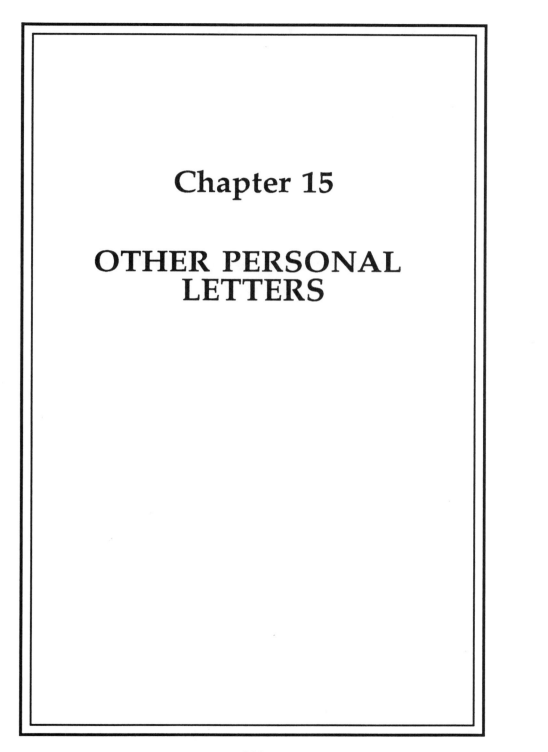

Chapter 15

OTHER PERSONAL
LETTERS

Because they contain elements of both, some letters are hard to classify as personal or business. A business letter should have a touch of personal friendliness. Even a letter containing only straightforward facts can be presented in a way that is more friendly and warm than cool. See Chapter 6, Information—Providing and Requesting, for suggestions. Going further, even a business letter of criticism or reprimand must show personal consideration for the reader or the reader will become disturbed, with the result that the letter does not accomplish its purpose. Should the person to whom you are writing a business letter be a personal friend, both your personal and business relationships can be enhanced with a sentence or two referring to some mutual, personal interest such as, "Give my regards to Alice," "How do you like your new city by now?" or "I'll call you next week about the Bowling Club dance."

On the other hand, a personal letter has some aspects of a business letter. When you wish to give information to a personal acquaintance, the same techniques of organizing and presenting facts will be used as in business letters. Again, the introductory remarks in Chapter 6 will help. If you are writing a get-well note to a co-worker, it may be a personal expression, but the fact that you work together keeps your business relationship from being completely excluded.

Whether you believe you are writing a business or personal letter, keep the reader uppermost in your mind. Write about what will interest the reader, what you want the reader to know and believe, what will appeal to the reader, and foremost, what will get the reader to react the way you want him to. A letter, even a friendly note, is written to accomplish a purpose, and the key to this accomplishment is to think the way the reader does. Put yourself in his or her place and ask, "How would I react to this letter if I were the reader?"

WELCOME

"Glad to have you here! You will find us friendly." This is the congenial mood that a letter of welcome should reveal to the reader. It is a gesture of courtesy and consideration.

Since a welcome letter is also a second cousin to a sales letter, you can mention something nice about your organization, place of work, or group. Let the reader know that you are proud to belong, hoping that he or she will be too.

Include some suggestion as to how the person can fit into your group, or how he or she can learn what is available, or what you will do to help orient the reader.

End the letter with a note of encouragement or a suggestion of how the reader can take the initial step.

How to Do It

1. Express pleasure at making the welcome.
2. Make complimentary remarks about your organization or place.
3. Draw a relationship between the person and the organization.
4. End with an encouraging comment.

To New Resident

Dear Mr. and Mrs. Webster:

Welcome to Seattle, the heart of the Evergreen State!

Coming from the East, you will especially enjoy our temperate climate, but you will not be leaving behind the thrill of the changing seasons. Most of all, you will enjoy the friendly, down-to-earth people here.

To help you get acquainted, please phone the New Residents Club at 000-0000. We will be happy to answer any questions you have, and we will suggest that someone call on you for a more personal discussion of how you can find your niche in this wonderful city.

Sincerely,

Dear Mr. and Mrs. Conrad:

Welcome to Sacramento!

We understand that you and your family plan to reside here, and we know you will find Sacramento a pleasant and friendly place in which to live and work.

If there is anything we can do to help you, come in and let us know. Our business requires us to keep completely informed about local conditions, and we may be able to help you in a number of ways, such as providing a street map, list of civic clubs, list of social clubs, bus routes and schedules, and answering questions about Sacramento.

If you can use our services, we will welcome the opportunity to include you among our clients.

Sincerely,

To New Member

Dear Ms. Wallace,

As president of the East Side Bridge Club, I want to extend a welcome to you.

I am sure you will be a great help to us in our annual, friendly competition with the West Side Bridge Club.

I also want to explain that our Club is involved in social activities as well as in playing bridge. We have parties, see stage plays, go on picnics, and have other activities that get families, and their friends, joining in a pleasant fellowship.

Welcome to our group, and I am sure you will enjoy the friendship.

Sincerely,

GOOD WISHES

A letter of good wishes is appropriate for a business friend who is also a personal friend, one to whom you can express your feelings in a friendly and natural way. It is a letter of sincerity combined with informality.

One special occasion for a letter of good wishes is the year-end holiday season. You can use this annual time of goodwill and good feeling to thank a customer for being *your* customer, to wish him or her well in the coming year, and to express pleasant thoughts to acquaintances and cheerful thoughts to friends.

Another occasion for sending good wishes is the convalescence of someone who has been ill or in an accident. A cheerful thought is great therapy, and all it takes is a short letter.

Whatever the occasion—even if there is no occasion—being remembered is always appreciated.

How to Do It

1. Mention the occasion for the good wishes.
2. Describe briefly some common topic or feeling or idea that is appropriate for the occasion.

Season's Greetings

Dear Mr. Allen:

As the magic of the holiday season approaches, our thoughts turn to those who have made our progress possible. We wish to express our appreciation for your goodwill—the very foundation of business success. In the spirit of friendship, we send you our hope for a continuing business relationship and best wishes for a pleasant holiday season.

Sincerely,

Dear Mr. Evans:

At this time of the year, many of us like to reminisce, and that led me back to that especially pleasant visit when you were here in September.

In the future, I hope we can have more of these interesting and stimulating meetings.

Have a relaxing holiday season—you have earned it—and we'll plan another get-together early next year.

Cordially,

Dear Mr. Elmers:

As the end of the year approaches, we'd like to take a moment or two from the usual rush of business to thank you for the fine relationship we have enjoyed this year and extend our best wishes for a happy holiday season and a good year ahead.

Sincerely,

Dear Mr. Cunard:

With the holiday season close at hand, let me say that all during the year I think of you more as a personal friend than as a business acquaintance. Your friendship is valued, and I hope we can continue it during the many years ahead.

Sincerely,

Convalescing

Dear Ethel,

How good it is to send a note to your home for a change. You must feel by now that you own the South Wing of the hospital.

I'm glad to hear that you are better and will be back to work soon.

Sincerely,

Dear Robert,

Being out of action can't be much fun these sunny autumn days, but for sure it's only temporary.

Remember our coach saying that being on the bench gave you a chance to see the whole field? Hang in there and make the most of it.

I'll keep in touch and come to see you soon.

Regards,

Dear Tim,

Now that your operation is over it is great to have you on the convalescent list.

A forced pause in a busy person's life can sometimes be a blessing. I am hoping this pause will turn into a blessing for you.

I know you like historical fiction, so I am sending you one of the latest books.

Happy hours of reading, resting, and pausing.

Your pal,

Dear Jean,

It's been a long, hard pull, but you made it! Your doctor tells me you're now on the way to recovery. All your friends are cheering for you. Believe me, we are full of admiration for your spirited determination to get well.

Sincerely,

ENCOURAGEMENT

Baseball players are not alone with their batting slumps. The rest of us have "batting slumps" too. That is when we need encouragement to try harder, to take a deep breath and hold on, to blink our eyes and take a new look. When you see a person feeling low or in a state of depression, a letter of encouragement may be just the needed stimulant.

Whatever (or whoever) the cause, admit that an adverse condition exists. Trying to offer help while avoiding mention of the problem that necessitates the help requires the type of thinking best left to politicians. If, however, a problem does not exist, and you wish to make your letter more of a compliment than an encouragement, please refer to the section on Compliments in this chapter.

Admit that a problem exists, and mention what it is so you and your reader are thinking together, but don't dwell on the problem.

If you are offering encouragement, you must be convinced that the adverse condition can be overcome. With this conviction in your mind, it will almost automatically show in the words and phrases you use.

The really helpful part of an encouragement letter is your suggestion of *how* an improvement can be made. Strong, forceful language or ideas are likely to create resistance of even discouragement. A more successful way is to make a clear and simple statement. For example:

> Encourage your staff to be more aggressive.
>
> Please reconsider, then I would appreciate discussing your decision.
>
> Consult your advisor about reorganizing your format.
>
> We will rework the equipment to provide you with better working conditions.
>
> You love challenges, and have met them before.
>
> Abe Lincoln found himself a defeated candidate for eight offices before being elected President.
>
> When you feel your rope is nearly played out, tie a big knot at the end; it will help you hold on.

How to Do It

1. Admit that an adverse condition exists.
2. Name the condition or problem.

3. Indicate your conviction that the condition can be overcome.
4. Suggest how to overcome the condition.

Sales Contest

Dear Ed,

You were second in our sales contest last year, and you had Sam working so hard to stay ahead that he was glad retirement came before this year's contest. I'm rooting for you to win this year.

Right now, you are neck and neck with Don. To keep ahead, it may take just a little more push on your part. I am sure you can make the special effort to become number one this year.

Sincerely,

Low Productivity

Dear Mr. Prescon:

Recent figures indicate that changes in the ventilation system have not resulted in the expected increase in productivity.

Work crews will be sent in to revamp the ductwork and other equipment on Tuesday.

We are fully confident that once the difficulties have been resolved, your production levels will meet and even exceed previous figures.

Sincerely,

Dear Mr. Waterman:

Recent reports indicate that productivity has dropped to an all-time low in your department. It appears that the new computer system is slowing the output of your daily reports.

Our estimate that installation of the system would result in improved efficiency was inaccurate. We will, therefore, remove the computer and make a study of alternate computer systems.

Your operation has been hampered for a time but I am certain that, in light of past performance, your department will not only resume normal promptness but get even more reports in ahead of the deadlines.

Sincerely,

Promotion

Dear Mr. Phillips:

The main office empowered me to offer you the position of CEO of its Wagner facility, with all of the accompanying difficulties the position entails. As you know, several recent strikes have literally crippled the plant and the Board has several times suggested shutting down the facility entirely.

Your continued strong growth with the company, and the abilities you have exhibited here in the last two years, recommend you as the ideal person to return the plant to a profitable operation.

Please consider the offer and let me know as soon as you have reached your decision.

Sincerely,

Research Paper

Dear Ms. Roback:

The committee did not approve your dissertation on Fulani mating habits. The manuscript was somewhat carelessly written and researched and the approach echoes Powder's view of the subject too closely.

Stop in and discuss the problem with me. Let's see where we can tighten up some of the writing and pull in a few more sources on the subject. It might be good for you to review both the style manual and the handbook of research before coming to see me.

With all the research you've already done and the recent papers you've presented, the corrections should pose no real problems. The committee should approve your efforts at their next review.

Sincerely,

Fund Drive

Dear Miss St. George:

Time is closing in on us and, with the end of the fund drive only two weeks away, the goal seems awfully hard to reach.

The early mix-ups in planning and scheduling delayed our moving ahead with much of the publicity and soliciting, but we still haven't picked up the proper momentum for getting people interested. A little more publicity in the area and some strong staff support should do it. But, we have to really begin moving to meet that goal.

The past few fund drives have been pulled through by your special talents, and we hope that this one will be the same. You just have to get your people moving.

Sincerely,

Teaching

Dear Ms. Silva:

Teaching at P.S. 24 is a difficult assignment for any teacher and even the most seasoned instructors often find that the integration process takes time. Therefore, it comes as no surprise that you have spoken of submitting your resignation at the end of the school year.

Discipline remains a problem for many new teachers here, as you have discovered. Students tend to "test" a teacher. However, once the test is passed, teachers often find themselves responding with enthusiasm to the challenge.

Please take a little time to reconsider your decision, then see me to discuss the matter at your earliest convenience.

Sincerely,

Dear Mr. Skiles:

Word has reached me that you are ready to hand in your resignation and to leave P.S. 24 at the end of the school year. I can't say that I blame you. A teacher can only take so much of the testing and of disciplining instead of teaching before throwing in the towel. P.S. 24 is the ultimate test.

Maybe, though, you're being a little hasty. The past months have been rough but this was what you wanted. You always spoke of the challenge of teaching in the inner city. Your face would glow as you anticipated giving children the thrill that you've found in learning.

The school was difficult to face but you've really brought out the talents of several students whose previous teachers had never given them a chance. These children may be difficult, often trying human beings, but they are also very grateful to you. You're a fine teacher and they've truly learned something from you.

Sincerely,

COMPLIMENTS

What is nicer to receive than a compliment? Not too many things, because everyone appreciates praise. A pat on the back can make new friends, cement old relationships, win admiration, and, furthermore, can be a powerful influence in making day-to-day relationships more pleasant and rewarding.

Sincerity must be at the heart of every compliment to make it acceptable to the other person as truth. Beware of flattery which can destroy an intended congratulatory remark and lower the esteem of the writer.

Above all, a compliment is an effective stimulant to those who are recognized for a job well done.

How to Do It

1. State what the compliment is for.
2. Comment on the action that led to the compliment.
3. Encourage continuance of that action.

Staff Help

Dear Allen:

Efficiency accompanied by courtesy is a rare combination in today's work world. The courtesy extended to me by your staff during the recent week of meetings and planning sessions was impressive because of its rarity.

Both office personnel and executive planners provided detailed explanations and personal assistance when needed.

Such concern is refreshing and should become more widespread.

Sincerely,

Expert Assistance

Dear Ted,

Just a note to express my sincere appreciation for the job both Pete and Tom performed while here in Baltimore. Between them they saved us untold thousands of dollars in material costs.

Tom just left after having spent most of the last twenty-four hours helping our people run tubing with a system that does not yet have sufficient power to maintain proper temperatures.

Without his help, it is doubtful that we would ever have identified the true magnitude of the problem.

Please let Pete and Tom know how much we appreciate their help.

Sincerely,

Orientation Help

Dear Ellen:

You've got quite an operation going, and your people are even more to rave about. They seem to love their work and carry out their duties both competently and enthusiastically. Certainly, productivity is high as the monthly report shows. Morale appears to be equally high.

During that round of meetings and brainstorming sessions last week, your people worked to fill me in on unfamiliar material. Without being asked, they pulled files, reports, and memos to justify items and to increase my knowledge of vagaries. They even supplied me with advice regarding several good restaurants and entertainment in town.

With your production rates and the quality of your people, you must be doing something right. Keep it up.

Sincerely,

Better Truck Loading

Dear Calvin:

The average weight of 28,297 pounds for each truckload shipped in July makes it a record month.

The increased business has helped, I'm sure, but most of the credit goes to you and your loading crews. Keep up the good work.

Regards,

Unusual Help

Dear Jerome,

Many thanks for the long hours, weekends away from home, and all the other inconveniences you've endured during the past months. The help you gave is much appreciated.

I have a fishing trip out of San Francisco scheduled for May 27. I'd like to invite you to join us if you can. Please let me know.

Best of everything to you in the future.

Sincerely,

Finding Error

Dear Mr. McAbee:

Tim Andrews, during his routine posting of energy usage for the month of July, noted an unusual increase and questioned me about this increased cost.

I investigated the procedure for recording electric power usage and found that an error in calculating the kilowatt hours used during July raised our costs by more than $4,000. An adjustment will be given to us next month.

I would like to compliment Tim for his alertness and thank him for the added $4,000 bottom-line profit.

Sincerely,

Getting the Facts

Dear Mr. Emory:

The city of Fairfield has just awarded us the contract for construction of the Municipal Plaza due to begin early next year.

Your involvement in gathering the data and presenting the proposal proved vital to our success.

Your expert approach made a formerly difficult task manageable. Such talent is indeed an asset to our firm.

Sincerely,

Construction Bid

Dear Tom,

Your proposal passed with flying colors and Fairfield has given us the Municipal Plaza job. Construction should start next fall, but we'll be needing your talents in the meantime for a few other bids we're working on.

Our specifications needed that extra polish that your way with words gave them. The Council looked at the proposals of a half-dozen other firms and accepted our offer faster than we'd anticipated.

Don't get too tied up in other work for a while. We'll be in touch in a week or two. Once again, we appreciate the great job.

Sincerely,

Good Salesman

Dear Torry,

The order from Easton arrived today and it alone raised our sales volume for the month by several points. Allen managed not only to sell a new account, but one that eluded us for several years despite serious work by several of our best people.

Allen's perseverance paid off. He spent several days trying to see Easton's president and finally caught him in the evening. Thanks to Allen's refusal to limit his working hours, the biggest account on the West Coast is ours.

You've got an eye for talent, and Allen is one man who is going to go far in this company.

Sincerely,

Sales Volume

Dear Bob,

John Harvey from our headquarters office reports that your sales volume for August was more than double July's volume.

We offer a good product to consumers, and equally important are the aggressive and competent employees like you who take our product before the public.

Continue the good work.

Sincerely,

Sales Increase

Dear Dave,

The latest issue of ACE had a circulation of over one million, a figure that no one thought we'd reach after the setbacks of the last three years.

A large part of the credit goes to you and the people you've chosen to rework what was once a dying publication. It looks like you've chosen a new format. Eliminating the "cute" departments and mindless quizzes has had its beneficial effect. You, Tom, Jean, and Dale have something to really gloat about in the industry. And ACE can look forward to increased profits in the months to come.

Please pass my appreciation on to your staff. Continue the good work.

Sincerely,

Dear Mr. Byran:

Circulation of ACE magazine has just passed the one million mark after a three-year lag in subscription sales. Although exposure has increased, your complete overhaul of the format and staff assignments have been key factors in this new success.

Keep up the good work.

Sincerely,

Vote Getter

Dear Wendell:

Rarely has a city experienced so high a percentage of voter turnout as in this last election. Well-planned publicity and careful scheduling brought out 72 percent of the registered voters who made their voices heard and their choice known.

Although the opposition often echoed the platform presented by our candidate, your work behind the scenes in managing the campaign made a major difference in voter reaction.

Local politics needs more dedicated workers like you.

Sincerely,

RECOMMENDATIONS

In a letter recommending one person to another, mention two or three points of strength. The person you are recommending should have more than one good quality, but if too many are listed, the authority of the letter is diminished.

Statements should be specific. Rather than saying, "Joan has a good attendance record," say, "Joan was absent only four days during the three years she worked here." Rather than saying, "Kathy is a good worker," say, "Kathy turns in her reports on time."

Assume a pleasant state of mind when writing the letter, because a cool or standoffish attitude will only harm the person you are trying to help. A feeling of warmth and enthusiasm should be felt by the reader.

Of course, mention the full name of the person you are recommending. Also state your relationship: employer, teacher, friend, and how long you have known him or her.

Usually the last sentence can be an affirmation that the person of your letter will fulfill the needs of the reader.

> I recommend her highly as a statistical clerk.
>
> I wish I had her back.
>
> She will rise to the top, whatever she tries.
>
> Tom was always a great help to me.
>
> He is one I can recommend with complete confidence.
>
> I know he will measure up to your expectations.
>
> He did so much to increase our sales, and I know he can do the same for you.
>
> She earned the confidence of all her customers.
>
> His enthusiastic hard work will be sorely missed here.
>
> Her efficiency may surprise you.

How to Do It

1. Mention the person's name and his or her most favorable trait.
2. State your association with the person—use specifics, not generalizations.
3. Reaffirm your recommendation.

Customer

Gentlemen:

This is to inform you that we have done business with our customer, Seymour Port Company, for more than five years. We are pleased to report that all business has been conducted by Mr. Seymour and his company in a highly satisfactory manner.

Mr. Seymour and his staff have always been most helpful in providing information and advice about both domestic and overseas packaging and packaging materials. In the specialized field of overseas shipments, we have found that he has a broad range of information that has been helpful to us.

If you wish further information, please write or phone.

Sincerely,

Domestic Service

Dear Mrs. Watson:

Annette Winton has worked for me two days a week for almost twelve years. She is punctual and a hard worker. In my opinion, her work is better than average. I have found her steady and cooperative—two qualities I appreciate.

I am sorry she is leaving, and I sincerely feel that whoever is fortunate enough to have her will be rewarded with work well done.

I have found Annette loyal to those she serves. My best wishes go with her.

Sincerely,

Inexperienced Worker

Dear Mr. Bishop:

I gladly recommend John Harley for work in your garage. He has been a neighbor all his life, is a hard and steady worker, and is a friendly person.

John has helped me with my car a few times and has demonstrated a good basic understanding of automobile mechanics.

Regards,

High School Graduate

Dear Ms. Wilson:

The best I can say may not be a sufficiently good recommendation for Joanne Grebner. She will be an excellent executive secretary trainee. She had the highest rating in my senior typing class during the five years I have taught here. Joanne is punctual, accurate, most willing, and quick to grasp new ideas.

In whatever she tries, she will rise to the top.

Sincerely,

REPRIMAND

A reprimand should include constructive criticism, and constructive criticism starts with a compliment. Show appreciation for some part of the other person's work that has been good or for some event he or she has participated in. A phrase like, "We appreciate your willing attitude," or "You have been with us a good many years," lets the person know that he or she is being treated with consideration. The complimentary attitude should not be overdone, however, or the turnabout to a reprimand will seem contradictory.

Make a letter of reprimand short: there is no reason to prolong the agony. Shortness will also prevent a tendency to ramble around the fringes of the subject. Make the fact of a reprimand direct, but in a tactful and considerate way, To keep criticism easy to take, criticize indirectly. Rather than saying, "Don't smoke in the lunchroom," say, "Please smoke outside." Replace, "You are late all the time," with "Please try to be more prompt."

The Eastern concept of saving face is applicable to a letter of criticism. Let the reader keep his or her ego; let the reader know that you too are not without fault—that you are human. A word or two of praise now and then in the letter will let the person retain his or her good image. This leads to a cooperative attitude on the part of both parties. Then, corrective action can be suggested. Tell the reader how errors can be corrected, what action needs to be taken, and how you will help.

Set goals that can be reached, not grand goals of improved self or a happier life ahead, but specific goals, as only 4 errors next month, or a chore completed by 4:00 p.m. each day. In a work environment, one person's accomplishing suggested goals can boost the morale of co-workers. In a personal situation, reaching goals makes you feel good. End your reprimand with encouragement.

How to Do It

1. Start with a compliment.
2. Use indirect criticism.
3. Set definite goals for improvement.
4. Offer encouragement.

Outside Activities at Work

Dear George:

Your work record in the past has been excellent, but now it has come to my attention that you have been spending a lot of working hours campaigning for new officers. I haven't been there to observe, but reports have come to me from several sources. Since this interferes with the amount of work you are doing, I would suggest you devote less time to campaigning and more to Company work.

Sincerely,

Lack of Cleanliness

Dear Betty,

You have a lot of good friends here. We all like your smile and your cheery greeting in the mornings. There is one area, however, in which we feel there is room for improvement. We would like to suggest a stronger deodorant and perhaps more frequent washing of your blouses. You no doubt have been unaware of this need, but your co-workers would appreciate your considering the problem.

Keep smiling and please hold on to your cheerful ways.

Sincerely,

Bad Behavior

Dear Employees:

We had a minor fender bender accident in the parking lot yesterday at quitting time between an employee and one of our customers. Our employee disregarded the directional arrows in his rush to leave.

Our customer was astounded that so many employees were dashing out against the arrows. He was more than unhappy, and threatened to take his business elsewhere.

Not only because of loss of business, but also for your own physical safety, DIRECTIONAL ARROWS IN THE PARKING LOT MUST BE OBEYED. If you cannot correct this type of behavior, strong measures will be taken to insure that you do.

Safety requires not only care but also courtesy and consideration for others.

Sincerely,

Travel Expense

Dear Ms. Rundell:

The executive committee has reviewed your travel expense account for the past year. Your overall expenses seem reasonable, and although we have not established a budget for each salesperson, we plan to have one developed for use next year.

One facet of your travel strikes us as probably uneconomical. You appear to be covering the western states in a disorganized way. For example, in May you made calls in cities in this order: Portland, San Francisco, Oakland, San Diego, Los Angeles, Boise, Denver, Portland, Seattle, Salt Lake City, Sacramento, and Oakland.

Looking at a map of the western states, this schedule involves a lot of skipping and backtracking. The Committee believes that money and travel time could be saved if you traveled in a roughly circular route to prevent backtracking. Is this thought correct, or is there a good reason for not following a more direct route from city to city?

Please let me have your comments on this by April 30.

Regards,

Lack of Cooperation

Dear Mr. Bell

Reports on the attractiveness of your displays in our midwestern stores and favorable comments by customers indicate you are doing an excellent job of displaying our merchandise.

These reports come to me from our department buyers who also bring up a situation that needs correcting. They report that you often appear on the selling floor during busy periods and request too much help from the salespeople. There is no reason why you should need help from the sales staff. Disruptions in the sales area could be minimized by organizing all your materials and tools in the work areas before bringing anything onto the selling floor. This will also lessen your time on the floor. You should be able to schedule your work on the sales floor so that most of it is done before customers arrive and after the store is closed.

Please give this some thought and let me know by March 20 your plans for closer cooperation with the department buyers. I know they tend to be difficult at times—but they do have a point.

Sincerely,

Unsafe Conditions

Dear Mr. Benjay:

I commend you for never having had a fire, but the January 31 report from our fire insurance company states that the fire insurance on the Belson plant will increase 30 percent next year. The reason stated is unsafe conditions, supported by two citations from the fire marshall for the *same* violation within four months.

This is poor management. You are risking the lives of the Belson employees.

By February 27, I want to have on my desk a compliance certification from the Belson County Fire Inspector.

Regards,

Exceeding Budget

Dear Mr. Harbor:

I have been studying the September and year-to-date cost statements for your plant. Overall, your cost-cutting has improved since my review of the first six months, but one thing disturbs me: the reductions have been in the small-cost categories. If you are to meet the budgeted goal by year-end, costs of finishing supplies and maintenance materials must be cut considerably. We discussed this in July. The time for action is fast disappearing. Please send me a plan by November 1 for reducing costs in the last two months.

Continue the good work on the small items; we can't lose any ground already gained.

Regards,

Trespassing

Dear Al:

A situation has recently come to my attention that must be corrected. Evidently some employees' families and friends are coming in to the plant, particularly on the second and third shifts.

As you know, this is strictly against company policy, because of the liability we could incur if someone were hurt. Any tours of the plant must be arranged through the Personnel Department.

Effective immediately, please take whatever steps are necessary to secure the manufacturing area from unauthorized persons.

Sincerely,

PRESENTING GIFTS

The purpose of sending a letter with a gift is to indicate that the giver is really a part of the gift; it is a way of giving oneself. Use individuality of expression as much as possible because it will put your own personality into the message. The letter should be short and friendly and reveal pleasure in the giving.

How to Do It

1. Mention the occasion for the gift.
2. Express pleasure in the giving.

Companionship

Dear Kathy,

This gift is only a token of how much your friendly companionship this summer has meant to me.

There will always be love in my thoughts of you.

With affection,

Friendship

Dear Don,

This gift is just a small thank-you for the friendship you showed me this summer.

I will always think of you as a kind friend who took a real interest in both my work and play.

Sincerely,

Advice

Dear David:

I am sending you a Chinese puzzle. It is a small thank-you for the consultation and advice you offered Tuesday. I felt much better about approaching the problem after discussing it with you. Your interest is appreciated.

Sincerely,

Funeral Officiating

Dear Reverend Thomas:

Please accept the enclosed check for conducting the funeral service for my father. We deeply appreciate the extra time and effort you devoted to making this a memorable service.

Sincerely,

Baptismal Officiating

Dear Reverend Thomas:

Thank you for the beautiful baptismal service for our daughter, Becky. Please accept the enclosed check as a personal gift for the thought and work you put into making the service so beautiful and meaningful.

Sincerely,

Hospital Patient

Dear Jo Ann,

Please accept this robe as a gift to someone special. I am sure that you will find use for the robe now that you are doing a little walking each day. I hope it buoys up your spirits enough for you to leave the hospital soon.

Sincerely,

Dear Joe,

Here is a book from your old friend Jack Hoskins. It should help to wile away the long daytime hours as you recuperate in the hospital. I'll drop by to see you next time I'm in town, and I hope that by then you will be home. If not, I'll stop by the hospital.

Regards,

Eightieth Birthday

Dear Mr. Winslow,

For your eightieth birthday, the bunch at the Neighborhood Center thought we would give you a reason to relax a little—about time.

The reclining chair you will receive this Thursday is a gift to show our appreciation for all the little things you do at the Center to make life more pleasant for your many friends.

Please enjoy the chair for many years to come.

Your friends,

Illness

Dear Ron,

Your friends at Elton Corporation are sorry to learn of your wife's serious illness. Please accept the flowers we have sent as sincere wishes that she will have a fast and complete recovery.

Sincerely,

Dear Alan:

Please accept this book from the office group. We hope it is not too exciting while you are recovering from your operation. If the book is too exciting, it is good enough to keep until your stitches heal over.

Sincerely,

Retirement

Dear Doug:

The Company, we are sure, will present you with a watch upon your retirement. If you are going to watch the time go by, we though we might appreciate a place to relax while doing so. That is why we in the Production Department are sending to your home a high-back reclining chair. Lean back and enjoy your retirement in comfort.

We have all benefitted from working with you and your presence will be sorely missed.

Congratulations,

ACCEPTING GIFTS

Accepting a gift graciously can be disquieting at times. The receiver may feel an obligation to reply while being unable to think of an appropriate expression of thanks for a gift that is really not wanted.

In spite of this seeming difficulty, one can write an appropriate gift acceptance letter by starting with a statement of what the thank-you is for:

> We wish to thank you for the book . . .
> Your box of goodies arrived yesterday . . .
> Your recent contribution of $ . . .
> The watercolor chosen by you for my office arrived today.

After the opening statement, make some comment about the gift; try to do a little better than merely saying, "It is just what I always wanted." Try to be original with a few words about the gift's desirability, beauty, usefulness, appropriateness, or some distinctive phase of the gift. For example:

> The refrigerator you gave us has upgraded the cooler department to the point where I may have to trade in the boat for a larger one.
> Your care in selecting a gift which coordinates so well with my office decor, serves to further increase my enthusiasm.
> Your gift of the finely crafted glass unicorn, so fragile in appearance yet strongly made, is distinctive.
> We shall treasure the gift for its beauty and craftsmanship, but even more as a constant reminder of your friendship.

The gift acceptance letter should express gratitude and pleasant expectancy in a courteous and tactful way.

How to Do It

1. Mention the gift received.
2. Make an original comment about the usefulness, desirability, beauty, or other distinctive phase of the gift.

Chess Set

Dear Mr. Danforth,

Your gift was waiting for us when we returned home. It reminded us of your gracious and pleasant hospitality.

We shall treasure the chess set for its beauty and craftsmanship, but even more as a constant reminder of your friendship.

Sincerely,

Food Snacks

Dear Len:

Your letter and box of goodies arrived yesterday and I have to return the thanks. It was nice of you to send along the snacks, and everyone here at Albany will partake of the treats.

We are glad you enjoyed the golf game with Brenner; he is a very personable young man.

Since I know you will forgive the photography, I am enclosing some photographs of you, Brenner, and the gang that played golf together.

Please let me know if you have a day while in San Francisco and maybe you and I can play golf at the Olympic Course.

Sincerely,

Book

Dear Ms. Vaughn,

The arrival of your gift was a pleasant beginning for my day, especially since the book was so unexpected. I admire greatly the works of Victorian authors but have never anticipated actually owning a signed first edition.

The volume will remain among my treasured displays to bring me pleasure and to remind me of your consideration.

Sincerely,

Dear Mrs. Kleinfeld,

The small brown package that came in today's mail was really an understated way in which to send such a valuable book. You must have known how thrilled I'd be as the wrappings were unfolded and the book appeared.

You know that I'll cherish this gift and you can expect to see it in a place of honor next time you visit. I'm not sure that I'll even dare read it—just look at it in wonder.

Thanks so much for indulging me. I'll take good care of my new treasure.

Sincerely,

Money

Dear Mr. Dodson:

Your recent contribution of $12,000 to the fund for aid to battered wives was a long-needed boost to our program. The money will be put to use in providing temporary shelter and protection to abused wives and their children, and in generating further contributions.

Your gift is an affirmation of the kindness and humanity that still exists in this world.

Sincerely,

Dear Mr. Gough:

Your gift to the battered wives' fund is a real start for us. A few months ago, none of us knew whether the project could even get off the ground, let alone survive all the red tape and expense.

Now, thanks to you, things will begin moving. We can do a lot with $12,000 to make people aware of the problem and to set up facilities.

Once the program has a real home, don't be surprised if we name it after you. Many women are in your debt.

A big thank you from them—and from me.

Sincerely,

Oil Painting

Dear Mr. Cowden:

While admiring your fine work last Wednesday, I never anticipated actually owning an original oil painting for my personal collection. You have an eye for color and proportion, and the work fits in beautifully with the decor of my office.

Stop by the office and see just how good a choice you made.

You can expect that whoever enters the office will notice the work and leave familiar with your name.

Thank you for your kindness.

Sincerely,

Watercolor Painting

Dear Ms. Meadows:

The watercolor that you chose for my office arrived today. The quality of your work, of the which the gift is an excellent example, has long been familiar to me.

Your care in selecting the gift, which coordinates so well with my personal work surroundings, serves to further increase my enthusiasm.

Thank you once again.

Sincerely,

Art Object

Dear Mrs. Skeen:

Although Annie is still too weak to thank you herself, I wanted you to know immediately how much your concern and your generous gift is appreciated.

Seriously ill children often receive many gifts from kind yet impersonal well-wishers. Your gift of the finely crafted glass unicorn, so fragile in appearance yet strongly made, was different. The care and love which you took in selecting the gift for Annie are visible, just as your concern for her well-being can be felt. It may only be our imagination, but we can see her gain strength daily as she gazes upon the tiny creature, knowing that many people love her.

Thank you for caring.

Sincerely,

Statuette

Dear Mrs. Skidmore:

Your considerate holiday gift arrived today and renewed my good feelings about our recent decision to collaborate.

The marble statuette, placed where it is always in my line of vision, remains a constant reminder of the quality and the enduring nature of our work.

I appreciate your effort.

Sincerely,

Free Product

Dear Mr. Bauer:

The shipment of cartons with a "No Charge" invoice and your best wishes arrived today. Rarely does one business provide anything, even merchandise that it doesn't need, to another fledgling company free of charge.

Your effort and the merchandise are both greatly appreciated.

Sincerely,

Cooler

Dear Don:

The food cooler for our boat arrived here in Sausalito yesterday, and I can't thank you enough for the wonderful gift. You have actually upgraded the cooler department to the point where I may have to trade the boat for something larger and more appropriate.

We are glad you enjoyed your day with us and hope you will return to San Francisco for some more sailing. Should Betty and I get to New Orleans, we will take you up on your offer to do some lake sailing.

Sincerely,

DECLINING GIFTS

Declining a gift is a delicate task, but at times a refusal may be necessary. Company policy may forbid gifts that could be valued at more than a very few dollars; a gift from a near stranger may be expensive; a gift may be a duplicate and of no use to you, but of value to the giver; you may feel your position could be compromised; or public opinion may be opposed to your accepting gifts.

Whether accepted or declined, a gift should always be acknowledged. However much you dislike the gift or the giver, never criticize either. You received the gift because of a kind thought, and there is no reason to indirectly criticize the thought by directly criticizing either the gift or the giver.

Make the letter brief to avoid drawing out the disappointment of a refusal.

How to Do It

1. Agree on some points with the giver, or apologize, or offer thanks for the thought.
2. State the refusal.
3. Offer an explanation.

Company Policy

Dear Ms. Sylvan:

I am sorry I cannot accept the case of champagne you sent me. Although the thought is gratefully accepted, company policy prevents me from accepting a gift of this value.

The gift has been returned, but not my appreciation of your thoughtfulness.

         Sincerely,

Dear Ms. Carrell:

The company appreciates your offer to provide free service and supplies for the copying equipment in return for an agreement to deal exclusively with Aabco.

Regrettably, the offer must be refused. Our long-standing policy is that no one company may be dealt with on an exclusive basis. While the reputation of Aabco and the quality of your product are well known, company policy must be followed.

         Sincerely,

Must Maintain Image

Dear Mr. Torres:

Your recent gift of appreciation as a result of the court decision last Tuesday was a kind gesture.

However, I must decline your offer, although I know it was well meant.

As a civil court judge, I take great pains to maintain my image of impartiality. Acceptance of gifts in this manner could compromise that image. Nonetheless, your kindness is appreciated.

         Sincerely,

Duplicate Gift

Dear Mr. Luddy:

Thank you for so thoughtful a gift. You are right. Every writer should have a typewriter of such quality.

I am sorry that I must return the typewriter, because, you see, my parents have the identical belief and good taste, and they bought a similar typewriter for my last birthday. Once again, thank you so much for caring.

Sincerely,

Gift Too Valuable

Dear Mr. Scott,

Once again you show that your taste in gifts is impeccable. Thank you so much for the lovely, and valuable, antique silver vase.

I regret that I must return it; a sincere regret because of its great beauty.

It is unfortunate but my frequent business trips make my home vulnerable, and several area homes have recently suffered burglaries. Although insurance would provide financial reimbursement, the irreplaceable nature of the vase would leave me forever guilty. Please allow me to return it.

Sincerely,

Expensive Gift

Dear Mrs. Byers:

The painting you sent is well suited to the decor and mood of the office.

I regret, however, that it must be returned.

It is my policy not to accept expensive gifts from clients, and an original painting by Picasso certainly fits the category of "expensive."

Sincerely,

TRIBUTE

Tribute to a Wife

Dear Pastor Jim,

You knew Peggy only during the time she was fighting for her life against cancer. Let me fill you in on our fifty-one years of marriage: 1937–1988.

We were married when our country was deep in the Great Depression. Only her careful management of my meager salary kept us going. I quit smoking even though my two packs a day cost only a quarter. We both made sacrifices.

Our three sons, born in 1939, 1942, and 1946, are all responsible, successful men because they were taught to be polite and respectful by their mother. I like to think I helped a little.

Peggy was known as "Mrs. Presbyterian" in our church in Dearborn, Michigan. She was a dedicated choir member for thirty years, taught Sunday School, held almost every church office, and took part in all aspects of church life.

Our move to Sun City West, Arizona didn't stop her activities. Of course choir was first; she was one of the first Elders and helped organize the women's association.

Even with all the problems we had after moving here: the loss of everything we owned in a moving van fire, her first bout with cancer and surgery, her two broken elbows—at the same time, and the recurrence of cancer in spite of chemotherapy and radiation, Peggy was as cheerful and gracious as she could be. She was a wonderful manager, mother, and mate, and was loved by all who knew her. I was fortunate to have been a part of her life and love.

We all miss her.

> Kindest regards to you
> and Betty,

Tribute to a Husband

Dear Joanne,

I am writing early this year. This note is going to a very divergent group of Al's and my friends. Some of you already know and to others it will be "news"—of a sort.

Al died July 31st in Quito, Ecuador at age 75. He was on his way to the Galapagos Islands on a nature safari with a small group of 14. He never got to his goal, to which he had aimed for many years, but he was doing what he loved—traveling. And, most importantly, he died without a long, lingering illness which had been a real worry to him for several years. I am most thankful for that. It was a heart attack and I am convinced that the over-9,000-foot elevation at Quito was his undoing. I had a Memorial Service and his ashes were scattered at sea outside the Golden Gate Bridge. (His many years in the Navy prompted that.)

The write-ups in the two San Francisco papers were well done, I thought. I am very proud of Al's many accomplishments in a broad spectrum of local, state, national, and international organizations and endeavors. He was still in practice after 42 years, and not too many doctors can say they have delivered more than 12,000 babies in their careers!

The past two months have been and continue to be hectic. Those who "have traveled this path" know only too well what I mean. But the outpouring of love and concern from hundreds of friends, and especially patients, has been most heart warming to me.

To those dear friends of Al's I wish a happy holiday season, its many blessings and good health. To my special friends I can only wish the same, and to all our mutual friends—"God bless us everyone."

Please keep in touch. I truly value the memories of all our past contacts and the friendships that ensued and have endured even though we may not have seen each other often or for many years.

My best wishes and love,

(With permission from Eleanor E. Long, wife of Dr. Albert E. Long, San Francisco.)

Index

A

Aabco, company, 419
Aames Company, 16
Aatel, company, 258
Abbott's, store, 30
Abel Paint Company, 381
Abelson Corporation, 355
Absentee record, 286
Academic assistance, 372
Accepting applicant, 249, 256
 How to Do It, 257
Accepting gifts, 414
 How to Do It, 414
 Sentences, 414
Accepting invitations, 374
Accepting resignation, 266
Account:
 Curent, 143
 Delinquent, 143
Accounting:
 Help, 358
 Manager, 239
 System, 184
Ace Manufacturing Company, 176
Ace Technical Academy, 245
Acknowledgment of gifts, 184
Action taken, 176
Action words, 49
Activities at work, 408
Adam-Sloop Company, 208
Additional information:
 Provided, 383
 Requested, 383
Address change, 181, 198
 Correction, 181
Adjustments, customer, 39
Advertising, 373
Advertising executive, 232
Advice, 351, 411
Agreeing while refusing, 23
Agreement, 24
 Ended, 367
 For signature, 380
Aid, financial, 46
Alameda Real Estate Board, 355
Alamo Business Women, 15
Alcove, J., Inc., 279

Alderwild Machine Shop, 180
Allen Company, 65
Allen's, business firm, 34
Allergies, 289
Alumni solicitation, 122
American Chicken, franchise, 36
American Heart Association, 93
American Veterans, 93
AMEX Life Assurance Company, 75
Amsterdam, Inc., 336
AMVETS, 93
Anderson Hardware Company, 246
Anniversary, 341
Ansell's, company, 357
Answer delayed, 321
Answering complaints, 214
Answering questions, 5
Antelope Machine Corporation, 269
A O pi, 27
Apology, 4, 24, 317
 How to Do It, 317
 Reasons, 318
 Sentences, 318
Appeal:
 Ego, 118
 Faith, 108
 Religious, 126
 Secular, 104
Appley Building Supplies, 41
Applicant:
 Accepting, 249, 256
 Data from, 251
 Recommended, 270
 Rejecting, 255, 271
Application letter:
 Computer systems manager, 241
 Private secretary, 240
Appointment:
 Making, 188
 Missed, 328
Appraisal, performance, 259
Appreciation, 347, 353
Arizona Authors' Association, 386
Article, magazine, 386
Art object, 73, 417
Ashton Warehouse Company, 380
Assistance, expert, 400
Assistant staff manager, 236
Association president, 342

Atchison project, 329
Atlanta, 371
Attending, 359
Attention devices, 49
    Collections, 136
    Opening sentences, 136
Attitude, 405
Australia, 360
Auto-10 camera, 63
Availability of information, 27
Award:
    Industry, 341
    Service, 339
AZE Corporation, 278, 283
AZE Shoe Company, 279
Aztec Hotel, 373

B

Bad behavior, 319, 408
Bad risk, 35
Baker's Dozen Bakery, 336
Bakery, 67, 336
Ball game, 374
Baltimore, 400
Bangladesh, 97
Baptismal offering, 412
Barking dog, 212
Barocchio's Bakery, 67
Barrow's:
    Business firm, 33
    College, 128
Basker Company, 309
Bastone Leather Company, 259
Beginning sentences:
    Accepting gifts, 414
    Accepting position, 377
    Complaint answer, 214
    Fund raising, 81, 127
    Sales, 50
    Thank you, 347
Behavior, bad, 408
Being our customer, 356
Belated condolences, 302
Belmont Boys Home, 37
Better truck loading, 401
BFG Shoe Company, 279
Bid:
    Construction, 402
    Price, 175
Billing error, 209, 223, 320
Birthday, 413
Birth defect, 310
Board a relative, 17
Boise, 409
Bonner Bridge, 300

Book, 415
    Club, 59
    Query, 385
Boulder River Hospital, 28
Bowen's Department Store, 30
Box manufacturer, 230
Boys:
    Homeless, 91
    Troubled, 87
Bradford Associates, 325
Brooklyn, 233, 322
Buchannan University, 126
Budget:
    Can be met, 107
    Exceeding, 410
    Limitations, 38
Building fund, 125
Bulletin, free, 365
Bullwright Construction, 274
Burns, school, 257
Business:
    Collection letters, 133
    Credit, 32
    Elders, 359
    Forecasts, 12
    Guidance, 11
    Letters, 363, 391
    Location, 13
    Magazines, 56
    Meetings, 43
    Opportunities, 13
    Statistics, 12
Buyer trainee, 230

C

California, 197
Camera, 63
Canada, 368
Cantebury Hospital, 117
Canvassing, fund drive, 107
Capper's, store, 30
CARE, 96, 97
Cash discount, 40
Catalog order, 209
Categories, 363
Celebration, football, 375
Central Freight Payments, Inc., 33
Central Trailer, 36
Centrex, company, 360
Cerebral Palsy Center, 94
Certificate of incorporation, 380
Chairperson, 378
Challenge, seeking, 287
Change address, 181
Change items used, 181

Change policy, 180
Change procedure, 192
Charge account, 145-149
    Inactive, 384
    Requested, 357
Charitable help, 84
Charity, disagree with, 39
Chemical hazards, 195
Chess set, 414
Chicago, 360
Chicago Tribune, 239
Chief accountant, 230
Children:
    Crippled, 89
    Destitute, 88
    Handicapped, 90
    Hungry, 90
    Runaway, 84
Children's Fund, 37
Child, sponsor, 98
Christmas Seals, 100
Churches, fund raising, 104
Cintex, company, 264
City councilman, 342
City information, 184
Claim:
    Against city, 178
    Follow-up, 197
    Freight, 45
    Review, 186
    Service evaluation, 198
Clarity, 171
Classroom:
    Performance, 285
    Procedure, 281
Cleanliness, lacking, 408
Cleveland Dental School, 123
Closing sentences
        (see Ending sentences)
Club, book, 59
Colfax, company, 95
Collection:
    Personal, 135
    Service, 70
Collection, humor, 136
Collection letters:
    Business, 133
    Final, 164-168
    First, 154
    Middle, 158-164
    Reminder, 140, 154
    Series, 140
College degree:
    Handicapped, 339
    Music, 338
College training, 288
Comair Service Systems, 77
Committee chairperson, 378
Commodity codes, 381

Companionship, 353, 411
Company:
    Cutbacks, 278
    Hotel room, 373
    Merger, 279
    Policy, 38, 419
    Procedure, 320
Complaint:
    Answering, 214
    Procedure, 224
    Making, 203
Compliments:
    Giving, 400
    How to Do It, 400
Comply with request, 175
Computer error, 209
Computer system, 64
Conditions, unsafe, 410
Condolence, 295
Confirmation, 176
Confusing word usage, 320
Congratulations, 335
    How to Do It, 335
    Promotion, 263, 272
    Retirement, 268, 274
Construction bid, 402
Consulting, income tax, 68
Consumer survey, 7
Contest, sales, 397
Continue procedure, 177
Contra Costa County Crippled Children's
        Society, Inc., 90
Contact, service, 69
Contribution, 369
Convalescing, 395
Cooler, 418
Cooperation, 182
    Lacking, 409
Cornwall, college, 129
Corporate name, 189
Correcting error, 191, 383
Corrugated box, 230
Costs, expansion, 113
Cost of purchases, 204
Cost savings, 75
Councilman, 342
Cover letters, 229, 378
    How to Do It, 230, 379
    Job applications, 231
    Resumes, 229
Credit:
    Business, 32
    Card, 187
    Delayed, 323
    Information, 29, 37, 186
    Late pay, 33
    Limited, 33
    Memo, 192
    Personal, 29, 72

Credit Union, 158, 290
Crippled children, 89
Crown Zellerbach Corp., 235
Current account, 143
Customer, 356, 405
    Adjustments, 39
    Disturbed, 215
    Ignored, 326
    Inactive, 69
    New, 336
    Specific, 65

                D

Damaged merchandise, 219
Damaged product, 40
Dartmouth Alumni Fund, 122
Dartnell, company, 66
Data for newsletter, 185
Data no longer needed, 175
Deadline:
    Meeting, 9
    Shorten, 9
Death:
    Belated father, 308
    Other, 306
    Business associate, 300
    Business firm, 300
    Business friend, 300
    Daughter, 304
    Father, 304
    Husband, 301
    Mother, 303
    Brother, 306
    Relative, 303
    Sister, 306
    Son, 305
    Spouse, 301
    Suicide, 308
    Use of the word, 295
    Wife, 302
Declining:
    Dinner invitation, 321
    Gifts, 418
    Invitation, 376
    Requests, 21
    Responsibilities, 222
Deer Valley Truck Supply, 75
Delayed answer, 321
Delayed credit, 323
Delayed dinner, 323
Delayed order, 218, 323
Delayed paper work, 324
Delayed return of item, 324
Delayed thank you, 325
Delinquent account, 152
Delinquent pledge, 108

Delivery late, 217
Delivery method, 218
Delivery person, 212
Deloitte, Haskins & Sells, 68
Delta Cost Accountants, 26
Dentistry, 59
Denver, 236, 328, 369, 409
Department store, 230
Destitute children, 88
Dinner:
    Declined, 321
    Delayed, 323
    Guest, 374
    Invitation, 352, 376
    Postponed, 323
    Retirement, 376
Direct mail solicitation, 83
Disadvantaged girl, 86
Disagree with goals, 290
Disease, lung, 100
Distribution of reports, 178
Disturbed retail customer, 215
Divorce, 311
Doctors:
    Business persons, 115
    Giving, 115
    Last appeal, 116
Documents valuable, 382
Dog, barking, 212
Domestic service, 406
Donation, 37
Dun & Bradstreet, 34
Duplicate gift, 420

                E

East Bay Accounting Society, 374
Easton, company, 403
Effect of strike, 179
Ego, appeal, 118
Eightieth birthday, 413
Election, public, 70
Elitist magazine, 56
Ellsworth College, 128
Elton Corporation, 299, 413
Emerson Society, 42
Emphatic position, 22
Employee:
    New, 258, 372
    Leaving notice, 267, 268
    Parents, 267
Welcome, 258
Employer letters, 249
    Data, 251
    How to Do It, 249
Employment, 229
    Letters from applicant, 229

Letters from employer, 249
Letters from third party, 270
Short record, 30
Encouragement, 25, 396
　How to Do It, 396
　Sentences, 396
Ending paragraph, 174
Ending sentences, 5
　Accepting gifts, 414
　Collection, 137-139
　Complaint answer, 215
　Information, 172, 183
　Invitation, 375
　Position acceptance, 371
　Recommendation, 405
　Refusal, 23
　Sales, 51, 53
　Thank you, 348
Enjoyed meeting you, 367
Entertaining a friend, 16
Equal Employment Opportunity
　　Commission, 277
Equipment:
　Hospital, 112
　Old, 188
　Replacing, 117
Error:
　Billing, 209, 223, 320
　Computer, 209
　Correction, 383
　Finding, 402
　Manufacturing, 207
　Pricing, 222
　Quote, 330
　Shipping, 208, 218, 330
　Statement, 224, 331
Etching, metal, 23
Evaluation:
　Performance, 260
　Personnel, 193
Every bit helps, 127
Every member canvass, 107
Exceeding budget, 410
Exceeding goal, 337
Executive recruiter, 71
Expansion costs, 113
Expenditures request, 379
Expense, travel, 409
Expensive gift, 420
Expert assistance, 400
Explanation, inadequate, 205

F

Facts, getting, 402
Failure of project, 329
Fairfield, city, 402

Faith appeal, 108
Fantasies, 364
Farnsworth, Inc., 259
Favors, 3
Fear, alleviating, 17
Fibreboard, company, 360
Fibre Containers, 340
Final collection letters, 164-168
Final sentences (*see* Ending sentences)
Financial aid, 46
Financial condition, 33
Financial disadvantage, 127
Financial problems, 279
Financial statements, 11
Finding error, 402
Firing, 277
First collection letter, 154
Fishing trip invitation, 368
Follow-up, 382
　Claim, 197
　How to Do It, 382
　Sales letter, 76
Food:
　Foreign object, 221
　Gift, 67
　Snacks, 414
Football:
　Celebration, 375
　Game, 27
Fordham's, store, 30
Ford Motor Company, 225
Ford's, store, 32
Foreign object in food, 221
Franchise refused, 36
Fredrick & Nelson, 231
Free bulletin, 365
Free product, 418
Freight bill, 142
Freight claim, 45
Friend, 371
　For sales position, 371
Friendship, 353, 411
Fruehauf Trailer Company, 236
Fund:
　Building, 125
　Drive, 398
Fund raising:
　Hospitals, 110
　Canvassing, 107
　Churches, 104
　Preparation, 105
　Sales techniques, 83
　Schools, 119
　Series of letters, 100
Funds limited, 37
Funeral officiating, 412
Furniture Mart, 8
Furniture, retail, 73

G

Gardening problem, 213
General Electric, 180
Getting the facts, 402
Gift, 349
  Accepting, 414
  Acknowledgment, 184
  Declining, 418
  Duplicate, 420
  Expensive, 420
  Food, 67
  Presenting, 411
  Received, 368
  Small, 128
  Valuable, 420
Gift accepting, How to Do It, 414
Gift declining, How to Do It, 419
Gift presenting, Hot to Do It, 411
Girl, disadvantaged, 86
Giving:
  Doctors, 115
  For love, 109
  Haven't yet, 122
  Increase, 105
  More, 119
Goal, exceeded, 337
Goals, 407
Going away party, 352
Golf invitation, 365
Golf tournament, 340
Good salesman, 403
Goodwill, 21, 363
  Collection, 138
  How to Do It, 364
Good wishes, 393
  How to Do It, 394
Good work, 365
Grace Foundation, 46
Graduation, 338
Grande Company, 18
Granger Graduate School, 124
Greetings, seasonal, 364, 394
Group, joining, 26
Guarantee, merchandise, 220
Guarantor, 34
Guest, dinner, 374

H

Hamilton Heavy Hardware, company, 356
Handicapped:
  Children, 90
  College graduates, 339
Hanukkah, 364
Harcourt College, 119

Harper Clean Air, company, 287
Harry and David, 67
Hastings-Allen, 328
Health:
  Illness, 288
  Insurance, 58
  Plan, 58
Heart:
  Fund, 92
  Disease, 92
  Problems, 289
Help, unusual, 401
Highland Estates, 360
High school graduate, 406
Homeless boys, 91
Honourman Medical Center, 28
Hoskins and Halloid, company, 287
Hospital:
  Equipment, 112
  Foundation, 118
  Fund Raising, 110
  Patient, 412
Hospitalized:
  Accident, 299
  Illness, 298
  Injury, 299
Hotel room, 373
Houston, 328
How to Do It:
  Accepting applicant, 257
  Accepting gift, 414
  Accepting position, 377
  Accepting resignation, 267
  Apology, 317
  Collection, 135
  Complaints, answering, 214
  Complaints, making, 204
  Compliments, 400
  Congratulations, 335
  Cover letters, 230, 379
  Declining gifts, 419
  Declining requests, 23
  Encouragement, 396
  Follow-up, 76, 382
  Fund raising, 84
  Goodwill, 364
  Good wishes, 394
  Introduction, 370
  Invitations, 373, 375
  Job application letters, 239
  Letters from employers, 249
  Performance appraisal, 259
  Presenting gifts, 411
  Providing information, 172
  Query letters, 385
  Recommendation, 405
  Refusing requests, 23
  Reprimand, 407

Requesting favors, 5
Requesting information, 183
Resignation, 286, 291
Sales, 51
Sympathy, 296
Termination, 277, 282
Thanking, 243, 349
Welcome, 392
Humboldt, college, 125
Humor in collection letters, 136
Humorous openings, 136
Hungry children, 90
Husband of saleswoman, 366
Husband, tribute, 421
Huston lawn mower, 384

I

Ignoring customer, 326
Ill health, 288
Illness, 299, 354, 413
Image, 419
Inactive charge account, 384
Inactive customer, 69
Inadequate explanation, 205
Income tax consulting, 68
Incomplete files, 190
Incomplete instructions, 216, 327
Incomplete project, 327
Incorporation certificate, 380
Incorrect mailings, 205
Increased sales, 403
Indiscretion, 280, 325
Individual Financing, 72
Industry award, 341
Inexperienced worker, 406
Inflation, fund raising, 105
Information, 350
    Additional, 5, 383
    City, 184
    Credit, 37, 186
    Exchange, 10
    Lacking, 32
    Not available, 27
    Provided, 171, 383
    Requested, 27, 182, 369, 387
    Sending, 369
    Wrong, 332
Inquiry, response, 7
Instructions:
    Incomplete, 216, 327
    Repeated, 178
Insurance:
    Fire, 410
    Health, 58
    Homeowners, 57
    Increase, 410

Life, 74
Mortgage, 57
Policy transfer, 179
Questions, 191
Renewal, 381
Intermediate collection letter, 158-164
Internal Revenue Service, 9
Interview:
    Accepting, 243
    Invitation, 253
    Obtaining, 14
    Thanking, 244
Introduction, How to Do It, 370
Inventory, physical, 196
Investigate, 190
Investment, real estate, 54
Invitation, 25, 372
    Accepting, 374
    Declining, 321, 376
    Dinner, 25, 352, 376
    Fishing trip, 368
    How to Do It, 373, 375
    Interview, 253
    Speak, 26
IRS, 9
Item not available, 27

J

Jacobs Company, 340
James and Holcomb, company, 252
Job:
    Application letter, 239
    For a relative, 18
    Hunting, 229
    Performance review, 260
    Well done, 336, 355
Job applicant's letters, 229
Job application letters, How to Do It, 239
Job offer:
    Accepting, 246
    Rejecting, 248
Job suggested, 242
Johnson Corporation, 65
Johnson's Hardware, 288
Join a group, 376
Jones & Johnson, 248
Junior Chamber of Commerce, 38
Just causes for termination, 277
Juvenile, 371

K

Keep records, 193

L

Labor law violation, 210
Lack of cleanliness, 408
Lack of cooperation, 409
Last collection letter, 164
Late delivery, 217
Late report, 327
Lawn mower purchase, 384
Layoff, 179
Lease instructions, 175
Letters:
    Declination, 42
    Sample, 14
    Series, fund raising, 100
Library, 100
    Campaign, 102
    Meadowvale, 100
    Needs, 121
    Volunteers, 103
Life insurance, 74, 191
Lions club, 378
Lists, 379
Loan paid, 342
Loan past due, 144
Long's Department Store, 357
Los Angeles, 409
Los Angeles Times, 230
Love is a reason for giving, 109
Low productivity, 397
Low sales, 206
Luncheon for friend, 373
Lung disease, 100

M

Magazine:
    Article, 386
    Business, 56
    Elitist, 56
    Query, 386
    Subscriber, 43
Mailings incorrect, 205
Mail misdirected, 217
Maintain image, 419
Maintain service, 114
Making appointment, 188
Making contribution, 369
Manufacturing, B. C., Inc., 189
Manufacturing errors, 207
Manufacturing plant visit, 10
Manufacturing problem, 208
Marin County Times, 15
Market research trainee, 240
Marriage, 343
    Separation, 311

Martinez Boy's Club, 350
Master Card, 74
Materials received, 350
Matson's Department Store, 31
Meadowvale Library, 100, 101, 102
Medical facility evaluation, 198
MEDICO, 97
Meeting:
    Missed, 328
    Out of control, 211
    You, 367
Member, new, 393
Menson Accounting System, 27
Mentally retarded, 88
Merchandise guarantee, 220
Messy work area, 206
Metal etching, 73
Middle collection letters, 158
Mills College, 338
Minneapolis, 371, 373
Minolta Corporation, 63
Minorities program, 124
Misdirected mail, 217
Misfortune, 311
Misrepresentation, 210
Missed appointment, 328
Missed caller, 329
Missed meeting, 328
Mistake, ours, 216
Misunderstanding, 36, 216
Money, 416
Monte-Atlanta Corporation, 185
Morgan Hill Toastmasters, 26
Morning Gazette, 240
Mortgage insurance, 57
Mountain Bell, company, 236
Mountain property, 62
Mt. Zion Health Systems, Inc., 110
Muddy newspaper, 212
Music, college degree, 338
Music Teacher's Conference, 352
Must maintain image, 419

N

Name used in fund raising, 37
National Labor Relations Board, 277
National Office for Social Responsibility, 85
Negative phrases, 214
Negative words, 134
New customer, 336
New employee, 372
New England, 350
New member, 393
Newport Beach, California, 237
Newport Harbor Art Museum, 237, 241
New position, 287, 339

New resident, 392
New sales representative, 370
Newsletter data, 185
Newspaper, muddy, 212
New York, city, 233, 234
Noisy driver, 211
Norcross Development Company, 288
Norfork University, 125
Norman's, store, 77
No, saying "no", 21
Notice:
    Employee leaving, 267
    Promotion, 263
Number code changes, 177

O

Oakland, 409
Occurrence, future, 180
Office:
    Furniture, 191
    Visit, 10
Official, public 70
Officiating:
    Baptismal, 412
    Funeral, 412
Oil painting, 416
Old equipment, 188
Olin College, 124
Onward Civic Club, 372
Opening sentences, sales, 51
Opening sentences (*see* Beginning
    sentences)
Openings, humorous, 136
Openings, store, 342
Operational fund, 125
Opinion asked, 196
Orders:
    Delayed, 218, 323
    Rescheduled, 8
Organization, 171
Orientation help, 401
Outside activities, 408

P

Pacific Northwest Medical Center, 114
Pacific Real Estate, 61
Painting:
    Oil, 416
    Watercolor, 417
Pallet, H. & H. Co., 265
Pamphlet, 350
Paper work delayed, 324

Paragraphs, ending, 174
Parents of employee, 367
Parking in driveway, 211
Parsons, store, 73, 258
Past due freight bill, 142
Patient, hospital, 412
Payment, 358
    Instructions, 177
    Loan, 342
    Slow, 331
    Terms, 164
Pay release and separation, 292
Performance, 281
    Classroom, 285
    Evaluation, 260
    Poor, 283
    Review, 260
Performance appraisal, How to Do It, 259
Personal collection letter, 135
Personal credit, 72
Personal friend, 280
Personal letters, 391
Personal problems, 282, 289
Personal reverses, 312
Personnel agency, 71
Personnel evaluation, 193
Persuasive words, 49
Phoenix, 233, 325, 355
Phrases:
    Negative, 214
    Positive, 214
Physical inventory, 196, 204
Pierce Tractor, company, 258
Plant accountant, 231
Plant closed, 278
Pleasant Hill Medical Center, 118
Please investigate, 190
Pledge:
    Delinquent, 108
    Not received, 128
Policy:
    Change, 180
    Company, 419
Politics, 70
Pollution check, 189
Poor pay, 34
Poor performance, 283
Portland, 409
Position, accepting, 376
Position, accepting, How to Do It, 377
Position, new, 339
Positive phrases, 214
Positive words, 135
Postponed dinner, 323
Postscript, 83
Power lawn mower purchase, 384
Power words, 49
Preparation for fund raising, 105

Presenting gifts, 411
President:
    Association, 342
    Rotary, 341
Price error, 222
Price increase, 173, 381
Price quote, 194
Primus book club, 59
Problem:
    Financial, 279
    Manufacturing, 208
    Personal, 282, 289, 396
Procedure:
    Change, 7, 173, 192
    Classroom, 281
    Company, 320
Product:
    Damage, 40
    Free, 418
    Slow selling, 41
    Special, 41
Productivity, low, 397
Project:
    Completed, 280
    Failure, 329
    Incomplete, 327
    Worthy, 129
Promotion, 398
    Congratulations, 263, 272
    Notice, 263
    Recommendation, 262
    Sales, 65
Prompt reply, 135
Property, mountain, 62
Providing information, 171
Psychology Association Workshop, 14
Publication:
    Editorial program, 44
    Needs reworking, 44
    Seeking, 384
    Specialized, 43
Public official, 70
Purchasing policy, 174

Q

Query letters, 384
    Article, 386
    Book, 385
    Hot to Do It, 385
Questionnaire, using, 6
Questions, answering, 5
Quote error, 330
Quote, requesting, 14

R

Ralph's, company, 357
Rankin's, 29
Reader:
    Consideration for, 22
    Interest, 4
    Save face, 22
Reader's viewpoint, 391
Real estate:
    Homes, 60
    Investment, 54
    Mountain property, 62
    Service, 368
Receiving hours, 191
Recent sales activity, 185
Recognition, 352
Recommendation, 351, 404
    Ending sentences, 405
    How to Do It, 405
    Job applicant, 270
Record:
    Address change, 198
    Telephone, 193
Recruiter, executive, 71
Redwood Furniture, company, 350
Redwood Girls Club, 21, 38
Reed & Barton, 73
Reference, data from, 251
Referral, 359
REFUGE, 84
Refusal, 24
    Agreement, 21
    Apology, 21
    Explain, 22
    Stated, 22
    Thank you, 21
Regan Department Store, 247
Rejecting:
    Applicants, 254, 271
    Job offer, 248
Relative, helping, 18
Reliance Trailer & Truck Company, 235
Religious appeal, 126
Reminder collection letter, 140
Ren Bearing Company, 380
Reorganization, 278
Repeated instructions, 178
Repetition, 171
Reply, prompt, 135
Report, 184
    Distribution, 178
    Late, 327
    Period changed, 193
Reprimand, 264, 407
    How to Do It, 407

Requests, 3
 Data, 250
 Declining, 21
 Information, 182, 369
 Miscellaneous, 45
Research paper, 398
Resident, new, 31, 392
Resignation, 249
 How to Do It, 286
Resignation acceptance, 266, 291
 How to Do It, 267, 291
Respect for reader, 295
Response:
 Positive, 4
 Willing, 3
Responsibility, declining, 222
Restricting receiving hours, 191
Resumes, 229, 231
 Advertising, 232
 Computer operator, 237
 Senior accountant, 234
 Telephone company, 236
Retail customer disturbed, 215
Retail furniture, 73
Retail Hardware Association, 13
Retarded, mentally, 88
Retirement, 413
 Congratulations, 268, 274
 Dinner, 376
Review, claim, 186
Reward, small, 331
Rio Salado College, 78
Risk:
 Bad, 35
 No hope, 35
Riverside Construction, 256
Riverside University, 121
Riverside University Library, 121
Rollins Consultants, 248
Roofing tile, 65
Rotary president, 341
Runaway children, 84

S

Sacramento, 392, 409
Safety news, 194
St. John's University, 39
Sales, 49
 Activity, 185
 Agreement ended, 367
 Christmas, 76
 Contest, 397
 Forecast, 206
 Increase, 403

Letter, 363
Low, 206
Position, 371
Presentation, 358
Representative, 230, 370
Store, 76
Volume, 336, 403
Salesman, good, 403
Salesperson, top, 337
Salesperson's spouse, 365
Sales Promotion Book, 65
Sales Promotion Handbook, 66
Salt Lake City, 409
Sample letter, 14, 42
Sampson's, 35
Samuelson Company, 355
Sanders Company, 190
San Diego, 369, 409
San Francisco, 16, 67, 236, 329, 371, 402, 409,
 415
San Jose, 358
Sano Company, 283
Saving face, 407
Savings:
 Cost, 75
 Statement, 381
Schools, fund raising, 119
Sear's Lumber, 300
Season's greetings, 364, 394
Seattle, 234, 392, 409
SEC, 176
Secretary, 231
Secular appeal, 104
Seeking new challenge, 287
Semiconductor Supplies, company, 274
Sending information, 369
Sentences:
 Accepting gifts, 414
 Apology, 318
 Encouragement, 396
 Ending, 372
 Invitation, 372, 374
 (*see also* Beginning sentences and Ending
  sentences)
Separation, marriage, 311
Separation pay, 292
Series collection letters, 140
Service award, 339
 Five years, 340
 Twenty years, 340
Service club, 352
Service contract, 69
Service, domestic, 406
Service, maintaining, 114
Seymour Port Company, 405
Share experience, 11
Sheraton Hotel, 15

Shipping:
  Error, 208, 218, 330
  Information, 173
Slow pay, 31, 150, 331
Slow-selling product, 41
Small reward, 331
Smith Manufacturing, company, 207
Snacks, 414
Society of Historical Businesses, 29
Sorority, honorary, 341
Speaker, requesting, 15, 16
Speaking, 375
Special assignment, 42
Specialized teacher, 339
Special product, 41
Specific customer, 65
Specific example, fund raising, 116
Sponsor a child, 98
Spouse of salesperson, 365
Spouse, tribute, 421
Staff help, 400
Stanford Construction, 256
Stanford, university, 338
Stanley Company, 383
Staples Family Store, 76
Starting sentences (*see* Beginning sentences)
Statement error, 224, 331
Statement, financial, 11
Statement of future occurrence, 180
Statement requested, 380
Statement, savings, 381
State of California, 197
Statuette, 417
Stewart City, 178
Stop light, 213
Store opening, 342
Store sale, 76
Strength analysis, 185
Strike, effect, 179
Strong close, collection, 137
Student Fund, 127
Student Union Building, 125
Style, wrong, 220
Subscriber, magazine, 43
Success story, fund raising, 111
Suggestions requested, 197
SunCor Development Co., 61
Sundstrom, J.P., company, 257
Sun Ray Distributors, 366
Sun Ridge, apartments, 78
Superintendent of Documents, 28
Support, continuing, 113
Surgery, fear, 17
Survey:
  Consumer, 7
  Consumption, 196
Sympathy, 295
  How to Do It, 296

  Sentences, 296
  Thanking, 297, 312
Systems administrator, 237

T

Tardiness, 285
Tatum Ranch, 61
Tax consulting, 68
Teacher, specialized, 339
Teaching, 399
Temporary Service, company, 270
Ten Keys to Money, 65
Termination, 266, 277
  How to Do It, 277
  Just causes, 277
  Warning, 266, 281
Termination warning, How to Do It, 282
Terms, payment, 164
Terry's Appliances, 69
Test run assigned, 180
Texon University, 122
Thank you, 102, 347
  Delayed, 325
  Employer, 243
  For interview, 244
  For recommendation, 246
  For sympathy, 312
  How to Do It, 243, 349
  In advance, 4
  Job help, 270
  With refusal, 23
Third party letters, 270
Time extension, 8
Token, A. J., company, 207
Tomkin's, company, 355
Top salesperson, 337
Tractor Mechanics, Inc., 27
Tragedy, 312
Transit damage, 204
Travel, 290
Travel expense, 409
Trespassing, 410
Tribute:
  Husband, 421
  Wife, 421
Troubled boys, 87
Truck loading, 401
Truck manufacturer, 230
Tylenol, 70

U

United Parcel, 358
United Way, 95

United Way Campaign, 95
University of California, 338
University of Michigan, 230
University of Oregon, 127
University of Pennsylvania, 292
University of Washington, 14, 73, 234, 372
Unusual tragedy, 312
Unsafe conditions, 410
Unsatisfactory chair, 221
Unsatisfactory recorder, 221
Unusual help, 401
Updating facilities, funding, 110
Using credit memo, 192

V

Valuable document, 381
Valuable gift, 420
Veterans Administration, 93
VA hospital, 93
Veterans, American, 93
Victory, 27
Viewpoint, reader's, 391
Visiting, 359
Visual aids, 49
Volume, sales, 336, 403
Volunteer, library, 103
Volunteer, refusing, 45
Vote getter, 404

W

Wadsworth University, 123
Walkup Corporation, 255
Wallingford Estates, 61
Ward Company, 324
Warehouse report, 380
Warner Bros., J & J, 384
Warning of termination, 266, 281
Warranty questions, 188
Washington, state, 360
Watch, wrist, 62
Watercolor painting, 417
Water Resources, State of California
    Department, 197

Watson Company, 182
Watson Corporation, 310
Webster Technical Institute, 127
Welcome, 392
    How to Do It, 392
    New employee, 258
Wellington College, 120
Wells Fargo Bank, 74
West Center Hospital, 117
Western Management Association, 342
Western States, cities, 409
Westminster Clothiers, 246
Wharton Industrial Research Unit, 292
Wheeler Hospital, 118
Where is report, 195
Whittington College, 125
Wife of salesman, 366
Wife, tribute, 421
Wiley Company, 287
Will contact you again, 182
Willow Pass Company, 206
Wilson Publishers, 44
Winston Developers, 255
Women's Hospital Auxiliary, 376
Woodstock & Sons, 274
Words:
    Negative, 134
    Positive, 135
    Power, 49
    Usage, confusing, 320
Work, good, 365
Work record lacking, 30
Workmanship, 41
Worthy project, 129
Wrist watch, 62
Wrong information, 332
Wrong style, 220

X

Xerox, 64

Y

"You" attitude, 363
Youth agency, 284